C000174080

BRITISH
Motor Cars

1950s

First published as three titles 1956 / 1957
Reprinted as a combined edition 2016

ISBN 978 0 7110 3853 0

© Ian Allan Publishing Ltd 1956 / 1957 / 2016

Published by Ian Allan Publishing

an imprint of Ian Allan Publishing Ltd, Addlestone, Surrey KT15 2SF.
Printed in Wales by Gomer Press.

This is a facsimilie reprint of two original editions first published in 1956/57,
and as such, all advertisements are no longer valid.

Visit the Ian Allan Publishing website at www.ianallanpublishing.com

abc
BRITISH CARS

Vauxhall Six

John Dudley
LONDON

Ian Allan Ltd

The new Jaguar XK 150 Drophead Coupé

Introduction

IT has been a year of consolidation in the British motor industry, and many of the big manufacturers have not added new models to the extensive ranges which they have developed since the war. There are, however, quite a number of interesting new cars—notably the Vauxhall 6-cylinder models which, with the 4-cylinder Victor, introduced after the last *ABC of British Cars* was published, make up a completely new range of Vauxhalls. The Riley Pathfinder is replaced by the 2·6-litre model—a Riley with a 6-cylinder engine after years of 4-cylinder tradition. Standards have restored the pre-war 14 h.p. model with the Ensign (on the Vanguard chassis) and have also introduced a new Ten—the Pennant. Between the last *ABC* and the 1957 Motor Show, the Wolseley 1500, the redesigned Humber Hawk and the Jaguar 3·4-litre, have made their appearance and are shown here for the first time.

There have been few major technical developments in the year. More cars are offered with automatic transmission, and output has been stepped up in some cases. The little Berkeley sports car, illustrated last year for the first time, has heralded a new wave of popularity of the " economy car "—the 4-wheeler with a motor cycle engine and room for two adults and often two children as well.

The new edition of the *ABC* shows a selection of these little cars. The main body of the booklet contains, as usual, quick reference panels to enable the salient features of each model to be spotted at a glance. Each model not shown in the 1957 *ABC of British Cars* is marked with an asterisk. Fuel consumption and maximum speed figures, where given, are approximate.

JOHN DUDLEY.

Allard

Allard Motor Co., Ltd.,

24/28 Clapham High Street,

London, S.W.4.

- PALM BEACH MARK II: 100 m.p.h. 6-cyl., 3½-litre o.h.v. Jaguar engine with 4-speed synchromesh gearbox and central control or 6-cyl 2½-litre Zodiac engine with 3-speed synchromesh gearbox and central control. Torsion bar i.f.s. Coil spring rear suspension. Overdrive or Borg-Warner automatic transmission optional extras. De Dion rear axle optional.
- *GRAN TURISMO: Same engine and chassis but 2-door fixed head body.

THE Allard Palm Beach is continued for 1958 with the choice of Jaguar 6-cylinder 3½-litre engine or Ford Zodiac 6-cylinder 2½-litre engine. The Jaguar engine is served by twin S.U. carburettors, and transmission is conventional 4-speed synchromesh. The Zodiac model has three Zenith carburettors and the usual Ford 3-speed synchromesh gearbox. The chassis frame consists of twin tubular side members joined by steel plate and the open two-seater body is of aluminium, with all-weather equipment which is stowed out of sight when not in use. Overdrive or the Borg-Warner automatic gearbox may be fitted as optional extras. Brakes are 12-inch Lockheed hydraulic.

The new Allard model for 1958 is the Gran Turismo, a two-door fixed head coupé on the Palm Beach chassis. The Jaguar or the Zodiac engine is available and, as on the Palm Beach, De Dion rear axle is an optional feature costing an extra £150. The Gran Turismo has two rear seats for children.

Allard Mk. II Palm Beach

4

For recognition purposes note the simple radiator opening with the letter " A " set in the centre.

Specifications

Model	c.c.	No. of Cyls.	Max. B.H.P.	Wheel Base	Max. Track	Length	Width	Turning Circle
PALM BEACH Mk.II ... ... (Jaguar)	3,442	6	210	8′	4′ 4″	13′	5′ 3″	35′
MARK II ... (Zodiac)	2,553	6	90	8′	4′ 4″	13′	5′ 3″	35′

Total U.K. Prices

PALM BEACH MK. II ZODIAC	£1,576	7s.	0d.
PALM BEACH MK. II JAGUAR	£1,951	7s.	0d.
GRAN TURISMO	£2,551	7s.	0d.

Alvis

Alvis, Ltd.,

Holyhead Road,

Coventry.

● T.C. 108/G: 100 m.p.h., 6-cyl. 3-litre o.h.v. engine with twin carbs. 4-speed synchromesh gearbox with central control. Coil spring and wishbone i.f.s. Semi-elliptic rear suspension. Hydraulic brakes. 2-door, 5-seater saloon or drophead coupé.*

THE Alvis Gran Turismo saloon with bodywork by the Swiss firm of Graber is joined by a drophead coupé version of the same model. This latest Alvis is a splendid looking fast sports tourer with a top speed of over 100 m.p.h. The 3-litre 6-cylinder engine is of the overhead valve type with pushrod operation. Transmission is conventional by a 4-speed synchromesh gearbox. An air conditioning unit is fitted as standard equipment. The Alvis radiator is vertically grilled and slightly pointed. The saloon has wire wheels and a two-door body. The drophead coupé has disc wheels and a hood which drops out of sight when not in use.

Alvis T.C. 108G Drophead Coupé

Specifications

Model	c.c.	No. of Cyls.	Max. B.H.P.	Wheel Base	Max. Track	Length	Width	Turning Circle
T.C. 108G ...	2,993	6	104	9' 3½"	4' 6⅝"	15' 9"	5' 6"	39' 6"

Total U.K. Prices

GRABER SALOON AND DROPHEAD COUPÉ .. £3,451 7s. 0d.

Alvis T.C. 108G Saloon

Armstrong Siddeley

**Armstrong Siddeley
            Motors, Ltd.,
Parkside,
Coventry.**

- SAPPHIRE 346: 100 m.p.h., 6-cyl. 3·4-litre o.h.v. engine. Twin carbs. optional. 4-speed synchromesh gearbox or automatic box. Coil spring i.f.s. Power steering optional. Adjustable ride control and power operated windows optional. 4-door 5/6 seater saloon or limousine.

ARMSTRONG SIDDELEYS are concentrating on the 346 Sapphire model with the 3½-litre engine in saloon and limousine form this year. The Sapphire 234 and 246 models are now discontinued. The Sapphire 346 has been established for some years and is continued for 1958 with only minor interior alterations in the limousine, designed to increase the passenger accommodation. Both saloon and limousine have the 6-cylinder 3·4-litre engine. With a single Stromberg carburettor this provides a top speed of around 95 m.p.h. With twin carburettors, an optional feature, the top speed is increased to over 100 m.p.h. Four-speed synchromesh is standard, but the saloon model is also offered with an automatic gearbox. At medium speeds petrol consumption is 18–22 miles per gallon. Note the slightly pointed vertical radiator grille and the traditional Sphinx mascot.

Armstrong Siddeley Sapphire 346

Model	c.c.	No. of Cyls.	Max B.H.P.	Wheel Base	Max. Track	Length	Width	Turning Circle
346 Saloon ...	3,435	6	125*	9′ 6″	4′ 9½″	16′ 1″	6′	42′ 6″
346 Limousine ...	3,435	6	125*	11′ 1″	4′ 9½″	17′ 8″	6′	45′

* 150 b.h.p. with twin-carbs

Total U.K. Prices

SAPPHIRE 346 SALOON	£1,651	7s.	0d.
SAPPHIRE 346 SALOON (Automatic)	£1,793	17s.	0d.
SAPPHIRE 346 LIMOUSINE	£2,866	7s.	0d.
SAPPHIRE 346 LIMOUSINE (Automatic)	£3,149	17s.	0d.

Aston Martin

**Aston Martin, Ltd.
(David Brown Group),
Feltham,
Middlesex.**

- *D.B. MARK III SALOON: 100 m.p.h., 6-cyl. twin o.h.c. 3-litre engine with twin S.U. carbs. 4-speed synchromesh close ratio gearbox with optional overdrive. Central control. Disc front brakes. Trailing link i.f.s. Also Drophead Coupé.

THE D.B. 2-4 Aston Martin sports saloon—a model with a high reputation among sports car enthusiasts—is succeeded for 1958 by the D.B. Mark III Saloon. The new model retains the classic body lines of the original D.B.2. The radiator grille is slightly altered, and shows the influence of the D.B. 3S competition car. The 3-litre engine has been redesigned and incorporates a new cylinder head with valves, ports and cam profiles all developed from the Aston Martin competition cars. The output is increased to 178 b.h.p. with twin exhausts. The new clutch is hydraulic, the David Brown close ratio synchromesh gearbox is retained, and Laycock overdrive is available at extra cost. This operates on top gear only. Girling disc brakes are fitted at the front and Alfin

Aston Martin D.B. Mark III Saloon

bi-metal drums at the rear. The D.B. Mark III has a top speed of 120 m.p.h. and over, and combines splendid road holding characteristics with roominess and luggage capacity. Essentially a two-seater, there are also two occasional rear seats. Note the stubby tail, the sloping rear window, and the competition type wire wheels.

Specifications

Model	c.c.	No. of Cyls.	Max. B.H.P.	Wheel Base	Max. Track	Length	Width	Turning Circle
D.B. MARK III	2,922	6	178	8′ 3″	4′ 6″	14′ 3½″	5′ 5″	35′

Total U.K. Prices

D.B. Mk. III Saloon	..	..	..	..	£3,076 7s. 0d.
D.B. Mk. III Drophead	..	..	..	..	£3,451 7s. 0d.

Austin

Austin Motor Co., Ltd.,

Longbridge,

Birmingham.

- A.35: 75 m.p.h., 4-cyl., 950 c.c. o.h.v. engine. 4-speed synchromesh gearbox with central control. Coil spring i.f.s. 2- and 4-door saloons and Countryman.

- *METROPOLITAN: 4-cyl., 1½-litre o.h.v. engine. 3-speed synchromesh transmission. Coil spring i.f.s. Hardtop or Convertible.

- *A.55 CAMBRIDGE: 80 m.p.h., 4-cyl., 1½-litre o.h.v. engine. 4-speed synchromesh gearbox with steering column control. Coil spring i.f.s. 4/5-seater saloon. Manumatic clutch optional. Overdrive optional.

- A.95 WESTMINSTER: 6-cyl., 2½-litre o.h.v. engine. 4-speed synchromesh gearbox or automatic transmission. Coil spring i.f.s. 5/6-seater or Countryman.

- A.105 WESTMINSTER: Specifications similar, but twin carb. engine.

- AUSTIN-HEALEY: 100 m.p.h., 2½-litre, 6-cyl. o.h.v. engine, 4-speed synchromesh gearbox with overdrive. 2-seater sports.

THERE are no changes in the Austin range for 1958—although the more powerful version of the A.50—the A.55—has been introduced since the last *A.B.C. British Cars* was published, and the Metropolitan is now available on the home market. The A.35—successor to the famous series of Austin Sevens—is equipped with the same engine as that used in the Morris Minor—the B.M.C. 4-cylinder 950 c.c. unit—and has a similar remote control gearbox. Externally there is very little change since the model was first introduced as the A.30 some years ago. The A.55 Cambridge is offered with Manumatic 2-pedal control as an optional extra. The A.95 Westminster is the 6-cylinder 2·6-litre model and, as the A.105, it has a more powerful twin-carburettor engine, and a number of luxury features.

The Metropolitan which is now offered on the home market was first produced some years ago as a joint venture by Nash and Austins. The cars are made at Longbridge for export to America, where they have proved very popular. The Metropolitan has a B.M.C. 1½-litre engine. It is available in two-door hardtop or two-door convertible form—and is typically American in appearance.

Austin A.35

Austin A.55 Cambridge

Austin A.105 Westminster

Austin A.95 Countryman

Austin Metropolitan 1500

The Austin-Healey Hundred Six model is continued without change. The 6-cylinder engine, introduced last year, provides 102 b.h.p., and overdrive is a standard fitting. Combined with the 4-speed gearbox this gives, in effect, six forward speeds. The oval Austin-Healey radiator grille is surmounted by a humped air scoop.

Specifications

Model	*c.c.*	*No. of Cyls.*	*Max. B.H.P.*	*Wheel Base*	*Max. Track*	*Length*	*Width*	*Turning Circle*
A.35	950	4	35	6′ 7½″	3′ 9¼″	11′ 4⅜″	4′ 7⅛″	33′
A.55	1,489	4	55	8′ 3¼″	4′ 1″	13′ 6¼″	5′ 1½″	36′
A.95	2,639	6	92	8′ 9¾″	4′ 3½″	15′ 0¾″	5′ 4″	40′
A.105	2,639	6	102	8′ 9¾″	4′ 3½″	15′ 0¾″	5′ 4″	40′
METROPOLITAN	1,489	4	47	7′ 1″	3′ 9 5/16″	12′ 5½″	5′ 1½″	—
AUSTIN-HEALEY ...	2,639	6	102	7′ 8″	4′ 2″	13′ 1½″	5′ 0½″	35′

Total U.K. Prices

A.35 Two-Door Saloon	£569 17s. 0d.
A.35 Two-Door (De Luxe)	£582 19s. 6d.
A.35 Four-Door Saloon	£596 2s. 0d.
A.35 Four-Door (De Luxe)	£601 7s. 0d.
A.35 Countryman	£667 7s. 0d.
A.55 Saloon..	£808 7s. 0d.
A.55 Saloon (De Luxe)	£856 7s. 0d.
A.95 Saloon..	£1,034 17s. 0d.
A.95 Saloon (De Luxe)	£1,079 17s. 0d.
A.95 Countryman	£1,252 7s. 0d.
A.105 Saloon	£1,235 17s. 0d.
Metropolitan Hardtop	£713 17s. 0d.
Metropolitan Convertible	£725 2s. 0d.
Austin-Healey	£1,144 7s. 0d.

Bentley S Series four-door Saloon

Bentley Continental Sports Saloon

Bentley Continental four-door Saloon

Bentley

Bentley Motors (1931),
Ltd.,
14-15 Conduit Street,
London, W.1.

- S SERIES: 100 m.p.h., 6-cyl. 4·9-litre engine. Automatic gearbox. Servo assisted brakes. Fitted heater and demister. Power steering optional. 5/6-seater 4-door saloon.
- CONTINENTAL: 100 m.p.h., 6-cyl., 4·9-litre engine. Automatic gearbox. Servo assisted brakes. Fitted heater and demister. Drophead coupé, 2-door and 4-door saloons.*

THE S Series Bentley is the sister car to the Rolls-Royce Silver Cloud and the only difference between the two cars is the radiator. The famous Bentley radiator is slightly pointed with a vertical grille. The 6-cylinder 5-litre engine is served by twin carburettors. Output of the engine is not released. On all Bentleys independent front suspension is by coil springs with hydraulic shock absorbers and anti-roll rod. At the rear semi-elliptic leaf springs are used with hydraulic shock dampers and a Z-type anti roll bar. The Continental is continued and in this series for 1958 there is a new 4-door Sports Saloon by Mulliner. The light alloy construction of this 4-door saloon has brought the weight down to within a few pounds of the 2-door Continental.

Specifications

Model	c.c.	No. of Cyls.	Max. B.H.P.	Wheel Base	Max. Track	Length	Width	Turning Circle
SERIES S ...	4,887	6	—	10′ 3″	5′	17′ 8″	6′ 2¾″	41′ 8″
CONTINENTAL	4,887	6	—	10′ 3″	5′	17′ 6″	5′ 11½″	41′ 8″

Total U.K. Prices

S SERIES SALOON	£5,543 17s.	0d.
HOOPER SALOON	£7,486 7s.	0d.
HOOPER LIMOUSINE	£7,786 7s.	0d.
MULLINER DROPHEAD	£8,183 17s.	0d.
MULLINER FOUR-DOOR SALOON	£8,033 17s.	0d.
JAMES YOUNG SALOON	£7,373 17s.	0d.
PARK WARD CONTINENTAL DROPHEAD OR FIXED HEAD	£7,493 17s.	0d.
MULLINER CONTINENTAL TWO-DOOR	£7,913 17s.	0d.

Bristol

**Bristol Cars, Ltd.,
Filton House,
Bristol.**

- BRISTOL 405: 100 m.p.h., 6-cyl. o.h.v. 2-litre engine with three Solex carbs. 4-speed synchromesh gearbox (freewheel inbuilt into first speed). Central control. Overdrive standard. Wishbone and transverse spring i.f.s. Heater–demister fitted. 4-seater, 4-door saloon.

PRODUCTION of Bristol Cars, Ltd., is now concentrated on the 405 saloon, which remains unchanged for 1958. Note the neat square radiator duct and the humped air scoop on top of the bonnet, and the typical Bristol wheels pierced for brake cooling. The Bristol 100B o.h.v. 6-cylinder engine puts the car into the 100 m.p.h. class. It gives the car a high cruising speed and fuel consumption of 24 miles per gallon at 60 m.p.h. A heating and ventilating unit which supplies fresh air to the interior of the car and provides air for windscreen demisting and defrosting is included in the equipment of each model. Laycock overdrive is a standard fitting with an automatic switch which returns direct to fourth gear after a lower gear has been engaged. A long-range spot lamp is mounted in the radiator duct.

Independent front suspension is by wishbone arms and a transverse multi-leaf spring. Rear suspension is by torsion bars running fore and aft. The Bristol 405 is a fine sports tourer of advanced aerodynamic design and luxurious fittings. The powerful engine has been well tried in competition work.

The Bristol 406 was shown at Earls Court for the first time. This model, which is for export only, is equipped with the new 2·2-litre Bristol engine, and has Dunlop disc brakes on all four wheels. It is a 4-seater, 2-door saloon by Gebr. Beutler, of Switzerland.

Specifications

Model	c.c.	No. of Cyls.	Max. B.H.P.	Wheel Base	Max. Track	Length	Width	Turning Circle
405	1,971	6	105	9′ 6″	4′ 6″	15′ 9¼″	5′ 8″	37½′

Total U.K. Price

BRISTOL 405 SALOON .. .. £3,586 7s. 0d.

Bristol 406 four-seater, two-door Saloon

Bristol 405 Saloon

Daimler 3½-litre One-O-Four Saloon

Daimler 4½-litre D.K. 400 Limousine

Daimler 4½-litre Hooper Limousine

Daimler

The Daimler Co., Ltd.,

Radford Works,

Coventry.

- CENTURY SALOON: 90 m.p.h., 6-cyl., 2½-litre o.h.v. engine with twin S.U. carbs. Automatic 4-speed gearbox. Torsion bar i.f.s. 4-door, 5-seater saloon.

- ONE-O-FOUR SALOON: 100 m.p.h., 6-cyl., 3½-litre o.h.v. engine with twin S.U. carbs. Fluid flywheel and 4-speed preselector gearbox or 4-speed automatic gearbox. Coil spring i.f.s. 4-door, 5/6-seater saloon.

- D.K. 400/A LIMOUSINE: 6-cyl., 4½-litre o.h.v. engine with twin S.U. carbs. Fluid flywheel and 4-speed preselector gearbox. Coil spring i.f.s. 8-seater luxury limousine.

- *D.K. 400/B LIMOUSINE: More luxurious version of same model.

- HOOPER LIMOUSINE: 6-cyl., 4½-litre o.h.v. engine with twin S.U. carbs. Fluid flywheel and 4-speed preselector gearbox. Coil spring i.f.s. Limousine body by Hooper.

THERE are very few changes in the Daimler series for 1958. All the 1957 models are continued but the D.K. 400 limousine is now available in two forms—known as the D.K. 400/A and the D.K. 400/B. The first is the model shown last year, primarily designed for high class hire trade, undertakers, etc. It has three occasional seats in addition to the 3-seat accommodation in the rear compartment, and two additional seats beside the

Daimler 2½-litre Century Saloon

driver in the front. The " B " version is trimmed and fitted in the rear compartment on a more luxurious scale and is intended for use as a private chauffeur-driven car, and for municipalities, corporations, firms and for ceremonial occasions. It has two occasional seats instead of three and a drop glass division between the front and rear compartments instead of a sliding partition.

The D.K. 400 has the 4½-litre engine. The One-O-Four models have the 3½-litre 6-cylinder engine which provides a top speed of over 100 m.p.h. This model is available with either the normal Daimler 4-speed preselector gearbox and fluid flywheel or the new automatic gearbox. The famous 2½-litre Century saloon is continued unchanged and this is now available with automatic transmission. The last model in the Daimler 1958 range is the Hooper limousine, on the 4½-litre chassis.

Specifications

Model	c.c.	No. of Cyls.	Max. B.H.P.	Wheel Base	Max. Track	Length	Width	Turning Circle
CENTURY ...	2,433	6	100	8′ 8″	4′ 4″	14′ 10½″	5′ 6″	33′
ONE-O-FOUR...	3,468	6	137	9′ 6″	4′ 9″	16′ 4″	5′ 10½″	42′
D.K.400 ...	4,617	6	167	10′ 10″	5′ 3″	18′ 1″	6′ 5″	44′
HOOPER LIMOUSINE...	4,617	6	167	10′ 10″	5′ 3″	18′ 5″	6′ 3″	44′

Total U.K. Prices

D.K. 400A	..	..	..	..	..	£4,195	0s. 0d.
D.K. 400B	..	..	..	..	..	£4,315	0s. 0d.
HOOPER LIMOUSINE ..	..	..	..	..	..	£6,578	0s. 0d.
ONE-O-FOUR ..	..	..	..	..	..	£2,395	0s. 0d.
CENTURY	..	..	..	..	..	£1,680	0s. 0d.

Ford

The Ford Motor Co, Ltd.,

Dagenham.

- POPULAR: 60 m.p.h., 4-cyl., 1·2-litre s.v. engine. 3-speed synchromesh gearbox with central control. Transverse leaf springs front and rear. 2-door, 4-light, 4-seater saloon.

- ANGLIA: 65 m.p.h., 4-cyl., 1·2-litre s.v. engine. 3-speed synchromesh gearbox with central control or 2-pedal control. Coil spring i.f.s. 2-door, 4-light, 4-seater saloon or de luxe saloon.

- PREFECT: 65 m.p.h., 4-cyl., 1·2-litre s.v. engine. 3-speed synchromesh gearbox with central control or 2-pedal control. Coil spring i.f.s. 4-door, 4-light, 4-seater saloon or de luxe saloon.

- ESCORT: Details as for Anglia but 2-door, 6-light, 4-seater estate car and 2-pedal control not available.

- SQUIRE: Details as for Prefect but 2-door, 4-light, 6-seater estate car and 2-pedal control not available.

- CONSUL: 4-cyl., 1·7-litre o.h.v. engine. 3-speed gearbox with steering column control. Coil spring i.f.s. 4-door, 4-light saloon, de luxe saloon, convertible or estate car.

- ZEPHYR: 6-cyl., 2½-litre o.h.v. engine. 3-speed synchromesh gearbox with steering column control. Coil spring i.f.s. 4-door, 4-light, 6-seater saloon, convertible or estate car.

- ZODIAC: Luxury version of Zephyr with optional overdrive, also Zodiac de ville convertible or estate car.

THE Anglia and Prefect models are shortly to be offered with 2-pedal control by means of a centrifugal clutch operated by engine vacuum and controlled by an electrical contact in the gear change lever knob. Contact is made by merely touching the lever knob in the normal gear change action. The Anglia has a new lattice type radiator grille for 1958, and this is chrome finished on the de luxe model. The Prefect grille is unchanged. Other minor changes include a larger rear window, restyled tail light units, a new facia panel, and the appearance of the model name in chromium script on the luggage compartment lid.

The Escort and Squire estate wagons are continued with minor changes. The Escort has the lattice work grille, and the wood side mouldings on the Squire are now replaced by chromium strips. Rear seats are set lower and constructed largely of foam rubber.

Ford Squire

Ford Zephyr

Ford Consul de luxe

Ford Anglia

Seating has been redesigned in the Consul, Zephyr and Zodiac saloons. The Zephyr has a redesigned grille and all these models have a new steering system. The only addition to the Ford range is the de luxe saloon version of the popular Consul. Special features on this model include two-tone body colours, windscreen washers, cigar lighter, coat hooks, and a Zephyr-type steering wheel with full horn ring.

The Popular—the cheapest of the Ford range—is continued unchanged.

Ford Prefect

Ford Zodiac Convertible

Specifications

Model	c.c.	*No. of Cyls.*	*Max. B.H.P.*	*Wheel Base*	*Max. Track*	*Length*	*Width*	*Turning Circle*
POPULAR ...	1,172	4	30	7′ 6″	3′ 9″	12′ 8¼″	4′ 8½″	34′ 9″
ANGLIA ...	1,172	4	36	7′ 3″	4′	12′ 5¾″	5′ 0¾″	32′ 9″
PREFECT ...	1,172	4	36	7′ 3″	4′	12′ 7¼″	5′ 0¾″	32′ 9″
ESCORT ...	1,172	4	36	7′ 2″	4′	11′ 9½″	5′ 0¾″	32′ 9″
SQUIRE ...	1,172	4	36	7′ 2″	4′	11′ 9¾″	5′ 0¾″	32′ 9″
CONSUL ...	1,703	4	59	8′ 8½″	4′ 5″	14′ 4″	5′ 8½″	35′
ZEPHYR ...	2,553	6	86	8′ 11″	4′ 5″	14′ 10½″	5′ 8½″	36′
ZODIAC ...	2,553	6	86	8′ 11″	4′ 5″	14′ 10½″	5′ 8½″	36′

Total U.K. Prices

Popular	£443	7s.	0d.
Anglia	£571	7s.	0d.
Anglia De Luxe	£601	7s.	0d.

PREFECT	..	..	..	..	..	..	£623 17s. 0d.
PREFECT DE LUXE ..	..	..	..	..	..	£658 7s. 0d.
ESCORT	..	..	..	..	..	..	£652 7s. 0d.
SQUIRE	..	..	..	..	..	..	£695 17s. 0d.
CONSUL SALOON	..	..	..	..	..	£818 17s. 0d.
CONSUL SALOON DE LUXE..	..	..	..	..	£871 7s. 0d.
CONSUL CONVERTIBLE	..	..	..	..	£991 7s. 0d.
ZEPHYR SALOON	..	..	..	..	..	£916 7s. 0d.
ZEPHYR CONVERTIBLE	..	..	..	..	£1,168 7s. 0d.
ZODIAC SALOON	..	..	..	..	..	£1,013 7s. 0d.
ZODIAC CONVERTIBLE	..	..	..	..	£1,310 17s. 0d.
CONSUL ESTATE CAR	..	..	..	..	£1,066 7s. 0d.
ZEPHYR ESTATE CAR	..	..	..	..	£1,163 17s. 0d.
ZODIAC ESTATE CAR	..	..	..	..	£1,268 17s. 0d.

Hillman

**Hillman Motor Co.,
Ltd.
(Rootes Group),
Ryton-on-Dunsmore,
Coventry.**

- MINX: 75 m.p.h., 4-cyl. 1·4-litre o.h.v. engine. 4-speed synchromesh gearbox with steering column change. Manumatic transmission optional on de luxe, convertible and estate models. Coil spring i.f.s. De luxe and special 4-door saloons, 2-door convertible, and estate car.

- HUSKY: 65 m.p.h., 4-cyl., 1·3-litre s.v. engine. 4-speed synchromesh gearbox, central control. Coil spring i.f.s. 2-door, 4-seater short wheelbase utility.

THE Jubilee Minx—commemorating 50 years of Hillman cars and 25 years of the Hillman Minx model—is the 1957 model with some modifications. For instance the de luxe saloon, the estate car and the convertible are now available with Manumatic transmission—giving 2-pedal control. The radiator grille has been changed slightly, and the thick central horizontal bar has given

Above : *Jubilee
Hillman Minx
Saloon*

Left : *Jubilee
Hillman Minx
Convertible*

26

Hillman Husky

place to a small square mesh. The engine is the powerful 1·4-litre o.h.v. unit which gives a top speed of over 75 m.p.h. and particularly lively acceleration. The special saloon—a lower-priced version of the Minx—has the same engine but is not offered with 2-pedal control. The Minx convertible is a 2-door model with a 3-position hood. The tough dual purpose Husky utility is continued without change. The engine is the old Hillman side valve 1·3-litre unit, which provides very favourable fuel consumption. The Husky retains the old Hillman oval radiator grille, and has a door at the rear. The more expensive Hillman estate car has the o.h.v. engine.

Specifications

Model	c.c.	No. of Cyls.	Max. B.H.P.	Wheel Base	Max. Track	Length	Width	Turning Circle
MINX	1,390	4	51	8'	4' 1"	13' 6"	5' 0¾"	34' 3"
ESTATE CAR ...	1,390	4	51	7' 9"	4' 0⅝"	13' 8"	5' 3½"	33'
HUSKY... ...	1,265	4	35	7'	4' 0⅝"	12' 2"	5' 2"	31'

Total U.K. Prices

MINX DE LUXE SALOON	£794 17s. 0d.
MINX CONVERTIBLE	£898 7s. 0d.
MINX SPECIAL SALOON	£748 7s. 0d.
ESTATE CAR	£938 17s. 0d.
HUSKY	£646 7s. 0d.

Hillman Minx Convertible

Humber

**Humber, Ltd.
(Rootes Group),
Ryton-on-Dunsmore,
Coventry.**

- *Hawk: 80 m.p.h., 4-cyl., 2¼-litre o.h.v. engine. 4-speed synchromesh gearbox with steering column control. Automatic transmission optional. Coil spring i.f.s. 5-seater touring limousine, saloon and estate car.

THE Humber factory is now concentrating on production of the new Hawk saloon and estate car. This model is offered with overdrive or Borg-Warner fully automatic transmission as an optional extra. The estate car is a 6-seater with a load carrying space of 56 square feet. It has a luxurious interior, and has a built-in ventilation system. Both the saloon and the estate car are powered by the 2¼-litre Humber Hawk o.h.v. engine with increased compression ratio. The radiator grille departs from Humber tradition for the first time and is wide with a horizontal grille under the winged badge. Note the hooded headlamps and the big overriders on the bumpers. The name " Hawk " is carried in chromium script on the front doors, and the rear lamps and traffic indicators are mounted in the stub-ended rear wings. The saloon is also offered in touring limousine form.

Humber Hawk Estate Car

Specifications

Model	c.c.	No. of Cyls.	Max B.H.P.	Wheel Base	Max. Track	Length	Width	Turning Circle
HAWK...	2,267	4	78	9′ 2″	4′ 8″	15′ 4¾″	5′ 9½″	39′

Total U.K. Prices

HAWK SALOON	..	..	..	..	..	£1,261	7s. 0d.
HAWK TOURING LIMOUSINE		..	..	..	£1,381	7s. 0d.
HAWK ESTATE CAR ..	..	..	..	..	£1,463	17s. 0d.

Humber Hawk six-seater

Jaguar

Jaguar Cars, Ltd.,

Coventry.

- MARK VIII SALOON: 120 m.p.h., 6-cyl., $3\frac{1}{2}$-litre twin o.h.c. engine with twin S.U. carbs. Borg-Warner automatic transmission optional, otherwise 4-speed synchromesh gearbox with optional overdrive and central control. Heater, demister and defroster fitted. 5-seater, 4-door saloon with sliding roof.

- *3·4-LITRE: 140 m.p.h., 6-cyl., 3·4-litre engine with twin S.U. carbs. Automatic or 4-speed synchromesh transmission with overdrive. Coil spring i.f.s. Disc brakes optional. Full 5-seater saloon.

- 2·4-LITRE: 100 m.p.h., 6-cyl., 2·4-litre twin o.h.c. engine with twin Solex carbs. 4-speed synchromesh gearbox with optional overdrive or automatic transmission. Disc brakes optional. Full 5-seater saloon.

- *X.K. 150: 150 m.p.h., 6-cyl., $3\frac{1}{2}$-litre twin o.h.c. engine with twin S.U. carbs. 4-speed synchromesh gearbox with optional overdrive or automatic transmission. Disc brakes optional. 2-door 2/3-seater fixed head coupé or 2-door 2/3-seater drophead coupé.

DISC brakes—perfected by Jaguars in a ong series of motor races—are now offered as optional equipment on all the Jaguar models except the Mark VIII saloon. The Dunlop type disc brake is used. All Jaguar models are now offered with a choice of 4-speed synchromesh gearbox—with or without overdrive—or Borg-Warner automatic transmission.

The range has undergone little change. The five models offered this year are the Mark VIII saloon, the 3·4-litre saloon, the 2·4-litre saloon, the XK 150 drophead coupé and the fixed head coupé. Special equipment models of the 2·4-litre and the XK 150 are available at extra cost.

The Mark VIII is continued without change. The $3\frac{1}{2}$-litre 6-cylinder engine develops 190 b.h.p. and has twin exhausts and twin carburettors. The slightly pointed vertically grilled radiator is retained. The 2·4-litre and the 3·4-litre models are now very similar in appearance. Both have a rounded pear-shaped grille with vertical bars. The only outward difference is that the spats over the rear wheels are all enveloping on the 2·4-litre and are cut away on the 3·4-litre. The 3·4-litre is powered by the famous

Jaguar Mk. VIII Saloon

Jaguar 3·4-litre Saloon

Jaguar 2·4-litre Saloon

Jaguar B-type engine which develops 210 b.h.p. and incorporates many of the features of the Jaguar competition engines. The 2·4-litre develops 112 b.h.p. and is basically similar to the larger Jaguar power units

The XK 150 models—successors to the XK 120 and XK 140 sports cars—have the sleek aerodynamic body of their predecessors, wire wheels, and a rounded pear-shaped radiator grille. The 3½-litre engine develops 210 b.h.p.

Specifications

Model	*c.c.*	*No. of Cyls.*	*Max. B.H.P.*	*Wheel Base*	*Max. Track*	*Length*	*Width*	*Turning Circle*
MARK VIII ...	3,442	6	210	10′	4′ 10″	16′ 4½″	6′ 1″	36′
3·4-LITRE ...	3,442	6	210	8′ 11⅜″	4′ 6⅝″	15′ 0¾″	5′ 6¾″	33′ 6″
2·4-LITRE ...	2,483	6	112	8′ 11⅜″	4′ 6⅝″	15′ 0¾″	5′ 6¾″	33′ 6″
XK150	3,442	6	210	8′ 6″	4′ 3⅝″	14′ 9″	5′ 4½″	33′

Total U.K. Prices

MARK VIII SALOON..	£1,829 17s. 0d.
MARK VIII (Automatic)	£1,997 17s. 0d.
3.4-LITRE	£1,672 7s. 0d.
3.4-LITRE (Automatic)	£1,864 7s. 0d.
2.4-LITRE	£1,495 7s. 0d.
2.4-LITRE (Automatic)	£1,709 17s. 0d.
XK 150 FIXED HEAD	£1,763 17s. 0d.
XK 150 FIXED HEAD (Automatic)	£1,955 17s. 0d.
XK 150 DROPHEAD..	£1,793 17s. 0d.
XK 150 DROPHEAD (Automatic)	£1,985 17s. 0d.

Jaguar XK 150 Fixed Head Coupé

3-litre Lagonda Saloon

Lagonda

Lagonda Ltd.
(David Brown Group),
Feltham, Middlesex.

- 3-LITRE SALOON: 100 m.p.h., 6-cyl., 3-litre o.h.c. engine with twin carbs. Fitted radio, heater, spotlights, windscreen washer, etc. 4-wheel independent suspension. 4-speed synchromesh gearbox. 4-door 4/5-seater saloon.

THE luxurious David Brown 3-litre Lagonda saloon is one of the few cars made in Britain with independent suspension in all four wheels. The 6-cylinder overhead camshaft engine is similar to that used on the Aston Martin cars. Radio, heater, windscreen washers, a hydraulic jacking system and twin spotlights are all offered as standard equipment—indeed there are no "extras" with this car. The chief recognition features are the long bonnet and curved nose with its pear-shaped radiator grille. The petrol tank holds 19 gallons and there is an electrically-operated reserve of 3½ gallons. Luggage accommodation is spacious and altogether the Lagonda is a comfortable and fast touring saloon designed to suit the tastes of the business man or the touring enthusiast.

Specifications

Model	c.c.	No. of Cyls.	Max B.H.P.	Wheel Base	Max. Track	Length	Width	Turning Circle
3-LITRE	2,922	6	140	9′ 5½″	4′ 8¾″	16′ 4″	5′ 9½″	38′

Total U.K. Price

3-LITRE SALOON   ..   ..   £2,993 17s. 0d.

M. G.

**M.G. Car Co., Ltd.
(Nuffield Organisation),
Abingdon-on-Thames,
Berkshire.**

- SERIES A: 90 m.p.h., 4-cyl., 1½-litre push-rod o.h.v. engine. Twin S.U. carbs. 4-speed synchromesh gearbox with central control. Coil spring i.f.s. 2-door, 2-seater sports or hardtop models.
- MAGNETTE: 85 m.p.h., 4-cyl., 1½-litre push-rod o.h.v. engine. Twin carbs. 4-speed synchromesh gearbox. Manumatic clutch control optional. Central Control. Coil spring i.f.s. 4-door, 4-seater saloon and Varitone saloon.

THERE are no changes in the M.G. models, and the two basic types—the Series A sports car and the Magnette saloon—are continued for 1958. Both have the British Motor Corporation " B " series engine with twin carburettors. The Series A has a separate chassis, but the Magnette saloon is of unitary construction. The Series A is, of course, the successor to the long series of successful M.G. Midget cars which date back to 1929. The famous octagonal M.G. nameplate is retained on the small oblong radiator grille.

The Magnette saloon is offered in two versions—standard or Varitone. The latter has a two-tone finish and a wrap-around rear screen. The 1½-litre engine is less highly tuned than the version used on the Series A sports car, and top speed is around 85 m.p.h. Manumatic clutch operation is offered as an optional extra. The radiator is vertically grilled and retains the traditional M.G. shape. The wheels are of the drilled disc type.

M.G. Magnette

M.G. Magnette Varitone

Specifications

Model		c.c.	No. of Cyls.	Max. B.H.P.	Wheel Base	Max. Track	Length	Width	Turning Circle
SERIES A	...	1,489	4	72	7' 10"	4' 0¾"	13'	4' 9¼"	28'
MAGNETTE	..	1,489	4	68	8' 6"	4' 3"	14' 1"	5' 3"	32'

Total U.K. Prices

M.G. " A " Two-Seater	..	..	..	..	£995	17s.	0d.
M.G. " A " Coupé	..	..	..	..	£1,087	7s.	0d.
Magnette	..	..	..	..	£1,072	7s.	0d.
Magnette Varitone	..	..	..	£1,111	7s.	0d.

M.G. Series " A " two-seater

Morris

Morris Motors, Ltd.

(Nuffield Organisation),

Cowley,

Oxford.

- MINOR 1,000: 75 m.p.h., 948 c.c., 4-cyl. o.h.v. engine. 4-speed synchromesh gearbox with central control. Torsion bar i.f.s. Semi-elliptic rear suspension. 2-door or 4-door saloons, convertible or Travellers car in standard or de luxe forms.

- OXFORD SERIES III: 85 m.p.h., $1\frac{1}{2}$-litre, 4-cyl. o.h.v. engine. 4-speed synchromesh gearbox with steering column control. Manumatic clutch optional on saloons. Torsion bar i.f.s. Semi-elliptic rear springing. 4-door, 6-seater saloon or newly designed Travellers Car.*

- COWLEY: Same details as for Oxford but less luxurious trim.

- ISIS SERIES III: 85 m.p.h., 6-cyl., $2\frac{1}{2}$-litre o.h.v. engine. 4-speed synchromesh gearbox with right hand lever. Automatic transmission optional. Torsion bar i.f.s., semi-elliptic rear suspension. 4-door, 6-seater saloon or Travellers Car.

THE only new model in the Morris range is the Oxford Traveller, which has a completely new all-steel estate wagon body. The new Traveller has four doors and a top hinged rear door which opens to reveal the luggage or goods space. Both front and rear seats are of the bench type. The $1\frac{1}{2}$-litre engine is basically similar to that used on all the Oxfords.

For the rest the Morris range consists of the ever popular Minor, the Oxford saloon, the Cowley—a less luxurious version of the

Morris Isis Series III

Morris Minor 1000 four-door Saloon

Oxford—and the 6-cylinder Isis. The Minor 1,000 had increased power and a new remote control gearbox last year. It is continued unchanged and is available in 2- or 4-door saloon form, as a convertible or as a Travellers Car.

The Oxfords were equipped with more power last year, and the Series III may be distinguished externally from previous Oxford models by the fluted radiator and the absence of the air scoop on

Morris Cowley 1500

Morris Oxford Series III

top of the bonnet. The Isis is continued unchanged in saloon or Traveller form. On this model overdrive or Borg-Warner automatic transmission is offered as an optional extra. Manumatic clutch control is offered as an extra on the Oxfords.

Specifications

Model	c.c.	No. of Cyls.	Max. B.H.P.	Wheel Base	Max. Track	Length	Width	Turning Circle
MINOR... ...	948	4	37	7' 2"	4' 2⅝"	12' 4"	5' 1"	33'
OXFORD & COWLEY ...	1,489	4	55	8' 1"	4' 5½"	14' 3"	5' 5"	35½'
ISIS	2,639	6	90	8' 11½"	4' 5⅝"	14' 10"	5' 5"	39¼'

Morris Oxford Traveller

MINOR SALOON (TWO-DOOR)	.. .. ..	£625 7s. 0d.
MINOR DE LUXE SALOON (TWO-DOOR) ..	..	£651 12s. 0d.
MINOR SALOON (FOUR-DOOR)	.. .. ..	£662 17s. 0d.
MINOR DE LUXE SALOON (FOUR-DOOR) ..	..	£694 7s. 0d.
MINOR CONVERTIBLE	.. ..	£625 7s. 0d.
MINOR CONVERTIBLE DE LUXE ..	.. ..	£651 12s. 0d.
MINOR TRAVELLER ..	.. ..	£708 12s. 0d.
MINOR TRAVELLER DE LUXE	.. .. ..	£734 2s. 0d.
COWLEY	.. ..	£834 12s. 0d.
OXFORD SALOON	.. ..	£884 17s. 0d.
OXFORD TRAVELLER	.. ..	£998 17s. 0d.
ISIS SALOON ..	.. ..	£911 17s. 0d.
ISIS DE LUXE SALOON	.. ..	£961 7s. 0d.
ISIS TRAVELLER	.. ..	£1,089 12s. 0d.

Princess

**B.M.C.,
Longbridge,
Birmingham.**

- PRINCESS IV: 6-cyl., 4-litre o.h.v. engine with twin S.U. carbs. Automatic transmission standard. Coil spring i.f.s. 6-seater, 4-door limousine or saloon.

THE Princess—largest of the Austin models which has been produced regularly since the war—is now marketed as a separate entity by the whole resources of the British Motor Corporation. The Princess IV has a 6-cylinder 4-litre engine with twin S.U. carburettors. The automatic gearbox is fitted as standard equipment, and another standard feature is power-assisted steering. The distinctive vertically grilled radiator is unchanged, and this car is offered in saloon, limousine, long wheelbase saloon and long wheelbase limousine forms.

Princess IV Saloon

Specifications

Model	c.c.	No. of Cyls.	Max. B.H.P.	Wheel Base	Max. Track	Length	Width	Turning Circle
PRINCESS IV SALOON ...	3,993	6	150	10' 1"	5'	16' 9"	6' 1"	43' 6"

Total U.K. Prices

PRINCESS SALOON	..	..	..	..	..	£3,376	7s.	0d.
PRINCESS LIMOUSINE		..	..	..	..	£3,541	7s.	0d.
PRINCESS LWB LIMOUSINE			..	..	..	£3,226	7s.	0d.
PRINCESS LWB SALOON	..		..	..	..	£3,226	7s.	0d.

Riley

**Riley Motors, Ltd.
(Nuffield Organisation),
Abingdon-on-Thames,
Berkshire.**

● *2·6-LITRE: 100 m.p.h., 2·6-litre
6-cyl. push-rod o.h.v. engine with
twin S.U. carbs. 4-speed synchromesh gearbox with right hand
control. Overdrive optional. Fully
automatic gearbox optional. Torsion
bar i.f.s., semi-elliptic rear springs.
4-door, 4/5-seater saloon.

THE Pathfinder is superseded by the Riley 2·6-litre model
which departs from Riley custom in recent years by being
equipped with a 6-cylinder power unit. In outward appearance
there is little change—the distinctive slightly pointed Riley radiator
is retained with its vertical grille and blue diamond-shaped nameplate. The dummy water filler cap which was a feature of the
Pathfinder is omitted. The 2·6 is slightly higher than its predecessor.
The engine is the B.M.C. " C " type, specially adapted with twin
S.U. carburettors. A conventional 4-speed gearbox may be equipped
with Borg-Warner overdrive, or the Borg-Warner automatic
transmission may be fitted at extra cost.

Riley 2·6-litre

Specifications

Model	c.c.	No. of Cyls.	Max B.H.P.	Wheel Base	Max. Track	Length	Width	Turning Circle
2·6-LITRE ...	2,639	6	101	9′ 5½″	4′ 6½″	15′ 5½″	5′ 7″	37½′

Total U.K. Price

2.6-LITRE   ..   ..   £1,411   7s.   0d.

Rolls - Royce

Rolls-Royce, Ltd.

(Motor Car Division),

4-15 Conduit Street,

London, W.1.

- SILVER CLOUD: 100 m.p.h., 6-cyl., 4·9-litre engine. Twin S.U. carbs. Automatic gearbox. Servo assisted brakes. Fitted heater and ventilator system. Power steering and refrigeration optional extras. 5/6-seater, 4-door saloon or long wheelbase model.*

- SILVER WRAITH: 100 m.p.h., 6-cyl. 4·9-litre engine. Automatic gearbox. Servo assisted brakes. Fitted heater and ventilator system. Power steering and refrigeration unit. Various coach built and saloon bodies.

THE Silver Cloud and Silver Wraith Rolls-Royce models are continued unchanged for 1958 and a new long wheelbase version of the Silver Cloud is added to the range. This is a car designed for the business executive. There is an electrically operated division between the front and rear compartments so that the business man may shut himself off from the chauffeur if he wishes to carry on a private conversation or work in the rear compartment as he drives from one appointment to another. The main specifications are the same as the Silver Cloud—6-cylinder 100 m.p.h. engine with twin carburettors, 4-speed automatic gearbox, independent front suspension with ride control, centralised chassis lubrication, and power steering as an extra. The Silver Wraith is available with a variety of saloon and limousine bodies by such famous coachbuilding firms as Hooper, Park Ward and Mulliner. A distinguished car easily recognisable by its traditional Rolls-Royce radiator and the well-known Goddess mascot.

43

*Rolls-Royce
Silver Cloud*

*Rolls-Royce
Silver Wraith*

44

Specifications

Model	c.c.	No. of Cyls.	Max. B.H.P.	Wheel Base	Max. Track	Length	Width	Turning Circle
SILVER CLOUD	4,887	6	—	10′ 3″	5′	17′ 8″	6′ 2¾″	41′ 8″
SILVER CLOUD L.W.B. ...	4,887	6	—	10′ 7″	5′	17′ 11¾″	6′ 2¾″	41′ 8″
SILVER WRAITH (Chassis)	4,887	6	—	11′ 1″	5′ 4″	18′ 2″	6′ 5″	45′ 6″

Total U.K. Prices

SILVER CLOUD SALOON	£5,693 17s. 0d.
SILVER CLOUD LWB	£6,893 17s. 0d.
JAMES YOUNG SALOON	£7,516 7s. 0d.
HOOPER SALOON	£7,628 17s. 0d.
HOOPER LIMOUSINE	£7,928 17s. 0d.
MULLINER DROPHEAD COUPÉ	£8,326 7s. 0d.
SILVER WRAITH PARK WARD TOURING SALOON	£8,243 17s. 0d.
PARK WARD TOURING LIMOUSINE	£8,318 17s. 0d.
PARK WARD ENCLOSED LIMOUSINE	£8,708 17s. 0d.
MULLINER TOURING LIMOUSINE	£8,438 17s. 0d.
MULLINER SEVEN-PASSENGER LIMOUSINE ..	£8,731 7s. 0d.
HOOPER SALOON	£8,371 7s. 0d.
HOOPER TOURING LIMOUSINE	£8,446 7s. 0d.
HOOPER SEVEN-PASSENGER LIMOUSINE	£8,708 17s. 0d.
JAMES YOUNG TOURING LIMOUSINE	£8,521 7s. 0d.

Long Wheelbase
Rolls-Royce
Silver Cloud

The luxuriously
upholstered rear
seating of the
Silver Cloud

Rover

Rover Co., Ltd.,

Solihull,

Birmingham.

- " 60 ": 4-cyl., 2-litre engine. Overhead inlet and side exhaust valves. 4-speed synchromesh gearbox with central control. Freewheel. Overdrive optional. 4/5-seater, 4-door saloon.
- " 75 ": 6-cyl., 2¼-litre engine of similar design.
- " 90 ": 6-cyl., 2½-litre engine of similar design.
- " 105S ": 100 m.p.h., 6-cyl., 2½-litre high performance engine with twin carbs. 4-speed synchromesh gearbox with overdrive.
- " 105R ": 100 m.p.h., 6-cyl., 2½-litre engine with high performance engine with twin carbs. Automatic transmission. De luxe model available.

THERE are no changes in the Rover range for 1958, although new colours are introduced this year, including a two-colour " Duotone " model. The 4-cylinder " 60 " has a 2-litre engine and normal 4-speed synchromesh transmission with the well-known Rover free-wheel system. (This is omitted when overdrive is fitted.) The " 75 " has a 6-cylinder 2¼-litre engine and the " 90 " a 6-cylinder 2½-litre engine. The latter has servo-assisted brakes and optional overdrive, but is not available with the freewheel system.

The two high performance models introduced last year—the 105S and the 105R—are continued. These both have the 6-cylinder 2½-litre engine with twin carburettors and a top speed of over 100 m.p.h. The 105S has a synchromesh gearbox and overdrive as standard equipment. Bucket type front seats, an extra on other Rovers, are standard on this model. The 105R has fully automatic transmission designed and manufactured by the Rover Company.

All the Rover models are similar in appearance. Recognition features are the square radiator with its vertical grille, the wide sloping bonnet, and the jutting boot. The Rover badge is a Norseman's sailing boat and the wheel hub plates carry a black spade design.

Rover " 105S "

Specifications

Model	c.c.	No. of Cyls.	Max. B.H.P.	Wheel Base	Max. Track	Length	Width	Turning Circle
" 60 "	1,997	4	60	9′ 3″	4′ 4″	14′ 10¼″	5′ 5⅝″	37′
" 75 "	2,230	6	80	9′ 3″	4′ 4″	14′ 10¼″	5′ 5⅝″	37′
" 90 "	2,638	6	93	9′ 3″	4′ 4″	14′ 10¼″	5′ 5⅝″	37′
105S & 105R ...	2,638	6	105	9′ 3″	4′ 4″	14′ 10¼″	5′ 5⅝″	37′

Total U.K. Prices

" 60 " Saloon	£1,325 17s. 0d.
" 75 " Saloon	£1,445 17s. 0d.
" 90 " Saloon	£1,499 17s. 0d.
" 105S " Saloon	£1,633 7s. 0d.
" 105R " Saloon	£1,687 7s. 0d.
" 105R " Saloon De Luxe	£1,733 17s. 0d.

Singer

**Singer Motors, Ltd.
(Rootes Group),
Birmingham.**

- GAZELLE: 80 m.p.h., 4-cyl., 1½-litre
  o.h.v. engine. 4-speed synchromesh
  gearbox with steering column control. Overdrive optional. Coil
  spring i.f.s. 4-door saloon, 2-door
  convertible, and estate car.*

T HE Rootes Group Singer Gazelle is offered for 1958 with
overdrive on third and top gears as an optional extra and the
Gazelle estate car is introduced this year to join the saloon
and the convertible models. Two-tone colour schemes are also
new this year, and there are other minor changes in external detail.
The engine is the 4-cylinder 1½-litre overhead camshaft unit originally used on the short lived Hunter. The fuel tank capacity has
been increased from 7¼ gallons to 10 gallons. A bench style front
seat is now fitted with enlarged arm rests. Tubeless tyres are
fitted as standard. The radiator grille is heart-shaped, with vertical
bars, and is flanked by two small horizontal grilles. The smart
interior fittings include walnut door panels and a walnut instrument panel. The new 4-door estate car will carry four adults and a
400 lb. load ; with the rear seat folded down the load capacity is
increased to 700 lb.

Specifications

Model	c.c.	No. of Cyls.	Max. B.H.P.	Wheel Base	Max. Track	Length	Width	Turning Circle
GAZELLE ...	1,496	4	52·5	8'	4' 1"	13' 7½"	5' 0¾"	34' 3"

Total U.K. Prices

GAZELLE SALOON	..	..	..	..	..	£898 7s. 0d.
GAZELLE CONVERTIBLE	..	..	..	..	£998 17s. 0d.
GAZELLE ESTATE CAR	..	..	..	..	£1,043 17s. 0d.

Singer Gazelle Estate Car

Singer Gazelle Saloon

Sunbeam

**Sunbeam Talbot Ltd.,
(Rootes Group),
Ryton-on-Dunsmore,
Coventry.**

- RAPIER: 90 m.p.h., 4-cyl., 1·4-litre o.h.v. engine with twin Zenith carbs. 4-speed synchromesh gearbox with steering column control. Overdrive standard. Coil spring i.f.s. 2-door, 4-seater hardtop saloon.

THE Rapier is the only representative of the Sunbeam range being produced for 1958—the famous 2½ litre Mark III saloon having been discontinued. There are no changes in the Rapier model which was first introduced two years ago and is rapidly establishing itself as a popular sports tourer with a fairly high top speed and a touring fuel consumption of about 30 m.p.g. The engine is a special edition of the Rootes 1,390 c.c. 4-cylinder unit with twin carburettors. Overdrive is standard equipment. The 2-door body has a wide radiator grille of horizontal chromium bars, and the Rapier—unlike the Mark III—is of unitary construction. The wheels are of chromium disc type and the Rapier is available in a wide range of single and dual colour schemes.

Sunbeam Rapier

A Sunbeam Rapier by the side of the Nahe river in Bad Kreuznach, with the town's famous old bridge in the background

Model	c.c.	No. of Cyls.	Max B.H.P.	Wheel Base	Max. Track	Length	Width	Turning Circle
RAPIER... ...	1,390	4	67·5	8'	4' 1"	13' 4"	5'	34' 3"

Total U.K. Price

RAPIER .. .. £1,043 17s. 0d.

Standard

Standard Motor Co.,
Ltd.,
Coventry.

- EIGHT: 60 m.p.h., 4-cyl., 800 c.c. o.h.v. engine. 4-speed synchromesh gearbox with central control. Coil spring and wishbone i.f.s. 4-door, 4-seater saloon.

- TEN: 70 m.p.h., 4-cyl., 950 c.c. " Gold Star " engine. 4-speed synchromesh gearbox with central control. Standrive 2-pedal control optional. Coil spring and wishbone i.f.s. 4-door, 4-seater saloon, and Companion estate car.

- * ENSIGN: 4-cyl., 1·6-litre o.h.v. engine. 4-speed T.R.3 sports type gearbox. 4-door, 4-seater saloon.

- *PENNANT: 4-cyl., 950 c.c. " Gold Star " engine. 4-speed synchromesh gearbox with central control. Standrive 2-pedal control optional. 4-door, 4-seater saloon.

- VANGUARD III: 80 m.p.h., 4-cyl., 2-litre o.h.v. engine. 3-speed synchromesh gearbox. Steering column control. Overdrive optional. 4-door, 5/6-seater saloon or Estate Car.

- SPORTSMAN: 95 m.p.h., 2-litre, 4-cyl. o.h.v. engine. Twin S.U. carbs. 3-speed synchromesh gearbox with overdrive. Coil spring and wishbone i.f.s. 4/5-seater sports saloon.

TWO entirely new Standard models are added to the range for 1958, the Pennant and the Ensign. The Ensign is basically similar to the long-established and popular Vanguard but has a 1,670 c.c. 14-horsepower engine and a 4-speed gearbox with

Standard Ensign Saloon

Standard Vanguard III Saloon de luxe

[Standard Eight Saloon

Standard Pennant Saloon

Standard Sportsman

Standard Vanguard Estate Car

a central gear lever. The radiator grille is the same shape as that of the Vanguard, but is a simple close mesh design. The Pennant is a 10-horsepower model, powered by a new " Gold Star " 950 c.c. engine giving a top speed of about 70 m.p.h. Petrol consumption is claimed to be 42 m.p.g. under normal road driving conditions.

The Vanguard III is continued with improved seating accommodation at the rear, smaller wheels and other minor modifications. The engine is the well tried 2-litre, and the 3-speed gearbox is operated by a shift lever on the steering wheel. The Vanguard is also offered with an attractive estate car body, and the Sportsman high performance sports saloon on the Vanguard chassis is also continued.

The Standard Eight and Ten models are continued with only minor changes. On both models there is a new rear bench seat which folds forward to allow access to the rear luggage boot. The Ten is also produced in estate car form—the Ten Companion.

Specifications

Model	c.c.	No. of Cyls.	Max. B.H.P.	Wheel Base	Max. Track	Length	Width	Turning Circle
EIGHT	803	4	30	7′	4′ 0½″	11′ 10″	4′ 10″	32′
TEN	948	4	37	7′	4′ 0½″	12′ 1″	4′ 10″	32′
PENNANT ...	948	4	37	7′	4′ 0½″	11′ 10″	4′ 10″	32′
ENSIGN ...	1,670	4	60	8′ 6″	4′ 3″	14′ 4″	5′ 7½″	35′
VANGUARD ...	2,088	4	68	8′ 6″	4′ 3″	14′ 4″	5′ 7½″	35′
SPORTSMAN ...	2,088	4	90	8′ 6″	4′ 3″	14′ 4″	5′ 7½″	35′

Total U.K. Prices

STANDARD EIGHT	.. ..	£638 17s. 0d.
STANDARD TEN	.. ..	£653 17s. 0d.
STANDARD PENNANT	.. .. ..	£728 17s. 0d.
STANDARD ENSIGN ..	.. .. ..	£899 17s. 0d.
STANDARD VANGUARD III ..	.. ..	£1,013 17s. 0d.
STANDARD SPORTSMAN	.. ..	£1,231 7s. 0d.
STANDARD III ESTATE CAR	.. ..	£1,148 17s. 0d.
STANDARD TEN COMPANION	.. .. ..	£743 17s. 0d.

Triumph

Triumph Motor Co.
      (1945), Ltd.,
Coventry.

- T.R.3 SPORTS: 100 m.p.h., 4-cyl. 2-litre pushrod o.h.v. engine. Twin carbs. 4-speed synchromesh sports type gearbox, optional overdrive. Central control. Coil spring i.f.s. Disc front brakes. 2-door, 2-seater open sports or hardtop models.

A POPULAR 2-seater sports car with a fine competition record, the Triumph T.R.3 remains the sole product of the Triumph section of Standards, and is continued without change for 1958. It is available in open or hardtop form. The 2-litre 4-cylinder engine is a linered down version of the famous 2-litre Vanguard unit, and top speed is about 110 m.p.h. Stopping power is provided by disc brakes on the front wheels and hydraulic at the rear. Wire wheels may be fitted at extra cost, and overdrive is also an optional extra. The neat square cut radiator with its thick square mesh grille is a good recognition feature.

Specifications

Model	c.c.	No. of Cyls.	Max B.H.P.	Wheel Base	Max. Track	Length	Width	Turning Circle
T.R.3	1,991	4	100	7' 4"	3' 9½"	12' 7"	4' 7½"	34'

Triumph T.R.3 Sports

T.R.3 Sports	..	..	..	..	..	£1,021	7s. 0d.
T.R.3 Hardtop	..	..	..	..	..	£1,073	17s. 0d.

Vauxhall

**Vauxhall Motors, Ltd.,
Luton,
Bedfordshire.**

- *Velox: 80 m.p.h., 6-cyl., 2·3-litre o.h.v. engine with choice of compression ratios. Single Zenith carb., 3-speed synchromesh gearbox with steering column control. Coil spring i.f.s. Semi-elliptic rear springs. 4-door, 5/6-seater saloon.

- *Cresta: Luxury version of Velox with fitted heater, etc.

- *Victor: 4-cyl., 1½-litre o.h.v. engine. 3-speed synchromesh gearbox with steering column control. Coil spring and wishbone i.f.s., semi-elliptic rear springs. 5/6-seater saloon.

A NEW 6-cylinder Vauxhall has now been introduced to join the 4-cylinder Victor in the 1958 range. The names of the two models—the Velox and the Cresta—are retained, but externally the new Sixes are quite different from the " E " type and they have new engines. These are of 2·3-litre capacity, of square design, with a single Zenith carburettor, and a brake horsepower of 82·5 at 4,400 r.p.m. The bonnet of the new Six is rather like that of the Victor, wide and flat, dropping in a sharp curve to the wide meshed radiator grille. Headlamps are hooded, and rear wings are finned on top. Windscreen and rear screen are curved. Brakes are hydraulic, and the gearbox is 3-speed synchromesh with a steering column control. The luxury Cresta is available with a heater as standard equipment and various other refinements.

The 4-cylinder Victor introduced after the last Motor Show is fast becoming as popular as its predecessor, the Wyvern. A tough, easy to handle, 4-door saloon with a lively 1½-litre engine, it is exceptionally roomy inside and has a pleasing appearance. The Grosvenor Estate Car and the Velox Dormobile are continued without change.

Above : *Vauxhall Victor Super*

Left : *Instruments and controls of the Velox and Cresta*

Below : *Vauxhall Cresta*

Specifications

Model	c.c.	No. of Cyls.	Max. B.H.P.	Wheel Base	Max. Track	Length	Width	Turning Circle
VELOX AND CRESTA ...	2,262	6	82·5	8' 9"	4' 6"	14' 9"	5' 8½"	36'
VICTOR ...	1,507	4	—	8' 2"	—	13' 10½"	5' 2"	—

Total U.K. Prices

VICTOR SALOON	..	..	..	..	..	£748	7s.	0d.
VICTOR SUPER SALOON	..	..	..	..	£781	7s.	0d.
VELOX	..	..	..	..	..	..	£983	17s.	0d.
CRESTA	..	..	..	..	..	..	£1,073	17s.	0d.
GROSVENOR ESTATE CAR	..	..	..	..	£1,126	7s.	0d.
VELOX DORMOBILE	..	..	..	..	..	£1,112	17s.	0d.

Wolseley

Wolseley Motors, Ltd.

(Nuffield Organization),

Cowley,

Oxford.

- *1500: 75 m.p.h., 4-cyl., 1½-litre o.h.v. engine. 4-speed synchromesh gearbox. Torsion bar i.f.s. 4-seater, 4-door saloon.
- FIFTEEN-FIFTY: 85 m.p.h., 4-cyl., 1½-litre o.h.v. engine. 4-speed synchromesh gearbox with central control. Coil spring i.f.s. Manumatic clutch optional. 4-door, 4/5-seater saloon.
- SIX-NINETY: 90 m.p.h., 6-cyl., 2½-litre o.h.v. engine. 4-speed synchromesh gearbox. Overdrive or automatic transmission optional. Right hand control. 4-door, 4/5-seater saloon.

THE three Wolseley models for 1958 are the 1500—introduced in April, 1957—the Fifteen-Fifty and the Six-Ninety. The 1500, with the same wheelbase as the ever popular Morris Minor, is powered by the 4-cylinder 1½-litre B-type B.M.C. engine which gives a top speed of over 75 m.p.h. combined with cruising

Wolseley 1500

Wolseley 15/50

fuel consumption of about 36 m.p.g. The traditional Wolseley radiator is retained, and the car has a full width 4-door body. The Fifteen-Fifty also has a 1½-litre engine with a higher output and a top speed of about 85 m.p.h. The 6-cylinder Six-Ninety is offered with either Borg-Warner automatic transmission or overdrive as an optional extra. The Fifteen-Fifty can be fitted with Manumatic clutch operation. The upright Wolseley radiator with its vertical grille and illuminated name plate is quite distinctive.

Specifications

Model	c.c.	No. of Cyls.	Max. B.H.P.	Wheel Base	Max. Track	Length	Width	Turning Circle
1500	1,489	4	50	7′ 2″	4′ 2⅞″	12′ 8½″	5′ 2″	34½′
FIFTEEN-FIFTY	1,489	4	55	8′ 6″	4′ 3″	14′ 5″	5′ 1″	32′
SIX-NINETY ...	2,639	6	97	9′ 5½″	4′ 6½″	15′ 8″	5′ 7″	37½′

Total U.K. Prices

1500 SALOON ..	..	..	..	..	..	£758 17s. 0d.
FIFTEEN-FIFTY	..	..	..	..	..	£991 7s. 0d.
SIX-NINETY ..	..	..	..	..	..	£1,276 7s. 0d.

Other types

A. C.

Built at Thames Ditton, the A.C. is a fine sports car with a growing export market in America. The marque gained second place in the 2-litre class at Le Mans in 1957. The ACE is equipped with either the 2-litre 6-cylinder A.C. engine or the more powerful 2-litre 6-cylinder Bristol engine. The ACECA is a 2-seater coupé version. New this year are disc brakes offered as optional equipment on all A.C. sports models. The 2-litre 6-cylinder saloon is made to special order.

Prices

SALOON £1,663 4s. 1d., ACE £1,651 3s. 0d., ACE-BRISTOL £2,111 17s. 0d., ACECA £2,063 17s. 0d., ACECA-BRISTOL £2,497 14s. 6d.

A.C. Aceca

*Astra

The little Astra utility is made by the British Anzani Engineering Co., Ltd., of Hampton Hill, Middlesex. The 322 c.c. twin cylinder 2-stroke motor cycle engine gives a top speed of about 58 m.p.h. with petrol consumption of 60 m.p.g. The vehicle weighs only 6½ cwt. It is made as a commercial utility or a private 2-seater station wagon.

Prices

COMMERCIAL £347 16s. 0d., STATION WAGON £471 16s. 0d.

Berkeley

First introduced in 1956, the Berkeley is an attractive and inexpensive sports car made by the Berkeley Coachwork Company, of Biggleswade. The standard and de luxe versions of the fibre glass bodied 2-seater sports are powered by a 328 c.c. Excelsior air cooled twin cylinder engine. New this year is a hardtop version powered by a 3-cylinder Excelsior 492 c.c. engine with a top speed of over 70 m.p.h. The Berkeley is a 2-seater, but with room for children in the boot.

Prices

STANDARD £499 18s. 3d., DE LUXE £574 19s. 9d., HARDTOP £573 19s. 10d.

Berkeley Sports

Frazer Nash

A long established firm with a reputation as makers of hand-built sports cars, A.F.N., Ltd., of Isleworth, continue to offer a wide range of models. The Continental for 1958 is available as a Gran Turismo fixed head coupé, a coupé or an open 2-seater. The V.8-cylinder 2½-litre engine gives 140 b.h.p. at 5,000 r.p.m., and there is a 4-speed synchromesh gearbox. A De Dion rear axle is employed. The other Frazer Nash models are the Sebring, the Le Mans Fixed Head and the Targa Florio Gran Sport.

Price

CONTINENTAL MODEL £3,751 7s. 0d.

* Frisky

Made by Henry Meadows, Ltd., of Wolverhampton, the Frisky is the latest addition to the range of British miniature cars. It is available in two forms—the open Friskysport (2-seater plus 1 child) or the Frisky saloon (2 adults and 3 children). The engine is a Villiers 325 c.c. 2-stroke and petrol consumption is 60 m.p.g., while a top speed of about 65 m.p.h. is possible.

Prices

FRISKY SALOON £450, FRISKY SPORT £484.

Jensen

The plastic bodied Jensen 541 saloon is a fast and economical car with fine handling characteristics. The Series R introduced for 1958 has an o.h.v. 6-cylinder 4-litre Austin DS 7 power unit. Overdrive is a standard fitting. The 541 standard and de luxe saloons are retained with the older A.130 4-litre power unit. The standard saloon has hydraulic brakes. The de luxe and Series R models are equipped with disc brakes.

Prices

541 STANDARD £2,153, 541 DE LUXE £2,626, SERIES R £2,866.

Jensen 541

Morgan

Successors to the famous air-cooled three-wheel Morgans of former years, the Morgan range for 1958 consists of two types—the Plus Four and the Four Four. In the Plus Four series there are six models, a 2-seater, a 4-seater and a drophead coupé, each offered with either the Standard 2-litre 4-cylinder Vanguard engine or the 2-litre Triumph T.R.3 engine (which has a greater output and a 100 m.p.h. top speed). In the Series II Four Four Morgan the engine is the 1,172 Ford Anglia with a 3-speed gearbox. Top speed is about 74 m.p.h., and this year a competition version is available with twin S.U. carburettors, an aluminium cylinder head, and a top speed of over 80 m.p.h.

4/4 SERIES II £748 7s. 0d., 4/4 SERIES II COMPETITION £826 7s. 0d., PLUS FOUR 2-Seater (Vanguard) £892 7s. 0d., PLUS FOUR 2-Seater T.R.3 £968 17s. 0d., PLUS FOUR COUPÉ (Vanguard) £962 17s. 0d., PLUS FOUR COUPE (T.R.3) £1,000 17s. 0d., PLUS FOUR 4-Seater (Vanguard) £914 17s. 0d., PLUS-FOUR 4-Seater (T.R.3) £991 7s. 0d.

Morgan two-seater Tourer

* Unicar

Another miniature motor car with a 2-stroke engine, and room for two adults and two children, is the Unicar, built by S. E. Opperman, Ltd., of Boreham Wood, Herts. The 328 c.c. Talisman twin engine gives a top speed of about 60 m.p.h. and 75 m.p.g. The body is made of reinforced fibre glass. There are two doors, and the rear wheels are partly covered.

Price

£399 10s. 0d. (including P.T.).

INTERNATIONAL
IDENTIFICATION LETTERS

WHEN a vehicle is taken abroad it carries an oval plate bearing the official identification mark of the country of origin. For instance, a British vehicle abroad would carry the letters " GB," and a French vehicle in Britain would carry the letter " F." Below you will find a complete list of these international identification letters. The registration letters QA, QB, etc., are issued from London to foreign vehicles temporarily imported and not carrying international identification plates.

Ident. Letters	Country	Ident. Letters	Country
A	Austria	EQ	Ecuador
ADN	Aden	ET	Egypt
AL	Albania		
AUS	Australia, Norfolk Islands	F	France, Algeria, Andorra, Corsica, French Equatorial Africa, French Guinea, French Morocco, French Somaliland, French West Africa, Guadeloupe, Madagascar, Martinique, Reunion, Tunisia
B	Belgium		
BA	Burma		
BG	Bulgaria		
BH	British Honduras		
BL	Basutoland		
BP	Bechuanaland		
BR	Brazil	FL	Liechtenstein
BRG	British Guiana	FM	Federation of Malaya (Johore, Kedah, Kelantan, Malacca, Negri Sembilan, Pehang, Penang, Perak, Perlis, Province Wellesley, Selangor)
BRN	Bahrain		
BS	Bahamas		
C	Cuba		
CA	Canada		
CB	Belgian Congo, Ruanda Urundi		
CH	Switzerland	G	Guatemala
CL	Ceylon	GB	Great Britain and Northern Ireland
CNB	British North Borneo, Labuan		
CO	Columbia	GBA	Alderney
CS	Czechoslovakia	GBG	Guernsey
CU	Curacao (Netherlands Antilles)	GBJ	Jersey
		GBM	Isle of Man
CY	Cyprus	GBY	Malta, Gozo
		GBZ	Gibraltar
D	Germany	GR	Greece, Crete, Dodecanese Islands
DK	Denmark, Faroe Islands		
DOM	Dominican Republic		
		H	Hungary
E	Spain, Balearic Islands, Canary Islands, Spanish Guinea, Spanish Morocco, Spanish Sahara	HK	Hong Kong
		I	Italy, Sardinia, Sicily, Eritrea
		IL	Israel
EAK	Kenya	IN	Indonesia
EAT	Tanganyika	IND	India
EAU	Uganda	IR	Iran (Persia)
EAZ	Zanzibar, Pemba	IRQ	Iraq
EIR	Republic of Ireland	IS	Iceland

Ident. Letters	Country	Ident. Letters	Country
JA	Jamaica, Cayman Islands, Turks and Caicos Islands	S	Sweden
		SD	Swaziland
		SF	Finland
KWT	Kuwait	SGP	Singapore
		SK	Sarawak
L	Luxemburg	SL	Syria
		SM	Siam (Thailand)
MC	Monaco	SME	Surinam
MEX	Mexico	SP	British Somaliland
MS	Mauritius	SR	Southern Rhodesia
MT	Tangier (Zone)	SU	Union of Soviet Socialist Republics
N	Norway	SWA	South West Africa
NGN	Netherlands New Guinea	SY	Seychelles
NIC	Nicaragua		
NL	Netherlands (Holland)	TD	Trinidad and Tobago
NP	Nyasaland	TR	Turkey
NR	Northern Rhodesia		
		U	Uruguay
P	Portugal, Azores, Cape Verde Islands, Madeira, Mozambique, Portuguese Guinea, Portuguese India, Portuguese West Africa (Angola)	USA	United States of America
		V	Vatican City
		WAC	Gold Coast, Ashanti, Northern Territories, British Togoland
PA	Panama		
PAK	Pakistan	WAG	Gambia
PE	Peru	WAL	Sierra Leone
PI	Philippine Islands	WAN	Nigeria, British Cameroons
PL	Poland	WD	Dominica (Windward Islands)
PY	Paraguay	WG	Grenada (Windward Islands)
		WL	St. Lucia (Windward Islands)
R	Roumania	WV	St. Vincent (Windward Islands)
RA	Argentina		
RC	China	YU	Yugoslavia
RCH	Chile		
RH	Haiti	ZA	Union of South Africa
RL	Lebanon		
RSM	San Marino		

BRITISH REGISTRATION LETTERS

THE letters on the number plate tell us by what County or County Borough a vehicle has been registered. It usually indicates the vehicle's first registration, but not always; for sometimes, after a licence has been allowed to lapse for some time, a vehicle is issued with a new number. Each Registration Authority has one or more two-letter index marks, and they are set out below. Most number plates today have three-letter registration marks, but only the last two letters will tell you where the vehicle was registered. For example, the index letters " KLX " indicate that the vehicle was registered by the London County Council (see " LX " in the following list). The first letter is merely to make more combinations of numbers available, but it is interesting to note that the further down the alphabet the first letter, the more lately registered was the vehicle. As these prefix letters are being used up in certain counties (Middlesex C.C. and Staffordshire C.C. being the first), a new system is being used whereby the number is shown first followed by the letter or letters of the licensing authority, e.g. 1076H and so on.

A	London C.C.	BH	Bucks. C.C.
AA	Southampton C.C.	BI	Monaghan C.C.
AB	Worcestershire C.C.	BJ	East Suffolk C.C.
AC	Warwick C.C.	BK	Portsmouth C.B.C.
AD	Gloucestershire C.C.	BL	Berks. C.C.
AE	Bristol C.C.	BM	Bedford C.C.
AF	Cornwall C.C.	BN	Bolton C.B.C.
AG	Ayr C.C.	BO	Cardiff C.B.C.
AH	Norfolk C.C.	BP	West Sussex C.C.
AI	Meath C.C.	BR	Sunderland C.B.C.
AJ	North Riding of York C.C.	BS	Orkney C.C.
AK	Bradford C.B.C.	BT	East Riding of Yorks. C.C.
AL	Nottinghamshire C.C.	BU	Oldham C.B.C.
AM	Wilts. C.C.	BV	Blackburn C.B.C.
AN	West Ham C.B.C.	BW	Oxfordshire C.C.
AO	Cumberland C.C.	BX	Carmarthen C.C.
AP	East Sussex C.C.	BY	Croydon C.B.C.
AR	Hertford C.C.	BZ	Down C.C.
AS	Nairn C.C.		
AT	Kingston-upon-Hull C.B.C.	**C**	West Riding of Yorks. C.C.
AU	Nottingham N.B.C.	CA	Denbigh C.C.
AV	Aberdeenshire C.C.	CB	Blackburn C.B.C.
AW	Salop C.C.	CC	Caernarvon C.C.
AX	Monmouth C.C.	CD	Brighton C.B.C.
AY	Leicestershire C.C.	CE	Cambridge C.C.
AZ	Belfast C.B.C.	CF	West Suffolk C.C.
		CG	Southampton C.C.
B	Lancashire C.C.	CH	Derby C.B.C.
BA	Salford C.B.C.	CI	Laoighis C.C.
BB	Newcastle-upon-Tyne C.B.C.	CJ	Hereford C.C.
		CK	Preston C.B.C.
BC	Leicester C.B.C.	CL	Norwich C.B.C.
BD	Northamptonshire C.C.	CM	Birkenhead C.B.C.
BE	Parts of Lindsey (Lincs.) C.C.	CN	Gateshead C.B.C.
BG	Birkenhead C.B.C.	CO	Plymouth C.B.C.

CP	Halifax C.B.C.		EY	Anglesey C.C.
CR	Southampton C.B.C.		EZ	Belfast C.B.C.
CS	Ayr C.C.			
CT	Parts of Kesteven (Lincs.) C.C.		**F**	Essex C.C.
			FA	Burton-on-Trent C.B.C.
CU	South Shields C.B.C.		FB	Bath C.B.C.
CV	Cornwall C.C.		FC	Oxford C.B.C.
CW	Burnley C.B.C.		FD	Dudley C.B.C.
CX	Huddersfield C.B.C.		FE	Lincoln C.B.C.
CY	Swansea C.B.C.		FF	Merioneth C.C.
CZ	Belfast C.B.C.		FG	Fife C.C.
			FH	Gloucester C.B.C.
D	Kent C.C.		FI	N. Riding of Tipperary C.C.
DA	Wolverhampton C.B.C		FJ	Exeter C.B..C.
DB	Stockport C.B.C.		FK	Worcester C.C.
DC	Middlesbrough C.B.C.		FL	Peterborough, Soke of, C.C.
DD	Gloucestershire C.C.		FM	Chester C.B.C.
DE	Pembroke C.C.		FN	Canterbury C.B.C.
DF	Gloucestershire C.C.		FO	Radnor C.C.
DG	Gloucestershire C.C.		FP	Rutland C.C.
DH	Walsall C.B.C.		FR	Blackpool C.B.C.
DI	Roscommon C.C.		FS	Edinburgh B.C.
DJ	St. Helens C.B.C.		FT	Tynemouth C.B.C.
DK	Rochdale C.B.C.		FU	Parts of Lindsey (Lincs.) C.C.
DL	Isle of Wight C.C.		FV	Blackpool C.B.C.
DM	Flint C.C.		FW	Parts of Lindsey (Lincs.) C.C
DN	York C.B.C.		FX	Dorset C.C.
DO	Parts of Holland (Lincs.) C.C.		FY	Southport B.C.
			FZ	Belfast C.B.C.
DP	Reading C.B.C.			
DR	Plymouth C.B.C.		**G**	Glasgow B.C.
DS	Peebles C.C.		GA	Glasgow B.C.
DT	Doncaster C.B.C.		GB	Glasgow B.C.
DU	Coventry C.B.C.		GC	London C.C.
DV	Devon C.C.		GD	Glasgow B.C.
DW	Newport (Mon.) C.B.C.		GE	Glasgow B.C.
DX	Ipswich C.B.C.		GF	London C.C.
DY	Hastings C.B.C.		GG	Glasgow B.C.
DZ	Antrim C.C.		GH	London C.C.
			GJ	London C.C.
E	Staffordshire C.C.		GK	London C.C.
EA	West Bromwich C.B.C.		GL	Bath C.B.C.
EB	Isle of Ely C.C.		GM	Motherwell & Wishaw B.C
EC	Westmorland C.C.		GN	London C.C.
ED	Warrington C.B.C.		GO	London C.C.
EE	Grimsby C.B.C.		GP	London C.C.
EF	West Hartlepool C.B.C.		GR	Sunderland C.B.C.
EG	Peterborough, Soke of, C.C.		GS	Perth C.C.
EH	Stoke-on-Trent C.B.C.		GT	London C.C.
EI	Sligo C.C.		GU	London C.C.
EJ	Cardigan C.C.		GV	West Suffolk C.C.
EK	Wigan C.B.C.		GW	London C.C.
EL	Bournemouth C.B.C.		GX	London C.C.
EM	Bootle C.B.C.		GY	London C.C.
EN	Bury C.B.C.		GZ	Belfast C.B.C.
EO	Barrow-in-Furness C.B.C.			
EP	Montgomery C.C.		**H**	Middlesex C.C.
ER	Cambridge C.C.		HA	Smethwick C.B.C.
ES	Perth C.C.		HB	Merthyr Tydfil C.B.C.
ET	Rotherham C.B.C.		HC	Eastbourne C.B.C.
EU	Breconshire C.C.		HD	Dewsbury C.B.C.
EV	Essex C.C.		HE	Barnsley C.B.C.
EW	Huntingdon C.C.		HF	Wallasey C.B.C.
EX	Great Yarmouth C.B.C.		HG	Burnley.C.B.C.
			HH	Carlisle C.BC.

HI	S. Riding of Tipperary C.C.	JY	Plymouth C.B.C.
HJ	Southend-on-Sea C.B.C.	JZ	Down C.C.
HK	Essex C.C.		
HL	Wakefield C.B.C.	**K**	Liverpool C B.C.
HM	East Ham C.B.C.	KA	Liverpool C.B.C.
HN	Darlington C.B.C.	KB	Liverpoo C.B.C.
HO	Southampton C.C.	KC	Liverpool C.B.C.
HP	Coventry C.B.C.	KD	Liverpool C.B.C.
HR	Wilts. C.C.	KE	Kent C.C.
HS	Renfrew C.C.	KF	Liverpool C.B.C.
HT	Bristol C.B.C.	KG	Cardiff C.B.C.
HU	Bristol C.B.C.	KH	Kingston-upon-Hull C.B.C
HV	East Ham C.B.C.	KI	Waterford C.C.
HW	Bristol C.B.C.	KJ	Kent C.C.
HX	Middlesex C.C.	KK	Kent C.C.
HY	Bristol C.B.C.	KL	Kent C.C.
HZ	Tyrone C.C.	KM	Kent C.C.
		KN	Kent C.C.
IA	Antrim C.C.	KO	Kent C.C.
IB	Armagh C.C.	KP	Kent C.C.
IC	Carlow C.C.	KR	Kent C.C.
ID	Cavan C.C.	KS	Roxburgh C.C.
IE	Clare C.C.	KT	Kent C.C.
IF	Cork C.C.	KU	Bradford C.B.C.
IH	Donegal C.C.	KV	Coventry C.B.C.
IJ	Down C.C.	KW	Bradford C.B.C.
IK	Dublin C.C.	KX	Bucks. C.C.
IL	Fermanagh C.C.	KY	Bradford C.B.C.
IM	Galway C.C.	KZ	Antrim C.C.
IN	Kerry C.C.		
IO	Kildare C.C.	**L**	Glamorgan C.C.
IP	Kilkenny C.C.	LA	London C.C.
IR	Offaly C.C.	LB	London C.C.
IT	Leitrim C.C.	LC	London C.C.
IU	Limerick C.C.	LD	London C.C.
IW	Londonderry C.C.	LE	London C.C.
IX	Longford C.C.	LF	London C.C.
IY	Louth C.C.	LG	Cheshire C.C.
IZ	Mayo C.C.	LH	London C.C.
		LI	Westmeath C.C.
J	Durham C.C.	LJ	Bournemouth C.B.C.
JA	Stockport C.B.C.	LK	London C.C.
JB	Berks. C.C.	LL	London C.C.
JC	Caernarvon C.C.	LM	London C.C.
JD	West Ham C.B.C.	LN	London C.C.
JE	Isle of Ely C.C.	LO	London C.C.
JF	Leicester C.B.C.	LP	London C.C.
JG	Canterbury C.B.C.	LR	London C.C.
JH	Hertford C.C.	LS	Selkirk C.C.
JI	Tyrone C.C.	LT	London C.C.
JJ	London C.C.	LU	London C.C.
JK	Eastbourne C.B.C.	LV	Liverpool C.B.C.
JL	Parts of Holland (Lincs.) C.C.	LW	London C.C.
JM	Westmorland C.C.	LX	London C.C.
JN	Southend C.B.C.	LY	London C.C.
JO	Oxford C.B.C.	LZ	Armagh C.C.
JP	Wigan C.B.C.		
JR	Northumberland C.C.	**M**	Cheshire C.C.
JS	Ross and Cromarty C.C.	MA	Cheshire C.C.
JT	Dorset C.C.	MB	Cheshire C.C.
JU	Leicestershire C.C.	MC	Middlesex C.C.
JV	Grimbsy C.B.C.	MD	Middlesex C.C.
JW	Wolverhampton C.B.C.	ME	Middlesex C.C.
JX	Halifax C.B.C.	MF	Middlesex C.C.
		MG	Middlesex C.C.

MH	Middlesex C.C.		OT	Southampton C.C.
MI	Wexford C.C.		OU	Southampton C.C.
MJ	Bedford C.C.		OV	Birmingham C.B.C.
MK	Middlesex C.C.		OW	Southampton C.B.C.
ML	Middlesex C.C.		OX	Birmingham C.B.C.
MM	Middlesex C.C.		OY	Croydon C.B.C.
MN	Isle of Man		OZ	Belfast C.B.C.
MO	Berks. C.C.			
MP	Middlesex C.C.		**P**	Surrey C.C.
MR	Wilts. C.C.		PA	Surrey C.C.
MS	Stirling C.C.		PB	Surrey C.C.
MT	Middlesex C.C.		PC	Surrey C.C.
MU	Middlesex C.C.		PD	Surrey C.C.
MV	Middlesex C.C.		PE	Surrey C.C.
MW	Wilts. C.C.		PF	Surrey C.C.
MX	Middlesex C.C.		PG	Surrey C.C.
MY	Middlesex C.C.		PH	Surrey C.C.
MZ	Belfast C.B.C.		PI	Cork C.B.C.
			PJ	Surrey C.C.
N	Manchester C.B.C.		PK	Surrey C.C.
NA	Manchester C.B.C.		PL	Surrey C.C.
NB	Manchester C.B.C.		PM	East Sussex C.C.
NC	Manchester C.B.C.		PN	East Sussex C.C.
ND	Manchester C.B.C.		PO	West Sussex C.C.
NE	Manchester C.B.C.			(GPO issued to L.C.C. for
NF	Manchester C.B.C.			G.P.O.)
NG	Norfolk C.C.		PP	Bucks. C.C.
NH	Northampton C.B.C.		PR	Dorset C.C.
NI	Wicklow C.C.		PS	Zetland C.C.
NJ	East Sussex C.C.		PT	Durham C.C.
NK	Hertford C.C.		PU	Essex C.C.
NL	Northumberland C.C.		PV	Ipswich C.B.C.
NM	Bedford C.C.		PW	Norfolk C.C.
NN	Nottinghamshire C.C.		PX	West Sussex C.C.
NO	Essex C.C.		PY	North Riding of Yorks. C.C.
NP	Worcestershire C.C.		PZ	Belfast C.B.C.
NR	Leicestershire C.C.			
NS	Sutherland C.C.		**QA**	London C.C.
NT	Salop C.C.		QB	London C.C.
NU	Derbyshire C.C.		QC	London C.C.
NV	Northamptonshire C.C.		QD	London C.C.
NW	Leeds C.B.C.		QE	London C.C.
NX	Warwick C.C.		QF	London C.C.
NY	Glamorgan C.C.		QG	London C.C.
NZ	Londonderry C.C.		QH	London C.C.
			QJ	London C.C.
O	Birmingham C.B.C.		QK	London C.C.
OA	Birmingham C.B.C.		QL	London C.C.
OB	Birmingham C.B.C.		QM	London C.C.
OC	Birmingham C.B.C.		QN	London C.C.
OD	Devon C.C.		QP	London C.C.
OE	Birmingham C.B.C.		QQ	London C.C.
OF	Birmingham C.B.C.		QS	London C.C.
OG	Birmingham C.B.C.			
OH	Birmingham C.B.C.		**R**	Derbyshire C.C.
OI	Belfast C.B.C.		RA	Derbyshire C.C.
OJ	Birmingham C.B.C.		RB	Derbyshire C.C.
OK	Birmingham C.B.C.		RC	Derby C.B.C.
OL	Birmingham C.B.C.		RD	Reading C.B.C.
OM	Birmingham C.B.C.		RE	Staffordshire C.C.
ON	Birmingham C.B.C.		RF	Staffordshire C.C.
OP	Birmingham C.B.C.		RG	Aberdeen B.C.
OR	Southampton C.C.		RH	Kingston-upon-Hull C.B.C.
OS	Wigtown C.C.		RI	Dublin C.B.C.

RJ	Salford C.B.C.	TR	Southampton C.B.C.
RK	Croydon C.B.C.	TS	Dundee B.C.
RL	Cornwall C.C.	TT	Devon C.C.
RM	Cumberland C.C.	TU	Cheshire C.C.
RN	Preston C.B.C.	TV	Nottingham C.B.C.
RO	Hertford C.C.	TW	Essex C.C.
RP	Northampton C.C.	TX	Glamorgan C.C.
RR	Nottinghamshire C.C.	TY	Northumberland C.C.
RS	Aberdeen B.C.	TZ	Belfast C.B.C.
RT	East Suffolk C.C.		
RU	Bournemouth C.B.C.	**U**	Leeds C.B.C.
RV	Portsmouth C.B.C.	UA	Leeds C.B.C.
RW	Coventry C.B.C.	UB	Leeds C.B.C.
RX	Berks. C.C.	UC	London C.C.
RY	Leicester C.B.C	UD	Oxfordshire C.C.
RZ	Antrim C.C.	UE	Warwick C.C.
		UF	Brighton C.B.C.
S	Edinburgh B.C.	UG	Leeds C.B.C.
SA	Aberdeenshire C.C.	UH	Cardiff C.B.C.
SB	Argyle C.C.	UI	Londonderry C.B.C.
SC	Edinburgh B.C.	UJ	Salop C.C.
SD	Ayr C.C.	UK	Wolverhampton C.B.C.
SE	Banff C.C.	UL	London C.C.
SF	Edinburgh B.C.	UM	Leeds C.B.C.
SG	Edinburgh B.C.	UN	Denbigh C.C.
SH	Berwick C.C.	UO	Devon C.C.
SJ	Bute C.C.	UP	Durham C.C.
SK	Caithness C.C.	UR	Hertford C.C.
SL	Clackmannan C.C.	US	Glasgow B.C.
SM	Dumfries C.C.	UT	Leicestershire C.C.
SN	Dunbarton C.C.	UU	London C.C.
	(USN London C.C.	UV	London C.C.
SO	Moray C.C.	UW	London C.C.
SP	Fife C.C.	UX	Salop C.C.
SR	Angus C.C.	UY	Worcestershire C.C.
SS	East Lothian C.C.	UZ	Belfast C.B.C.
ST	Inverness C.C.		
SU	Kincardine C.C.	**V**	Lanark C.C.
SV	Kinross C.C.	VA	Lanark C.C.
SW	Kirkcudbright C.C.	VB	Croydon C.B.C.
SX	West Lothian C.C.	VC	Coventry C.B.C.
SY	Midlothian C.C.	VD	Lanark C.C.
SZ	Down C.C.	VE	Cambridge C.C.
		VF	Norfolk C.C.
T	Devon C.C.	VG	Norwich C.B.C.
TA	Devon C.C.	VH	Huddersfield C.B.C.
TB	Lancashire C.C.	VJ	Hereford C.C.
TC	Lancashire C.C.	VK	Newcastle-upon-Tyne
TD	Lancashire C.C.		C.B.C.
TE	Lancashire C.C.		
TF	Lancashire C.C.	VL	Lincoln C.B.C.
TG	Glamorgan C.C.	VM	Manchester C.B.C.
TH	Carmarthen C.C.	VN	North Riding of Yorks. C.C.
TI	Limerick C.B.C.	VO	Nottinghamshire C.C.
TJ	Lancashire C.C.	VP	Birmingham C.B.C.
TK	Dorset C.C.	VR	Manchester C.B.C.
TL	Parts of Kesteven (Lincs.)	VS	Greenock P.C.
	C.C.	VT	Stoke-on-Trent C.B.C.
TM	Bedford C.C.	VU	Manchester C.B.C.
TN	Newcastle-upon-Tyne	VV	Northampton C.B.C.
	C.B.C	VW	Essex C.C.
TO	Nottingham C.B.C.	VX	Essex C.C.
TP	Portsmouth C.B.C.	VY	York C.B.C.

W	Sheffield C.B.C.	**Y**	Somerset C.C.
WA	Sheffield C.B.C.	YA	Somerset C.C.
WB	Sheffield C.B.C.	YB	Somerset C.C.
WD	Warwick C.C.	YC	Somerset C.C.
WE	Sheffield C.B.C.	YD	Somerset C.C.
WF	East Riding of Yorks. C.C.	YE	London C.C.
WG	Stirling C.C.	YF	London C.C.
WH	Bolton C.B.C.	YG	West Riding of Yorks. C.C.
WI	Waterford C.B.C.	YH	London C.C.
WJ	Sheffield C.B.C.	YI	Dublin C.B.C.
WK	Coventry C.B.C.	YJ	Dundee B.C.
WL	Oxford C.B.C.	YK	London C.C.
WM	Southport C.B.C.	YL	London C.C.
WN	Swansea C.B.C.	YM	London C.C.
WO	Monmouth C.C.	YN	London C.C.
WP	Worcestershire C.C.	YO	London C.C.
WR	West Riding of Yorks. C.C.	YP	London C.C.
WS	Edinburgh B.C.	YR	London C.C.
WT	West Riding of Yorks. C.C.	YS	Glasgow B.C.
WU	West Riding of Yorks. C.C.	YT	London C.C.
WV	Wilts. C.C.	YU	London C.C.
WW	West Riding of Yorks. C.C.	YV	London C.C.
WX	West Riding of Yorks. C.C.	YW	London C.C.
WY	West Riding of Yorks. C.C.	YX	London C.C.
		YY	London C.C.
X	Northumberland C.C.	**Z**	Dublin C.C.
XA	London C.C.	ZA	Dublin C.B.C.
XB	London C.C.	ZB	Cork C.C.
XC	London C.C.	ZC	Dublin C.B.C.
XD	London C.C.	ZD	Dublin C.B.C.
XE	London C.C.	ZE	Dublin C.C.
XF	London C.C.	ZF	Cork C.B.C.
XG	Middlesbrough C.B.C.	ZH	Dublin C.B.C.
XH	London C.C.	ZI	Dublin C.C.
XI	Belfast C.B.C.	ZJ	Dublin C.B.C.
XJ	Manchester C.B.C.	ZK	Cork C.C.
XK	London C.C.	ZL	Dublin C.B.C.
XL	London C.C.	ZM	Galway C.C.
XM	London C.C.	ZN	Meath C.C.
XN	London C.C.	ZO	Dublin C.C.
XO	London C.C.	ZP	Donegal C.C.
XP	London C.C.	ZR	Wexford C.C.
XR	London C.C.	ZU	City and County of Dublin
XS	Paisley B.C.		Dublin C.B.C.
XT	London C.C.		The Council of any County which adjoins N. Ireland.
XU	London C.C.	ZZ	The Royal Irish Automobile Club, Dublin.
XV	London C.C.		The Automobile Association, Dublin.
XW	London C.C.		
XX	London C.C.		
XY	London C.C.		

The Number Game

H ERE is a game which you can play whenever you see a motor vehicle. The object is to spot registration numbers in numerical order from 1-999. Challenge a friend to a race, and remember that neither of you can claim to have begun until you have spotted a number plate with the number 1. Then go on to 2 and 3, and so on to 999. You can use the pages which follow to keep a record of your progress.

1	38	75	112
2	39	76	113
3	40	77	114
4	41	78	115
5	42	79	116
6	43	80	117
7	44	81	118
8	45	82	119
9	46	83	120
10	47	84	121
11	48	85	122
12	49	86	123
13	50	87	124
14	51	88	125
15	52	89	126
16	53	90	127
17	54	91	128
18	55	92	129
19	56	93	130
20	57	94	131
21	58	95	132
22	59	96	133
23	60	97	134
24	61	98	135
25	62	99	136
26	63	100	137
27	64	101	138
28	65	102	139
29	66	103	140
30	67	104	141
31	68	105	142
32	69	106	143
33	70	107	144
34	71	108	145
35	72	109	146
36	73	110	147
37	74	111	148

149	195	241	287
150	196	242	288
151	197	243	289
152	198	244	290
153	199	245	291
154	200	246	292
155	201	247	293
156	202	248	294
157	203	249	295
158	204	250	296
159	205	251	297
160	206	252	298
161	207	253	299
162	208	254	300
163	209	255	301
164	210	256	302
165	211	257	303
166	212	258	304
167	213	259	305
168	214	260	306
169	215	261	307
170	216	262	308
171	217	263	309
172	218	264	310
173	219	265	311
174	220	266	312
175	221	267	313
176	222	268	314
177	223	269	315
178	224	270	316
179	225	271	317
180	226	272	318
181	227	273	319
182	228	274	320
183	229	275	321
184	230	276	322
185	231	277	323
186	232	278	324
187	233	279	325
188	234	280	326
189	235	281	327
190	236	282	328
191	237	283	329
192	238	284	330
193	239	285	331
194	240	286	332

333	379	425	471
334	380	426	472
335	381	427	473
336	382	428	474
337	383	429	475
338	384	430	476
339	385	431	477
340	386	432	478
341	387	433	479
342	388	434	480
343	389	435	481
344	390	436	482
345	391	437	483
346	392	438	484
347	393	439	485
348	394	440	486
349	395	441	487
350	396	442	488
351	397	443	489
352	398	444	490
353	399	445	491
354	400	446	492
355	401	447	493
356	402	448	494
357	403	449	495
358	404	450	496
359	405	451	497
360	406	452	498
361	407	453	499
362	408	454	500
363	409	455	501
364	410	456	502
365	411	457	503
366	412	458	504
367	413	459	505
368	414	460	506
369	415	461	507
370	416	462	508
371	417	463	509
372	418	464	510
373	419	465	511
374	420	466	512
375	421	467	513
376	422	468	514
377	423	469	515
378	424	470	516

517	563	609	655
518	564	610	656
519	565	611	657
520	566	612	658
521	567	613	659
522	568	614	660
523	569	615	661
524	570	616	662
525	571	617	663
526	572	618	664
527	573	619	665
528	574	620	666
529	575	621	667
530	576	622	668
531	577	623	669
532	578	624	670
533	579	625	671
534	580	626	672
535	581	627	673
536	582	628	674
537	583	629	675
538	584	630	676
539	585	631	677
540	586	632	678
541	587	633	679
542	588	634	680
543	589	635	681
544	590	636	682
545	591	637	683
546	592	638	684
547	593	639	685
548	594	640	686
549	595	641	687
550	596	642	688
551	597	643	689
552	598	644	690
553	599	645	691
554	600	646	692
555	601	647	693
556	602	648	694
557	603	649	695
558	604	650	696
559	605	651	697
560	606	652	698
561	607	653	699
562	608	654	700

701	747	793	839
702	748	794	840
703	749	795	841
704	750	796	842
705	751	797	843
706	752	798	844
707	753	799	845
708	754	800	846
709	755	801	847
710	756	802	848
711	757	803	849
712	758	804	850
713	759	805	851
714	760	806	852
715	761	807	853
716	762	808	854
717	763	809	855
718	764	810	856
719	765	811	857
720	766	812	858
721	767	813	859
722	768	814	860
723	769	815	861
724	770	816	862
725	771	817	863
726	772	818	864
727	773	819	865
728	774	820	866
729	775	821	867
730	776	822	868
731	777	823	869
732	778	824	870
733	779	825	871
734	780	826	872
735	781	827	873
736	782	828	874
737	783	829	875
738	784	830	876
739	785	831	877
740	786	832	878
741	787	833	879
742	788	834	880
743	789	835	881
744	790	836	882
745	791	837	883
746	792	838	884

885	914	943	972
886	915	944	973
887	916	945	974
888	917	946	975
889	918	947	976
890	919	948	977
891	920	949	978
892	921	950	979
893	922	951	980
894	923	952	981
895	924	953	982
896	925	954	983
897	926	955	984
898	927	956	985
899	928	957	986
900	929	958	987
901	930	959	988
902	931	960	989
903	932	961	990
904	933	962	991
905	934	963	992
906	935	964	993
907	936	965	994
908	937	966	995
909	938	967	996
910	939	968	997
911	940	969	998
912	941	970	999
913	942	971	

abc
historic
cars

JOHN LLOYD, A.F.C.

a new addition to the Ian Allan range
of abc books, giving details, specifications
and illustrations of a selection of cars
which have made history through the
ages, including—

- **VETERANS**   1896 — 1904
- **EDWARDIANS**   1907 — 1914
- **VINTAGE**   1919 — 1930
- **POST VINTAGE**   1931 — 1937
- **POST WAR**   1949 — 1956

Over 50 illustrations	**2/6**	64 pages 7½″ × 5½″

another   *Ian Allan*   car   book

abc

SPORTS CARS

Works 'D'-type Jaguars

Albert Douglas

LONDON :

Ian Allan Ltd.

*Out in the country with
the Bristol 405 Saloon*

Contents

Introduction

THE British Motor Industry, now in its sixtieth year, has long recognised the commercial value of the sports car. For over thirty-five years, British manufacturers have produced sporting cars—cars which are fun to drive, not merely transport—and have sold them successfully to enthusiasts at home and abroad. It is extraordinary that for years this country, in spite of its uncertain climate, has made many more open sporting cars than any other country. Even Italy, home of speed and sunshine, confines most of its non-competition sports car designs to enclosed types.

America, land of nearly every climate, has rediscovered the sports car after an interval of many years, and it is to that country that Britain is shipping fast "machinery" in ever-increasing numbers The export of these cars materially assists in the earning of dollar currency so sorely needed for the nations' economy and to maintain our standard of living.

British sports cars cater for every taste and pocket. Currently the smallest is the 322 c.c. Berkeley, with handsome plastic bodywork and twin-cylinder, two-stroke engine. At the other end of the scale are the beautiful Aston Martin and Jaguar models, both with a string of international race and rally successes behind them. In this issue of the *ABC of British Sports Cars* is included the Rover T3 Gas-Turbine car. This fantastic machine could easily be the type of car that the sporting motorist will be driving within the next ten years. The Rover Company are well versed in turbine technology and they can be relied upon to keep Britain to the fore in this new form of motor engineering.

The enthusiasm in these islands for the sporting type of car has played its part in producing such a large number of super drivers. Every week-end throughout the summer months there are racing and speed events all over the country run by hundreds of different motor clubs. Hundreds of young men take part in them, some of whom are destined to reach the top. Stirling Moss, Mike Hawthorn and Peter Collins are examples of top-flight British drivers whose services are sought by the world's leading racing teams.

In the *ABC of British Sports Cars* for 1957 we deal with no less than 28 makes of car, providing salient features, historic and competition background, and, it is hoped, interesting reading.

ALBERT DOUGLAS.

AUSTIN-HEALEY

The Donald Healey Motor Co. Ltd., The Cape, Warwick

IN four years the Austin-Healey has become one of the world's most popular sports cars. Using a four-cylinder B.M.C. engine, basically the same as the old Austin A90, the production costs were kept to a reasonable level, yet the car was capable of well over 100 m.p.h., and had an excellent competiton record.

The latest Austin-Healey adheres to the same principles as the original model. The power-unit is still of 2.6-litres, and is derived from the Austin A90 (currently A95) Westminster saloon. The new engine has six-cylinders and is consequently smoother and more flexible than the unit which it replaces; also it is more powerful in basic form—102 b.h.p. compared with the 90 b.h.p. of the standard four-cylinder engine. The six-cylinder B.M.C. engine is also used in the Morris Isis, and Wolseley 6/90 saloons.

To meet the requests of many potential buyers, particularly from America, the two-seater body has been cleverly redesigned to accommodate two small additional seats behind the main ones. The family man can thus enjoy the thrills of a sports car without having to leave his family behind, or alternatively the car will carry four adults for short journeys. Wheel-base is increased only 2 inches to gain this extra body room.

Basically the Austin-Healey 100-Six, as the new model is called, looks very similar to the earlier machines, but has slightly wider doors, acetate side-screens with sliding panels, and a radiator grille of "crinkly" plated strip (similar to last year's Austins). A modification that will not perhaps be so popular with some enthusiasts is the dropping of the folding windscreen for a fixed type.

A four-speed gearbox with a short "floor" type lever is fitted, and this provides the quick, satisfying gear-changes from which the keen motorist gains so much enjoyment. With the standard four-speed gearbox, the car is geared at 18.9 m.p.h. at 1,000 r.p.m., but a switch-controlled overdrive is available which gears the 100-Six even higher with consequent effortless performance. It operates in third as well as top gear, giving in effect a 5-speed gearbox.

To drive the new model is a most exhilarating experience—good roadholding and good braking, comfortable seats, plus a hundred miles an hour whenever a reasonably straight piece of road presents itself.

Donald Healey, erstwhile racing driver and one-time winner of the Monte Carlo Rally, believes in subjecting his products to plenty of

Austin-Healey 100-six

hard testing. Late in 1956 he took two 100-Sixes to the Bonneville Salt Flats at Utah, U.S.A. to attack records and to see what his new cars would do. One of the cars, which had a streamlined nose, small windscreen, and covered passenger's seat, broke several records, and in doing so covered 1,000 kilometres at over 150 m.p.h. It was unsupercharged.

The other car, which had special aerodynamic bodywork and a supercharged engine (still the B.M.C. "Six"), covered a measured mile at over 203 m.p.h. In this way Donald Healey demonstrated that the basic engine parts, transmission and chassis components can stand up to heavy punishment.

The special competition Austin-Healey with 132 b.h.p. four-cylinder engine and disc-brakes is available for export only.

ALLARD

Allard Motor Co. Ltd., 24-28 Clapham High Street, London S.W.4

A FTER making a variety of models for many years based on large Ford engines, and chassis components, Sidney Allard has introduced a new version of his Palm Beach 2/3 seater with a

Allard Mk. II Palm Beach

choice of Jaguar XK 140 (3½-litre) or Ford Zodiac (2.6-litre) engines. His traditional swing-axle front suspension has disappeared, and in its place is a wishbone layout with laminated torsion bars. Rear suspension is normal "live" axle with hypoid bevels, suspended on coil springs and located by trailing and radius arms.

The idea behind the Palm Beach Mark II is to provide one basic model with a medium-size engine and three-speed gearbox for the buyer who desires a brisk roadster that does not ask for a great deal of gear-changing, or alternatively a sports car of tremendous power and performance with a "quick" four-speed gearbox to extract the utmost from the car.

Both cars have attractive open bodywork with all-weather equipment, and well-finished interior trim. Knock-on wire wheels are fitted and the brake drums on the Mark II have been increased in size to 12 inches diameter to cope with the high performance. A dis-

Allard J.2.R. with Cadillac engine

tinguishing "A" motif is inserted in the mouth of the radiator air-intake.

At one ton, the Zodiac-engined model weighs 1½ cwt. less than the Jaguar-powered car. The Ford engine develops 90 b.h.p. in standard trim whereas the XK140 develops 190 b.h.p. It can be realised that both cars are capable of exceeding 100 m.p.h., the last-named model having a potential of 120 m.p.h. plus.

Made to special order and intended mainly for export is the well-proved J2/R Sports/Racing 2-seater. Even this old favourite has been fitted with the wishbone and laminated torsion bar front suspension (it had swing-axles for a number of years), but it retains its very effective De Dion rear suspension with coil springs, located by trailing and radius arms. A useful feature for the competition motorist on this model is the "quick-change" final-drive. This enables changes of final-drive ratio to be speedily carried out by easily "swapped" spur gears. Ratios are available from 2.8 to 1—5.1 to 1.

Invariably fitted with an American Cadillac V8 engine of some 5½-litres, the J2/R's power to weight ratio is impressive. The engine develops 270 b.h.p. at a mere 4,800 r.p.m. and the car weighs one ton. Normally fitted with a three-speed gearbox, it can be supplied with a fully automatic transmission which makes lightning gear-changes with no assistance from the driver.

The bodywork of the J2/R can be described as functional rather than beautiful. It is fitted with a full-width "touring" windscreen which can be detached for racing. Knock-on wire wheels are fitted and the rear brakes are mounted inboard to reduce unsprung weight to the minimum and so enhance roadholding. Every car in the Allard range has 198 square inches of braking area, so their stopping power should be in keeping with their aptitude for "Go."

ALVIS

Alvis Ltd., Holyhead Road, Coventry

THE old-established house of Alvis now concentrates on one model, the TC108/G, usually known as the "Graber." This is a beautifully styled 3-litre six-cylinder model with two-door coupe coachwork designed by the celebrated Swiss coachbuilder Graber.

Originally the TC108/G was an Alvis TC21/100 (now obsolete) which was fitted with a special body by Graber for exhibition at the Continental motor shows. It was similar in design to the current production car, but had a plain radiator air-intake instead of the handsome facsimile of the traditional Alvis radiator which blends

Alvis T.C. 108G 3-litre Saloon

nto the nose of the latest car. Graber, like many Continental coach-builders, is more than just a bodybuilder; he is also an artist *and* an engineer. So that the car's performance would live up to its new appearance, he included a new, stiffened scuttle section, which, attached to the steel body framework, imparted immense rigidity to the entire chassis structure. This modification played its part in improving roadholding and making the TC108/G a real *Gran Turismo* model.

The original car produced such favourable comment from motoring journalists and the public in general that Alvis Ltd. decided to make available a certain number of replicas which Graber built for them. Those cars had the Alvis radiator grille.

Now it is the sole Alvis model, and the bodywork is built in England by Willowbrooks of Loughborough, who make a very fine job of this unusually handsome car. Although a large machine, it feels quite small from the driving seat, due to the excellent driving

9

position and the pronounced downward slope of the bonnet. The windscreen pillars are slim, and this feature coupled with the large wrap-around rear window makes for first-class visibility.

Performance is in keeping with Alvis tradition and its background of racing successes—over 100 m.p.h. in comparative silence, superb roadholding and braking, and a slick gear-change by a short, central lever. Knock-on wire wheels are standard equipment, and the interior finish of soft hide and polished wood is of the highest quality.

For some time the Company were engaged on the design of a completely new Alvis under the direction of Alec Issigonis, who joined the firm as designer. It was to have been a very advanced machine with stressed-skin (chassisless) design of extreme light weight, powered by a 3-litre V8 engine. Unfortunately the project was abandoned after a great deal of work and experiment as the Company ultimately regarded the production programme as too expensive.

Alvis Ltd. also manufacture radial air-cooled and helicopter engines.

ASTON MARTIN

The David Brown Corporation (Sales) Ltd., 96 Piccadilly London, W.1

FOR four years the famous Aston Martin Company have raced a team of DB3S works cars in all important sports car races with outstanding success. In 1956 they took second place in general classification at Le Mans (also a class win), first, second and third places in the British Empire Trophy race at Oulton Park besides several wins in international races at Silverstone, Aintree and elsewhere.

Aston Martin DB3S with coupe body

Aston Martin DBR1/250

Two new cars are included in the 1957 team, and both are based on the DBR1/250 prototype which was entered in the 1956 Le Mans race where it ran with great regularity until a universal-joint broke after 22-hours. The DBR1/250 had a 2½-litre engine with dry-sump lubrication, and light-alloy cylinder-block, but the new DBR1/300 has a 3-litre engine of similar basic design. Bore and stroke of the new six-cylinder unit is 83 m.m. by 90 m.m. respectively which gives a precise capacity of 2,922 c.c. It develops 250 b.h.p. at 6,300 r.p.m., which is ten more horse-power than the DB3S even though the new engine is still in the initial stages of development.

A new lightweight "space-frame" is used, built up of small diameter chrome-molybdenum steel tubes, unlike the DB3S which uses two large-diameter tubes for its frame. Each of the two cars have different forms of front suspension. One car uses the almost traditional Aston Martin trailing link/torsion bar layout, but the other has a wishbone/torsion bar arrangement. In this way the

Aston Martin DB2/4 Mk. II

The system of interlocking stops on the five-speed gear-box 'gate' of the DBR1/250.

Aston Martin Company try out new schemes under racing conditions and learn many lessons, some of which are ultimately embodied in their production machines.

Rear suspension is by lateral torsion bars and De Dion tube located by Watts linkage—a most effective method first used by James Watt on his steam locomotives over 100 years ago ! The DBR1/300's gearbox is a David Brown production which is made in one unit with the final-drive. It has five forward speeds with the gear running transversely across the casing. The whole unit is mounted at the rear of the car where it is has been instrumental in improving weight distribution and wheelgrip. Its disposition has also resulted in a lower car with reduced frontal area which results in greater speed from a given power-output.

The slim bodywork is of magnesium light-alloy, and its excellent shape contributes to the cars maximum of about 170 m.p.h.

The DB2/4 is made as Saloon, Hard-Top or Drop-head coupe, and like the DB3S it is of 2,922 c.c. Twin overhead camshafts actuate the valves of this 140 b.h.p. engine and two S.U. carburetters are standard equipment. The chassis is a novel one of square-section steel tubing which is formed into an extremely rigid structure. Front suspension is by coil springs and trailing arms, but at the rear a normal "live" axle is located by a parallelogram linkage and sprung coil springs.

The beautiful bodies fitted to these cars are made by Tickfords of Newport Pagnell, Bucks. (part of the David Brown group of companies), and their well-streamlined shapes play no small part in the high maximum speed and surprising fuel economy of the Aston Martin range. All the DB2/4's are capable of over 120 m.p.h., and the luxury of the interior and fittings makes long journeys a pleasure. A four-speed gearbox is fitted in unit with the engine and gear-changes are effected by a short "remote" lever which falls naturally to the driver's left hand (right hand on export models).

Introduced at the 1956 Earls Court Motor Show was a DB2/4 with *Superleggera* (superlight-weight) open two-seater bodywork by the Italian coachbuilder Touring of Milan. It is available to special order, and is a worthy addition to the range.

A.C.

A.C. Cars Ltd., High Street, Thames Ditton, Surrey

RIGHT from the 'twenties when they first introduced cars with sporting attributes, the A.C. Company have always made "good-lookers." Their current Ace and Aceca models have that beauty of line that is usually associated with the Italian school of coachbuilders. The Ace is the open two-seater and the Aceca is a two-seater coupe with two occasional seats behind the main ones which can alternatively be utilised as extra luggage space.

No pretty body ever made a car a good one, however, but the A.C. has a very advanced chassis also. Designed by John Tojeiro (maker of Tojeiro sports/racing cars) it has two massive steel tubes as the main longitudinal members, and independent suspension to all four wheels. Only a very few British cars have this desirable feature which makes for superb roadholding, and handling.

For over thirty years A.C. cars have been propelled by a most advanced 2-litre engine of their own design and construction. The "Light Six" as it is called, has a light-alloy cylinder-block, removable cylinder liners, and a single overhead camshaft. In its latest form it

A.C. Ace

13

LEFT: *The Bristol 2-litre engine installed in the A.C. Ace.*

BELOW: *The A.C. Aceca.*

develops 90 b.h.p. at 4,500 r.p.m. and has most impressive torque (power at low and medium revs.) for a 2-litre engine. This engine is capable of providing either A.C. model with a top speed of over 100 m.p.h., coupled with sweetness of running and great flexibility. In addition to the A.C. "Light Six" engine, both the Ace and Aceca are available at extra cost with the well-proved 2-litre Bristol unit.

This engine develops 120 b.h.p. at 5,750 r.p.m. making the A.C. a 120 m.p.h. plus car. The Bristol does not have the torque figures of the "Light Six", but it has a wonderful ability to rev, and in conjunction with the four-speed Bristol gearbox is a delight to use.

The little factory at Thames Ditton in Surrey is working to capacity to make enough of these fine cars for home use and for export to all parts of the world. The Bristol-engined models are enjoying considerable competition success in the hands of private owners, particularly in the United States.

The Company was founded over fifty years ago, when the initials A.C. stood for Auto Carrier, a small commercial motor tricycle which they then manufactured. Currently the Company manufactures motor invalid carriages, three-wheeled "Petite" economy cars and the famous 2-litre A.C. Saloon, now to special order only.

There have been rumours for some time now of a "new" A.C. with a horizontally-opposed four-cylinder engine. It is said to adhere to the A.C. "size" of 2-litres, but so far no details have been released.

BENTLEY

Bentley Motors (1931) Ltd., 14–15 Conduit Street, London, W.1

THE modern Bentley carries the same badge and classic radiator shape as the roaring, evergreen Bentleys of the 'twenties and early 'thirties. In those days they built up a second to none reputation in sports car racing—their successes among countless others included no less than five wins in the world-famous and gruelling 24-hours race at Le Mans, France.

In 1931 the original Company was bought by Rolls-Royce Ltd., the racing policy was dropped completely, and the new company embarked on a "Silent Sports Car" policy which they have continued to the present day. Every Bentley produced since that date (excluding a handful of new "Vintage-type" cars which were assembled by the new company) has been based on a contemporary Rolls-Royce model.

The first Rolls-Bentley was produced in late 1932 and was based on the 20/25 h.p. Rolls-Royce of the period. It had a 3½-litre six-cylinder engine with overhead valves, and was capable of over 90 m.p.h. in uncanny silence. With their very first car, the new company had lived up to the newly-adopted slogan of "The Silent Sports Car."

Bentley Continental Sports Saloon

By the beginning of World War II, the Bentley had grown to 4¼-litres, and a handful of a new model, the Mark V, had been built with independent front suspension by coil springs and wishbones. The war suspended production of such cars, but when hostilities ceased a new Bentley, the Mark VI, appeared with the independent suspension and a completely new 4¼-litre engine with an unusual type of cylinder-head which employed overhead inlet and side exhaust valves.

Over the intervening years the engine has been stepped-up in size until the latest versions have a capacity of nearly 4.9-litres. All current Bentley models are capable of over 100 m.p.h., but the Continental has a top speed of over 125 m.p.h. This superb car is the high-performance model of the range, and is available with a choice of a two-door Mulliner saloon body or with a drop-head coupe or saloon by Park Ward. All are perfect examples of the coachbuilder's art, and are of extreme aerodynamic efficiency.

For 1957 the power-output has been increased by the adoption of a new cylinder-head with six inlet ports and fitted with twin S.U.

Bentley Continental Drophead Coupe

carburetters. The inlet valves have been enlarged and the compression ratio has been raised to 8 to 1 (from 7.25 to 1). Bentley Motors, in common with Rolls-Royce, never divulge the power-output of their car engines, but it is safe to assess the Bentley Continental unit at over 200 b.h.p.

All current Bentley cars are fitted with a fully-automatic transmission which has been developed from the American Hydramatic gearbox (made under General Motors licence). This ingenious mechanism makes for the most effortless driving, the driver merely having to depress the accelerator. The gearbox then makes lightning gear changes at intervals dependent on the driver's mood, a fully depressed pedal causing the car to accelerate like a racing car, a light pressure resulting in "lazy" changes. An over-riding control on the steering column enables 2nd or 3rd gear to be held-on to if maximum performance is desired. In addition, hard pressure on the accelerator to the full extent of its travel brings into operation a kick-down change into a lower gear for overtaking, or when maximum acceleration is required.

These superb cars with their impeccable finish and "manners," represent the pinnacle of luxury high-speed travel. They are to be found, and coveted, in all parts of the world.

BERKELEY

Berkeley Coachwork Ltd., Hitchin Street, Biggleswade, Herts.

NORMALLY a car with an engine capacity of only 322 c.c. would be classified as an economy type, but the Berkeley, with its British Anzani two-stroke engine, fully deserves its title of sports car. It is a beautifully proportioned two-seater with space behind the seat for small children or extra luggage. The space normally contains the spare wheel but this component can be carried on a special shelf under the dashboard when the occasion arises.

The "chassis" of the Berkeley is an ingenious piece of work, and is in fact the world's first car to employ a system of stressed plastic for the main frame. Designed by Laurence Bond, who was also responsible for the Bond Minicar, Minibyk and 500 c.c. racing car, the Berkeley uses moulded plastic sections for its very handsome bodywork, reinforced by aluminium members. The parent company, Berkeley Caravans Ltd., have had the experience of thousands of plastic-bodied caravans of their own design and construction, so they are fully competent to handle such an unusual project.

The 322 c.c. Berkeley Sports car.

The roadholding and handling of the car is exceptionally good, being definitely of the sports car variety. Stirling Moss, who carried out extensive tests with it on its introduction, was most enthusiastic. The exceptional roadholding for so light a car (it weighs 5½ cwt.) is largely due to the independent suspension on all four wheels. At the front it is by coil springs and wishbones but at the rear coil springs are used in conjunction with swinging half-axles. The hydraulic dampers are incorporated in the suspension units.

The power for this amazing little car is supplied by a 322 c.c. parallel twin-cylinder two-stroke engine which is installed at the front of the

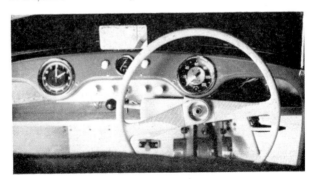

ABOVE:
Front suspension and shaft drive.

RIGHT:
The Anzani twin-cylinder two-stroke engine which drives the front wheels.

FACING PAGE:
Motor cycle gearchange lever is mounted under the steering wheel.

car where it drives the front wheels. It has rotary inlet valves in the crankcase and develops 15 b.h.p. at 5,000 r.p.m., which gives it a top speed of just over 70 m.p.h. The three-speed and reverse gear-box is controlled by a short lever in a motor-cycle type quadrant mounted under the steering wheel where it comes nicely to hand. Final drive to the front wheels is by roller-chain and universally-jointed half-shafts.

So good is the roadholding and handling of the current 322 c.c. model that the manufacturers are expected to offer alternative engines of greater capacity in the near future. A detachable coupe "hard-top" is available at extra charge.

BRISTOL

Bristol Cars Ltd., Filton, Bristol

PART of the great Bristol aircraft and aero-engine manufacturing organisation, it is hardly surprising that the Bristol car is a product of high-quality and high performance. Made for the motoring connoisseur, each one is virtually hand-built, and subjected to innumerable tests before being released to the purchaser.

For several years since the war (Bristol cars have only been made since 1947), the Company took part in a strenuous racing programme to prove and develop their products. This they can safely be said to have done with 2-litre class wins at Le Mans in 1954 and 1955, Rheims in 1953, and with a series of records at Montlhery in 1953. They retired from works-entered racing in 1956, and they currently make one basic model with two available body styles.

A great deal of their racing experience had been built in to their production cars. For instance, the original 2-litre Bristol engine developed 85 b.h.p. installed in the Type 400 saloon. The current Type 405 has an output of 105 b.h.p. from an externally similar engine. Since 1947 there have been types 400, 401, 402, 403, 404, and now 405, as well as the competition Type 450 which was never available to the public.

The Type 405 is available with a choice of two body styles, four-door saloon or two-door convertible. Both have considerable beauty of line and have been the subject of much wind-tunnel research—the legacy of an aircraft and racing background. Due in no small measure to the excellent aerodynamic qualities of the bodies, the cars are capable of returning fuel consumption figures of around 24 m.p.g. at a constant 60 m.p.h.

Both models have a Bristol-manufactured four-speed gearbox with a rigid central gear-lever which makes changing a pleasure. A good gearbox is an essential feature of the Bristol, for it is a "driver's car." That is to say, it has a powerful engine which revels in high revs, and to get the best out of the car, it must be driven with enthusiasm—and that is easy with a Bristol. To complete the pleasure of driving this outstanding car there is a switch-controlled Laycock overdrive which permits high-speed cruising with relatively low engine revs. It also saves wear and tear on the engine and reduces fuel consumption.

The bodies are beautifully finished by craftsmen who apply over twenty coats of cellulose, then polish by hand. The interior trim is of the finest grade hide, and there is every instrument and accessory to appeal to the keenest driver.

Although the Company do not now support racing, they produce a special model primarily for the American market known as the Arnolt-Bristol which has an imposing list of successes in the United States. It is marketed by the Arnolt Corporation, a company which specialises in sports cars and equipment, and whose principal, "Wacky" Arnolt, is himself a racing driver. The Arnolt-Bristol has a special chassis and 130 b.h.p. Bristol 2-litre engine. Body is by Bertone of Turin, Italy. They are supplied with left-hand drive only in open or coupe form.

Bristol engines are still supplied to a great many sports car and "special" builders like Frazer-Nash, A.C., Tojeiro, Lister, Lotus and so on.

BUCKLER

Bucklers, 67 Caversham Road, Reading, Berks.

ORIGINATOR of the "do it yourself" sports car some nine years ago, Derek Buckler now makes a range of several models, all of advanced design, and all capable of a good showing in a variety of competitive events.

Buckler Mk. V

The tubular frame of the Buckler DD2

Hundreds of Bucklers have been constructed, and a formidable list of competition successes has been built-up over the last few years. Performance "recipe" is to provide an ultra-light, rigid chassis frame that will ensure well above average sprightliness, even from an engine of "family" power-output.

The average young motor sporting enthusiast is impecunious, and with him in mind Derek Buckler has made use of a great many Ford suspension and transmission parts. This not only ensures that components are obtainable at reasonable cost, it also means that the potential Buckler constructor will have no difficulty in getting spares from the hundreds of Ford stockists all over the British Isles. In addition the materials used for the components are of the highest quality.

Buckler sports cars are made in several types, but all have a light-weight tubular "space-frame," triangulated in all planes. Front suspension on all models is independent on the swinging "half-axle" principle. This system, designed and manufactured by Buck-lers, consists of a Ford Popular type front axle cut in half, then modified and each half attached to a central pivot point. The axle beams are lightened, and the finished job gives very effective suspension at most reasonable cost. On all models except DDI and DDII (DD stands for De Dion rear suspension) the front suspension has a Ford transverse leaf spring.

Rear suspension is also by Ford transverse leaf spring, and Ford "live" axle. Fitted with a tuned Ford Anglia or Prefect engine of the current series (1,172 c.c.) and with one of the several available bodies (including plastic), the Buckler 2-seater can be made to provide performance comparable to cars costing many times their purchase price. They are economical too. A Buckler has several times put up some noteworthy performances in the International Mobilgas Economy Run. Even with a fully tuned Ford 1,172 c.c.

engine a Buckler will return fuel consumption figures of 35-45 m.p.g.

The DDI and DDII models have the same swinging half-axles for the front suspension but instead of the single transverse leaf spring, a pair of coil spring/damper units are employed. The De Dion rear-end also utilises similar damper units. These cars can be fitted with a choice of 1,100 c.c. or 1,500 c.c. Coventry-Climax, Ford Consul or M.G.A. engines. All give the Buckler a speed in excess of 100 m.p.h., but the 1,500 c.c. Coventry-Climax is capable of propelling it at 130 m.p.h. The Buckler "construction kit" can be assembled by anyone with a reasonable engineering knowledge, and in addition to the necessary parts, Bucklers also manufacture special components to enhance the performance of their own and other products, i.e., close-ratio gears, cylinder-heads, crown wheels and pinions, etc.

COOPER

The Cooper Car Co. Ltd., 243 Ewell Road, Surbiton, Surrey

IN ten years the little Cooper works at Surbiton, Surrey has made over 700 racing cars—more than any other organisation in the world. Father and son, Charles and John Cooper, have between them been right in the thick of the racing game for many years. Cooper Senior was racing mechanic in pre-war days to race and record-man Kaye Don, and John Cooper, besides building racing cars in association with his father, was a very successful racing driver a few years back driving Cooper products varying from 500 c.c. up to two-litres. A background such as this is certain to produce cars of outstanding merit, and Cooper racing and sports/racing machines certainly come into that category.

Cooper-Climax prototype   [GEOFFREY GODDARD

24

Multi-tube chassis frame of Cooper-Climax   [GEOFFREY GODDARD

Although the bulk of Cooper products over the last ten years have
been 500 c.c., single-cylinder-engined racing cars, the Company
have produced several front-engined sports cars with Rover, M.G.,
Bristol and Jaguar engines. Over the last two years, however, they
have built in some quantity a very successful rear-engined sports/
racing machine with 1,100 and 1,500 c.c. Coventry-Climax engine.
Know as the Cooper-Climax, this potent machine has upheld British
prestige in all corners of the Earth, and has formed the basis of the
new Cooper Formula 2 single-seater racing car.

Like the ubiquitous Cooper 500 c.c. racing car, the Cooper-Climax
has its engine at the rear, and also employs a transverse leaf spring
front and rear for the all-independent suspension. The springs are
used in conjunction with single (per wheel) tubular wishbones. The
chassis frame is a simple tubular structure weighing only 65 lb.

Magnesium wheels with an unusual spoke layout are employed.
These "dished" spokes are shaped to promote air turbulence around
the separate brake drums and so provide the necessary cooling.
Fuel tanks are side-mounted, and the radiator is in the nose of the
all-enveloping body. It lifts with the hinged front panelling, rubber
water connections running the entire length of the car.

The Coventry-Climax engine fits snugly between the rear frame tubes,
and the four-speed gearbox is attached at the rear-end of the engine.
A modified Citroen gearbox with French E.R.S.A. gears is usually
fitted, but the Cooper Company is currently experimenting with
several alternatives.

Maximum speed of the 1,100 c.c. model with Coventry-Climax
single overhead camshaft engine is in excess of 130 m.p.h., so the
performance of the new model with 1,500 c.c. twin overhead camshaft engine is awaited with more than usual interest.

DELLOW

Dellow Engineering Co. Ltd., Albert Street, Oldbury, Nr. Birmingham

THE Dellow is a small lightweight sports car originally conceived after World War II by noted trials drivers Delingpole and Lowe. It made a big name for itself in reliability trials in 1949 and 1950, but was gradually superseded as an awards winner in this type of event by the highly specialised machines which hold sway today.

The Company has now changed hands, and production is concentrated on a small range of sports cars which, although based on the original design, are suitable for almost any sporting event, and general motoring and touring.

Dellows are, and always have been, constructed of a great many Ford components. This feature keeps down the price and also makes possible cheap spare parts of high-quality and well-proven reliability.

There are two models, the Mark II and the Mark V. Both have simple but very stiff A-shaped chassis frames with Ford Eight/Ten front and rear axles. The Mark II has a Ford transverse leaf spring

Dellow Mk. II

26

at the front, but the Mark V utilises a pair of coil spring/damper units which materially assists in reducing the frontal height of the car. Coil springs are used at the rear of both cars.

Power-units can be either Ford Eight or Ten in varying degrees of tune, with or without superchargers, or other engines up to 1½-litres to special order. Three-speed Ford gearboxes are fitted when Ford power-units are specified.

The simple but easily maintained bodies can be had with one, two, or with no doors at all. The hand-brake can be mounted inside or outside the bodywork. Full all-weather equipment comes with every Dellow.

ELVA

Elva Engineering Co. Ltd., London Road, Bexhill-on-Sea, Sussex

THIS comparatively new name in sports cars has come very much to the fore in the last year or two. Numerous competition successes have been gained by such well-known drivers as Archie Scott-Brown, "Robbie" Mackenzie-Low, Peter Gammon and "Dizzy" Addicot driving Elva cars, which are becoming increasingly popular in the U.S. and in Canada where their competition score is also high.

The Elva (derived from Elle Va, French for "She Goes") can be bought either in complete form or as a "running chassis." The latter specification means that the buyer has to instal engine, transmission, etc., and generally finish off the car.

The design is delightfully simple, but remarkably effective. Chassis is a space-frame built up of welded steel tubes with a complete Standard Eight front suspension assembly. This front-end consists of a rigid but light steel pressing (which bolts on to the Elva frame) with independent suspension by coil springs and wishbones. It is efficient, light, and readily obtainable. Front brakes are Triumph Mayflower, another product of the Standard Motor Company. Steering is by Elva-produced rack and pinion.

Elva Chief Frank Nichols has made a point of keeping the cost of the car to a minimum by using production components which can easily be obtained. He was himself a racing driver until a couple of seasons back, and is thus well qualified to choose the right components for a competition car.

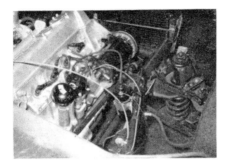

Coventry-Climax engine in the Elva sports car.

A Ford Anglia/Prefect rear axle is used for the Elva and is suspended on coil springs. Both types are interchangeable. Bodywork can be aluminium-panelled or plastic.

Usual power-unit to be found in Elva competition cars is the 1,100 c.c. Coventry-Climax which endows the car with a fantastic performance. It is capable of around 120 m.p.h. with leech-like road-holding properties, and wonderfully sensitive steering. Brakes are first-class, and it is small wonder that many drivers are turning towards this excellent Sussex-built product for the season's racing. A Mark II model is also available with a lighter frame and De Dion rear suspension, which has an even higher performance. Based on

An Elva in action [GEOFFREY GODDARD

the 1956 works racing prototype, the chassis front-end is of welded-up steel tubes, and does not employ the steel pressing of the Mark I model.

Alternative engine is the 1,172 c.c. Ford Anglia/Prefect unit which can be installed either in standard form or with the Elva cylinder-head, yet another Elva product which increases the power-output to over 70 b.h.p.—double that of the standard unit. The Elva head will also fit normal Ford saloons and transforms them into real *Gran Turismo* machines with top speeds around 90 m.p.h.

FRAZER-NASH

A.F.N. Ltd., Falcon Works, London Road, Isleworth, Middx.

THE name Frazer-Nash has meant thoroughbred for practically as long as sports cars have been built. Started by racing driver Archie Frazer-Nash, the Company was acquired by the Aldington Brothers in the mid-twenties, and they really put the marque on the motor sporting map. H. J. Aldington, the present managing director of the firm, became a racing driver of some note and had great success with the early chain-driven cars and the later pre-war Frazer-Nash-B.M.W. machines.

The post-war Frazer-Nash cars have a great deal in common with the immediate pre-war German B.M.W's (which A.F.N. Ltd. marketed in Britain under the name of Frazer-Nash-B.M.W.).

Frazer-Nash Sebring   [GEOFFREY GODDARD

29

Frazer-Nash Le Mans Coupe [GEOFFREY GODDARD

Usual engine to be fitted is the 2-litre Bristol which is of the same basic design as the Type 328 B.M.W. unit. It has an unusual type of cylinder-head which by clever use of long and short pushrods, and bellcrank rockers, enables a hemispherical combustion-chamber to be used without the heavy production expense of the customary twin overhead camshafts.

The engine has been developed a great deal by Bristol's and by Frazer-Nash. The pre-war unit produced 85 b.h.p. but the current version can be had in varying degrees of tune from 100 to 140 b.h.p. Frazer-Nash have notched-up an impressive list of competition successes since the war with Bristol-engined cars, notably a first at Sebring, a third place at Le Mans, two third places in Tourist Trophy races, first in the Silverstone International Production Car race, second in the Jersey Road Race, third in the Prix de Monte Carlo and first in the Sicilian Targa Florio. It will be observed that most of these events are of a long and gruelling nature, ample testimony of Frazer-Nash speed and stamina.

The chassis is a beautifully constructed tubular structure which employs two large diameter tubes as the main longitudinal members. Front suspension is by transverse leaf spring and wishbones. Steering is by rack and pinion.

For the rear suspension the customer has the choice of De Dion or "live" axle both with torsion bars as the springing medium. Wheels can be perforated disc or wire, knock-on or bolt-on and brakes can be of different sizes, in fact the Frazer-Nash is a hand-built thoroughbred that is made to the customer's own ideas and fancies.

They are available with a choice of beautifully made bodies—the Sebring, and Targa Florio Gran Sport open 2-seaters, and the Le Mans fixed-head Coupe. New addition to the range is the Continental open 2-seater which marks the marque's return to an association with the German B.M.W. Company of Munich. It follows the general chassis lines of the Bristol-engined cars but is powered by a B.M.W. V8 of $2\frac{1}{2}$-litres capacity. Although details of power-output have not yet been released, this will be a Frazer-Nash developed engine and it will be surprising if something over 140 b.h.p. is not achieved. The B.M.W. V8 engine is famous for its outstanding torque figures, so the acceleration of the Continental will undoubtedly be exceptional. An unusual feature of the car due to the "snug fit" of the V8 engine in the compact chassis is the lack of an oil dipstick. Instead a neat oil indicator is fitted on the dashboard.

FAIRTHORPE ELECTRON

Fairthorpe Ltd., Market Place, Chalfont St. Peter, Bucks.

MADE by Air-Vice Marshal "Pathfinder" Bennett of World War II fame, the Fairthorpe Electron is a lightweight sporting two-seater with a maximum speed of over 120 m.p.h. It is powered by the wonderful little Coventry-Climax single overhead camshaft engine of only 1,100 c.c., originally designed (and made in great quantity) as a lightweight, portable fire-pump unit.

The Electron is eminently suitable for competition work—racing, rallies, speed trials, hill-climbs, but is equally at home on long-distance tours or on shopping expeditions. Air-Vice Marshal Bennett, a keen racing motorist, has raced the prototype model on several British circuits besides carrying out long-distance trials in the Alps.

Fairthorpe Electron

Although the car has a really high performance, it covers 35 to 45 m.p.g. according to the way in which it is driven.

The chassis frame consists basically of two large diameter steel tubes with tubular cross members. Front suspension is by unequal length wishbones and coil springs in conjunction with hydraulic double-acting dampers. Rear suspension is by coil springs and trailing arms with similar dampers. Steering gear is worm and bevel.

The Electron has high cornering power and can be fairly hurled into fast curves with complete assurance. The four-speed gearbox has a neat remote-control lever which adds to the pleasure of driving it. Body is a neat, but roomy two-door, two-seater made of re-inforced glass-fibre.

Fairthorpe Ltd. also produce an interesting miniature saloon car with four wheels called the Atom. It has two-door plastic body capable of accommodating three adults, or two adults and two children. Comfort and good roadholding are assured by the use of independent suspension to all four wheels by coil springs and double acting dampers. A single steel tube forms the basis of the "back-bone" type frame. The engine is rear-mounted and final-drive is through an Albion three-speed and reverse gearbox.

The Atom is available with a choice of engine types, varying in capacity from 250 to 650 c.c. All are air-cooled motor-cycle types which are produced in great quantity, a fact which enables the Atom to be turned out at a reasonable price and makes spare parts a matter of small expense. The prospective purchaser of an Atom thus has choice from an 11 b.h.p. economy car up to a 40 b.h.p. high-performance machine. All models will return m.p.g. figures in the region of 60 m.p.g. if driven accordingly, and a convertible body is an alternative style.

H.W.M.

H.W. Motors Ltd., New Zealand Avenue, Walton-on-Thames, Surrey

MADE in only very small quantities, the H.W.M. is a pure competition car based on the very successful H.W.M. Formula 2 single-seater racing cars of a few years back. Chassis frame has two large-diameter steel tubes for the main longitudinal members with tubular cross-members, and a further steel tube structure to carry the very handsome two-seater bodywork.

H.W.M. Jaguar [GEOFFREY GODDARD

Front suspension is by coil springs and double wishbones, but the rear suspension is by the well-proven De Dion system. The final-drive unit is rigidly attached to the chassis frame with inboard brake drums mounted close-up to the final-drive casing. This system ensures that unsprung weight is kept to the minimum and makes for fine roadholding.

Several engines have been installed in these cars which are made to special order, but the usual "wear" is a 3½-litre XK Jaguar unit which endows the car with a power to weight ratio of around 320 b.h.p. per ton. Its maximum speed is probably in the region of 160 m.p.h.

Driving force behind the H.W.M. is George Abecassis, himself a well-known racing driver of twenty years experience.

H.R.G.

H.R.G. Engineering Co. Ltd., Oakcroft Road, Tolworth, Surrey

A PRECISION engineering company which yearly turns out a small quantity of high-grade, technically-advanced sports cars, the H.R.G. Company has been making cars of this type for over twenty years. The Managing Director of the firm is H. R. Godfrey who was a partner over forty years ago with "Archie" Frazer-Nash in the design and production of the famous and phenomenally successful G.N. car, first with belt and then with chain-drive.

H.R.G. [GEOFFREY GODDARD

The pre-war and immediately post-war H.R.G.'s had a front axle layout that was similar in many respects to the old G.N., and until the "era" of independent front suspension arrived, it was considered a very good suspension indeed.

When the Company decided to proceed with a new model, they designed one with not only independent front suspension but with "independence" at the rear also. The chassis bristles with novel ideas. It has a very wide transverse leaf spring mounted below the "two-tube" chassis at the front and a similar spring above the chassis at the rear. Used in conjunction with single wishbones this provides a very effective system of "all-independent" suspension. In addition it has the unique arrangement of supplementary suspension to all four wheels by the use of coil spring/damper units (one per wheel) which enables the owner to easily substitute springs of different rates and so "tune" his suspension to suit his needs, e.g., for racing, touring and so on.

The engine is a highly efficient unit based on the four-cylinder 1½-litre Singer, but with an H.R.G.-designed and manufactured cylinder-head. This has twin overhead camshafts and it makes the already powerful Singer unit into a 110-plus b.h.p. engine. Special crankshaft and connecting-rods are also fitted, and the Singer gearbox is specially strengthened to withstand the extra power.

H.R.G.'s are not seen on the road in large numbers as they are made to special order for the super-enthusiast who likes a technically interesting car with well above average performance and is prepared to pay for the privilege. Another unusual feature of the H.R.G. is its disc-brakes which can be relined in the fantastic time of ten minutes per brake. Latest cars have very pretty bodies and can easily be recognised by the unusual "spider" wheels with exposed nuts on the rims and hubs.

JAGUAR

Jaguar Cars Ltd., Coventry

THE progress of this famous company has been phenomenal. Before the war it was registered as S.S. Cars Ltd., and was well-known for its fast and luxurious cars, but not for its racing successes. Late in 1935 Mr. William Lyons (now Sir William), founder and chief of the firm, announced a new model, the Jaguar. It represented wonderful value for money and brought such repute and prestige to the Company that after the war the trading name was changed to Jaguar Cars Ltd.

The immediate post-war Jaguars were practically identical to the pre-war cars, except that the open two-seater Jaguar 100 model was no longer made. While the old-type cars were still being produced, Jaguar's brilliant design team were working on a new engine which was to make such a mark in competition—the $3\frac{1}{2}$-litre twin over-head camshaft XK unit.

It was introduced in 1949 in the beautiful 130 m.p.h. XK120 two-seater. Developing 160 b.h.p. it began a new era in sports car manufacture. In two years the same basic engine in the then new "C"-type sports/racing Jaguar had won the famous French Grand Prix d'Endurance at Le Mans. A "C"-type won it again in 1953, and a "D"-type, still with similar but more highly developed engine, won the race in 1955 and 1956. Over the years the power-output had gone from 160 to more than 250 b.h.p. Besides the 24-hours events at Le Mans Jaguar's won the 12-hour races at Rheims, France in 1953-54-56 (there was no race in 1955), the American 12-hour race at Sebring, the Tourist Trophy Race, International races at Silverstone, and many others. In addition they have won Monte Carlo, Tulip, Liege-Rome-Liege, R.A.C. International, Du Soleil and Lyons-Charbonniere Rallies, not to mention best performance in the Alpine Trial for several years.

The XK120 engine has now become the XK140, and although similar to the older unit, it now develops 190 b.h.p. in standard form, and 210 b.h.p. with special equipment which can be supplied by the Jaguar Company. This extra power has been extracted as a direct result of the lessons learned in a strenuous racing programme.

The same engine in one form or another powers every car in the seven-model range, from the shapely 2.4-litre saloon (with short-ened stroke) to the 190 m.p.h. "D"-type sports/racing machine. Actual sports models are the XK140s with 190 or 210 b.h.p. engines and a choice of open two-seater, drop-head or fixed-head coupe bodywork of great luxury and elegance. The "XK's" are all

Jaguar XK140 open 2-seater

---

capable of over 130 m.p.h. and all are available with four-speed gearbox and overdrive, or with fully-automatic transmission.

The new XK "SS" is an ultra-high speed two-seater at present for export only. It is a luxury version of the D-type with the same engine specification, disc brakes, light-alloy wheels and so on. A neat hood, windscreen, sidescreens and even bumpers are included in the specification, and top speed with the high axle ratio (3.54) is around 170 m.p.h.

In October 1956 the Jaguar Company announced their intention of giving up racing so that their technical staff could concentrate more on the production cars. It is hoped that their withdrawal is merely temporary, and that 1958 will see them back in the classic sports car races with a new design. In the meantime that great Scottish team "Ecurie Ecosse" who won the 1956 Le Mans race carries the Jaguar banner in important races with the assistance of the Company.

Jaguar XK140 2/3 seater

36

JENSEN

Jensen Motors Ltd., West Bromwich

FOR about twenty years the Jensen Company, besides making a technically advanced range of large commercial vehicles, have produced high-performance cars of quality and elegance. They have always championed the use of large engines with exceptional pulling powers in conjunction with high gearing and body shape of aerodynamic efficiency. This policy has resulted in some cars of high maximum speed, but allied with very reasonable fuel consumption and long life.

Jensen Interceptor

Currently two models are produced, the Interceptor and the "541." Both are powered by the 4-litre six-cylinder Austin engine as fitted to the Austin Princess Saloon and Limousine. The Interceptor has the 130 b.h.p. unit with 6.8 to 1 compression ratio, but the "541" is available with this or the 150 b.h.p. version with 7.4 to 1 compression ration. Three horizontal S.U. carburetters are fitted to the more powerful engine, the other one having a single Zenith-Stromberg instrument.

Both models have four-speed gearboxes with remote control and both are available with overdrive, in which case the lower axle ratio is employed. The better-streamlined "541" has less passenger room than the full four-seater Interceptor, and will exceed 120 m.p.h. with the big engine turning over in lazy fashion, assisted by the overdrive.

Dunlop disc brakes fitted to the Jensen 541.

The Interceptor has a conventional metal-panelled saloon or convertible body, but the "541" has beautifully finished plastic coachwork. The latest cars are available with disc brakes—the first production saloon to be so equipped as standard. Another unusual feature of the "541" is its variable radiator air-intake which gives the car such a distinctive appearance. With this fitting the driver is able to dashboard-control the water temperature, also to effect full streamlining for speed bursts.

Both models have the same basic chassis which uses many Austin suspension components, but the larger Interceptor weighs about 4 cwt. more than the "541". Even so they will both average around 25 m.p.g. at high speeds.

LOTUS

Lotus Engineering Co. Ltd., 7 Tottenham Lane, Hornsey, London, N.8

ALTHOUGH this marque has been in existence only a few years it already has a performance and competition record that is second to none. From a starting point of building cars for his own amusement, Lotus-Chief Colin Chapman now has a steady production line of sports and racing cars that are despatched to all parts of the world. Over 300 Lotus cars have been built.

The latest model, the Lotus Eleven is the result of a keen racing programme and intensive development. Many important racing successes have been attained by this model including the winning of the 1,100 c.c. class in the 1956 Le Mans 24-hour race, and a 1st, 2nd and 3rd in the Rouen 1,500 c.c. sports car race, and many others. Mark Eleven's have been successfully raced by such famous drivers as Mike Hawthorn, Ivor Bueb, Ron Flockhart and Harry Schell, to name just a few.

Chapman is managing director of the Lotus Company, chief designer and No. 1 driver in the works racing team. He is an extremely fast driver and has innumerable successes to his credit, and in this way he is able to assess the potentialities of his cars and to develop and improve them.

Currently under the heading of "Series Eleven" there are four basic types, the Le Mans 75, Le Mans 85, Sports and Club. Both the Le Mans models are fitted with the amazing 1,100 c.c. Coventry-Climax engine in different stages of tune, the first-mentioned with 75 b.h.p. at 6,250 r.p.m. and the latter with 83 b.h.p. at 6,800 r.p.m. Both models have disc brakes (inboard at the rear), De Dion rear axle, four-speed gearbox and aerodynamic bodywork which has been evolved after much research and wind-tunnel testing. Even with an engine of only 1,100 c.c. Lotus Eleven is capable of over 130 m.p.h.

Coventry-Climax engine in the Lotus Eleven

39

Lotus Eleven Sports (left) *and Le Mans*

Designer Colin Chapman at the wheel of a Lotus Eleven

Lotus Elevens at Le Mans

The Sports model is a simplified machine for the enthusiast who wants to enter the more impecunious "club" race meetings, and who perhaps cannot afford the higher price of the Le Mans models. The Sports model is powered by a 1,172 c.c. Ford Anglia/Prefect engine which can be brought to a very advanced stage of tune, and can propel this efficiently streamlined machine at well over a hundred miles per hour and with astonishingly low fuel consumption.

It has a Ford rear axle, normal drum brakes, and a Ford three-speed gearbox, but the lucky owner can ultimately convert the car to Le Mans specification if he so wishes, as all the Le Mans components are interchangeable.

The Club model is another "simplified" type, but is powered by the 1,100 c.c. Coventry-Climax engine.

Late in 1956 Chapman introduced his new Lotus Formula 2 single-seater, the first "racing" car to emerge from his little Hornsey works. It is powered by the new 1,500 c.c. Coventry-Climax FPF engine with twin overhead camshafts, and an output of over 140 b.h.p. There is little doubt that the Lotus Eleven will be seen in competition with this promising new power-unit when a sufficient quantity are being produced by the works.

LAGONDA

**The David Brown Corporation (Sales) Ltd.,
Lagonda Division, 96 Piccadilly, London, W.1.**

ALTHOUGH not an "out and out" sports car, the David Brown Lagonda is a genuine high-performance machine with the same engine type as its close relation, the Aston Martin, also a product of the David Brown group. It has a top speed of over a hundred miles per hour and its advanced and unique chassis and engine were designed by none other than W. O. Bentley.

The chassis is of most unusual design and is of the cruciform pattern, i.e., the two main members form the shape of a cross. It is one of the few British cars with independent suspension to all four wheels, and consequently magnificent roadholding is combined with an unusually comfortable ride. The front suspension is orthodox with coil springs and wishbones but the rear suspension is by long torsion bars and swing-axle located each side by two splayed tubular radius arms. The rear brake drums are mounted close up to the final-drive unit, this feature keeping the unsprung weight to a minimum and substantially contributing towards the excellent roadholding.

Unusual X-shaped chassis frame of the 2.9-litre Lagonda

Lagonda 4-door Saloon

The 2.9-litre, six-cylinder engine has twin overhead camshafts and two S.U. carburetters and develops over 140 b.h.p. It is in unit with a David Brown gearbox which is available with "floor" mounted or steering-column gear-change lever. The power is transmitted through a two-piece propellor-shaft to a hypoid bevel rear-axle.

Two elegant bodies are available as standard on the Lagonda, a Drop-head Coupe or Saloon, both of which are built by Tickford of Newport Pagnell, Bucks., a subsidiary of the David Brown Group. It is the saloon model which is run by H.R.H. The Duke of Edinburgh who is a most enthusiastic motorist.

LISTER

Brian Lister (Light Engineering) Ltd., Abbey Road, Cambridge

THE Lister is a product of a subsidiary company of a famous firm of ornamental gate-makers, and engineers, in the old university city of Cambridge. Founded over sixty-five years ago, there are beautiful examples of their intricate gates in and around Cambridge and other historic cities. The same painstaking skill and attention to detail that goes into their age-old craft is lavished on the sports and racing cars that are the products of the smaller company.

Driving force behind the Lister car project is Brian Lister, grandson of the founder of the parent firm. He has been building "specials"

Lister-Maserati

for years, but in 1954 he decided to put the family name into a new branch of engineering. The word engineering is stressed rather than car production as the Lister car is usually sold in "partly assembled form," the customer supplying his own engine and gearbox. In this way the new owner is not liable to pay Purchase Tax as he installs the engine and transmission, and generally finishes the car.

Besides selling his cars, Brian Lister also believes in racing a works machine, for in this way he can try out new ideas and gain valuable advertising from any successes which may be collected. Success certainly has come the way of the works Lister, and the many other cars in the hands of private owners. The official works driver is Archie Scott-Brown who has enjoyed innumerable race wins with M.G., Bristol, and Maserati-engined versions of the marque.

Private owners have installed various types of power-units in their cars, but so far nothing exceeding 2-litres has been used. The 1956 works car had a 2-litre six-cylinder Maserati engine, an Italian unit developing around 170 b.h.p. This car is undoubtedly one of the fastest 2-litres in the country, and with its dry weight of $10\frac{1}{2}$ cwt. has startling acceleration. It measures a mere 27 inches to the top of the scuttle with the driver aboard.

Since 1954 all Lister sports cars have had a very rigid chassis frame consisting of two tubular longitudinal members. There are three tubular cross-members. Front suspension is by wishbones and coil spring/damper units, and rear suspension is by De Dion tube and coil spring/damper units. Girling disc-brakes are employed, outboard at the front and inboard at the rear. Steering is by MG rack and pinion gear.

The shapely body was designed by Brian Lister, and it has a frontal area comparable with many racing cars of much smaller capacity.

Air entries and exhausts have been the subject of much study on the Lister. There are three in the nose which feed the radiator, oil-cooler and front brakes, and two in the scuttle which feed air to the rear brakes, final-drive and carburetters.

Several replicas of the works car are now racing, powered by Bristol and Alta engines. The works car has its engine prepared by Don Moore of Cambridge, a tuner who is rapidly making a name for himself as being unusually proficient in wringing extra power from already potent engines.

MORGAN

Morgan Motor Co. Ltd., Pickersleigh Road, Malvern Link, Worcs.

A PIONEER name in British cars, the first Morgan was marketed in 1912 and was a three-wheeler. Not only did it quickly acquire for itself a name as a first-class cyclecar (as ultra-light cars of the period were known) but it was soon winning races and reliability trials. Although introduced in 1912 the Morgan had many advanced features including independent front suspension by means of coil springs and sliding pillars. The system is still used today on Morgan four-wheelers, in slightly modified form.

Modern Morgans are made in two basic models, the 4/4 Series 2 and the Plus-Four with Standard Vanguard or Triumph TR3 engine. The 4/4 has opened up great possibilities for the enthusiast who requires a real sports car at a reasonable price with unlimited

Morgan Plus Four

45

LEFT: *Instrument panel of the Morgan 4-4.*

BELOW: *Morgan Plus 4 Drophead Coupe.*

LEFT: *Rear suspension of the Morgan Plus 4.*

Morgan 4-4 two seater

tuning potentialities. This neat, nippy car is powered by the ubiquitous 1,172 c.c. Ford "Ten" engine which in completely standard form develops 36 b.h.p. This output in a machine weighing only 13 cwt. dry ensures excellent acceleration and a good maximum coupled with reasonable fuel consumption.

A great deal more power can be wrung from the Ford engine by adding the many accessories and components that can currently be obtained from the many "Speed Shops" that have sprung up to cater for the sporting motorist. In this way the owner can buy a high-performance car at low initial cost and then gradually increase his performance "out of income." Even with a greatly increased power output the Ford-engined Morgan is still a miserly petrol-user.

The 4/4 is available as an open two-seater only, but the Plus-Four comes with two-seater, four-seater or drop-head coupe bodywork. All but the two-seater are available with Vanguard or TR3 engine, and this is powered by the 95 b.h.p. TR3 unit which makes it the least-expensive 100 m.p.h.-plus car obtainable.

All Morgans have a firm, almost Vintage ride, but they are noted for excellent handling and accurate steering. The TR3-engined models are already firm favourites in America where they have enjoyed considerable success in sports car races.

The 4/4 model has a three-speed Ford gearbox in unit with the engine, and an unusual gear lever which protrudes through the scuttle and comes "nicely to hand" under the dashboard. The Plus-Four has a separate four-speed gearbox which is installed some distance from the engine and which permits the use of a short, remote gear-lever in an ideal position near the driver's thigh.

ABOVE: *An M.G.A. racing in the United States.*

LEFT: *Facia panel of the M.G. Magnette.*

BELOW: *M.G.A. Hardtop.*

M.G.

The M.G. Car Co. Ltd., Abingdon-on-Thames, Berks.

ONE of the world's most popular sports cars, the M.G. has a racing record that goes back over twenty five years. Right from the Company's beginnings in the early twenties, M.G. models have been derived from Lord Nuffield's more everyday machines. For example, the original M.G. (Morris Garages) was a modified and tuned Morris Oxford, the "M"-type Midget was a super Morris Minor, the TA Midget was based on the contemporary Morris Ten engine and so on.

Latest of the line, the M.G.A., and the Magnette Saloon both have modified versions of the 1½-litre "B" series engine which are produced by and for the British Motor Corporation. The less potent units are installed in Morris Cowley, Oxford, Wolseley Fifteen-Fifty, Austin A40, A50 and several B.M.C. commercial vehicles and estate cars.

As fitted to the M.G.A. the "B" series engine develops 72 b.h.p. at 5,500 r.p.m. and endows the handsome little two-seater with an extremely lively performance. With the car in absolutely standard form it is possible to attain nearly 100 miles per hour with acceleration to match. It is a delightful car to drive with precise handling, perfect roadholding and a gearbox that is a joy to use. It is no car for ordinary motoring excursions like shopping, etc., (although it performs this task admirably), but a real little thoroughbred which revels in being *driven*. Very high averages can be set up with the M.G.A., but not with any great thirst for fuel.

Another view of the M.G.A. Hardtop showing top being easily detached.

M.G. Magnette

The shapely bodywork which can be had as open two-seater or as hard-top coupe either fixed or detachable has been the subject of much aerodynamic study, and it exerts negligible drag at high speeds. Secret of its incredible roadholding is the massive and rigid box-section steel frame which was developed from the record-breaking "EX 179" which made a series of ultra-high-speed runs at the Bonneville Salt Flats, U.S.A. in 1954. Since those publicity-making runs, a new car has been to the Salt Flats, in September 1956, where it broke sixteen International Class records ranging from 50 kilometres at 148.39 m.p.h. to 12 hours at 141.70 m.p.h., a phenomenal performance for a 1½-litre machine.

Although the chassis frame of the new record-breaker was the same as "EX 179", its engine had a new twin overhead camshaft cylinder-head which develops well over 100 b.h.p. The combustion-chamber and port design is the work of gas-flow expert Harry Weslake who was responsible for similar development work on the sports and racing Jaguars. It is likely that the new cylinder-head will ultimately become optional equipment on production M.G.s.

The Magnette Saloon has a similar engine to the M.G.A. and is eminently suitable for the enthusiast who must have four doors and seats, and greater luggage space than the smaller, more sporting car can offer. It is also an excellent rally car.

THE FRONT COVER *drawing shows Colin Chapman, British racing driver, at the wheel of a Lotus, winning a* Grand Prix *event at Rouen, France.*

ROVER

The Rover Co. Ltd., Meteor Works, Solihull, Warwickshire

ALTHOUGH not strictly speaking a production sports car, the Rover T.3 with gas-turbine power-unit has such an interesting specification, and may well prove to be the sort of car that the sporting motorist of a few years hence will be clamouring to acquire. There can be little doubt that the Rover Company's knowledge of turbine-propelled cars is second to none, and their latest version of a line of "jet-cars" is obviously nearer to a production machine than anything that has yet appeared from any of the world's factories.

The latest machine, the T.3 has the smallest turbine yet of any Rover turbine-car. Based on their highly successful portable industrial unit it produces about 110 horse-power at its maximum of 52,000 r.p.m. Even in its experimental stages the T.3 was lapping the Lindley research track at well over 100 m.p.h. Its fuel consumption figures, due to an efficient surface-type contra-flow heat exchanger, can be compared favourably with a sports car of equal performance. At a steady 80 m.p.h. it can average 12.8 m.p.g. This turbine runs on Diesel oil.

Acceleration is immense, and to gain full advantage of the tremendous engine torque, four-wheel drive is used in conjunction with free-wheels on the front road wheels. This feature ensures good cornering capabilities. The turbine is installed at the rear of the car in what could almost be taken for a luggage boot on a conventional car. A De Dion rear axle is employed.

Rover T.3 Turbine Car

The compact two-door, two-seater *Gran Turismo* type body is of reinforced glass-fibre and is impeccably finished and equipped. Two pedals only, i.e., accelerator and brake are necessary with this advanced car of the future.

SUNBEAM

Sunbeam-Talbot Ltd., Ryton-on-Dunsmore, near Coventry

ALTHOUGH open sports Sunbeams are no longer produced, the current range of Rapier and Mark III saloons are high-performance cars in every sense of the word, and are very popular with rally drivers. They have gained many awards in this type of event and it is to the great credit of the Rootes Group, manufacturers of the Sunbeam, that they entered a team of cars in the gruelling Italian Mille Miglia (Thousand Miles) Race which finished first and second in their class.

Cars used were Rapier saloons, and new modifications have been embodied in the latest models which are a direct result of lessons learned in that race. The 1,390 c.c. four-cylinder engine which is based on the Hillman Minx (produced by the same group) now has twin Zenith downdraught carburetters which has resulted in a power increase to 67 b.h.p. at 5,400 r.p.m. With a dry weight of

Sunbeam Mk. III Sports Saloon

Sunbeam Rapier with famous rally driver Sheila Van Damm

just over one ton, the Rapier has a very brisk performance, and aided by its overdrive will reach approximately 90 m.p.h.

The Mark III with its larger engine of 2,267 c.c. will top 95 m.p.h. Overdrive is an optional extra on this model, and if this is fitted it provides effortless, high-speed cruising on an effective rear axle ratio of 3.28 to 1. The clean, aerodynamic lines of the bodywork substantially contribute to the high speed and economy of running of the Mark III.

Both models are well-finished and beautifully appointed for long-distance motoring in superb comfort and with a minimum of fatigue.

Another Mk. III in Alpine Trials form

TOJEIRO

Tojeiro Automotive Products Ltd.
Middle Garage, Barkway, Nr. Royston, Herts.

FROM a little works in a Hertfordshire village near Cambridge comes a line of competition sports cars built by John Tojeiro. Revered in sports cars circles, the latest cars have multi-tube space frames with independent front suspension by wishbones and coil spring/damper units. Rear suspension also has coil spring/damper units but is non-independent by De Dion axle tube—perhaps the most efficient form of rear suspension for competition machines.

Tojeiro cars are hand-made and are virtually built to the customer's needs. There are two basic models, the large one which will accommodate engines like 3½-litre Jaguar, 2-litre Bristol, etc., and the small one which will take 1,100 c.c.-1,500 c.c. units such as the Coventry-Climax and so on. Both frames are constructed on the same jigs, the smaller diameter steel tubing of the Climax chassis being fitted into reducing collars before the welding takes place.

The frames are welded electrically, as are the wishbones and many other components for the cars. Workmanship is of a very high order, and a high degree of frame rigidity is obtained. Disc or drum brakes can be specified. They are fitted inboard at the rear and outboard at the front.

Tojeiro-Jaguar

Jaguar engine installed in the Tojeiro Sports car.

The Tojeiro-Jaguar works car driven by John Ogier and ex-test pilot Dick Protheroe has had many racing successes in the British Isles. It is a very powerful machine with 3½-litre Jaguar engine and gearbox, and capable of over 160 m.p.h. The engine is a "C" type unit with "D" type cylinder-head and three Italian Weber carburetters, and its power-output is somewhere in the region of 230 b.h.p., with a dry weight of 15 cwt. for the complete car. Chassis frame weight is a mere 96 lb., yet this will resist the torque of a Jaguar engine developing over 200 b.h.p.! The 1,100 c.c. frame weighs 15 lb. less.

Besides the current models, John "Toj," as he is known to racing drivers and personalities, was responsible for the design of the chassis frame of the current A.C. Ace and Aceca. He also has some very interesting ideas on inexpensive high-speed cars which may ultimately go into production.

TURNER

Turner Sports Car (Wolverhampton) Ltd.
Pendeford Airport, Wolverhampton

THE Turner Company are to be congratulated on their praise-worthy efforts in producing a really effective and fast sports car at a reasonable price. It has many other attributes too. The whole design is simple but strong, and many of its components are of Austin manufacture which makes them easily replaced or serviced by any Austin agent. In addition the Turner can be purchased as a complete car, as a chassisless engine and gearbox, or as a chassis frame complete with steering, suspension, and wheels. In this way the car can be bought ready to drive, or it can be built up by degrees.

Basis of the whole car is the Turner-designed and built chassis frame which is built of two 3 inch diameter steel tubes to T.45 specification. It has three cross-members which render it a stiff yet light structure. The two main cross-members extend beyond the width of the longitudinal members where they support the shapely 2/3 seater body which is constructed of steel inner panels and a glass-fibre skin. The cross-members are further strengthened by perforated channel-section steel strips which are welded longitudinally between the extensions.

Turner Sports Car

Front suspension is a complete Austin A30/A35 assembly, as is the rear axle. Unlike the Austin, however, the Turner has its rear axle suspended by trailing arms and transverse laminated torsion bars. Front dampers are built-in to the top wishbones but the rear-end has telescopic dampers which are attached to angled box-section extensions at the rear of the chassis tubes. Hydraulic brakes (two-leading-shoe at the front) are fitted to all four wheels, and rack and pinion steering is standardised. Road wheels are standard Austin A30/35.

Early production models were powered by the Austin A30 engine, but although this is still available, the latest models have the current A35 engine. This is fitted in completely standard form except for twin carburetters and although the output is a modest 34 b.h.p. at 4,750 r.p.m., the Turner has an astonishing fuss-free performance. A maximum speed of 90 m.p.h. is easily attained with over 70 m.p.h. available on the close-ratio third gear. The gear-change is delightful with the latest Austin remote-control lever, and the handling is first-class.

In spite of the Turner's lively performance, it will return 50 m.p.g. if driven in a reasonable manner. It will accelerate to 50 m.p.h. from a standstill in 13 seconds. Anyone desiring to obtain ultra-high performance would find it an easy proposition to fit the many available "Speed shop" accessories to the Austin engine, making it a 100 m.p.h.-plus sports car.

It is hardly surprising that the car has such a high performance and excellent handling when it is realised that Jack Turner, the driving force behind the Turner project, was responsible for the super-charged single-seater Turner, and Formula 2 Turner (2-litre) racing cars, the last-named with fuel-injection. Another of his brain-children was the 500 c.c. four-cylinder Turner Formula 3 racing engine. His co-director is John Webb who was third in the 1951 Manx Cup Race with a Turner.

TRIUMPH

Triumph Motor Co. (1954) Ltd., Coventry

THE Triumph Motor Co. made a sound decision five years ago when they decided to market a 100 m.p.h. sports car based on the engine components of the Standard Vanguard saloon, a pro-duct of the same manufacturing group. Called the TR2, the new car was an immediate success and has since earned thousands of dollars in export orders.

*Interior of the
T.R.3*

The original TR2's developed 90 b.h.p., a step up of 22 b.h.p. on the Vanguard unit in spite of reducing the capacity of the Triumph to bring it into the 2-litre competition class. Latest version of the TR2 is known as the TR3 and this has larger carburetters and higher compression ratio (8.5 to 1) than the older model. Power is now up to 100 b.h.p. at 5,000 r.p.m.—a notably high figure for a "simple" four-cylinder, pushrod o.h.v. engine.

A great deal of development has gone into this willing "punchy" engine. It has leadindium bearings which will withstand merciless driving on track, mountain, or autobahn, yet it will regularly return figures of over 30 m.p.g. under the most arduous conditions.

Nearside view of the Triumph T.R.3

The stiff chassis frame is of box-section construction and is based on the now obsolete Standard Eight. It is admirably suited to the job, and used in conjunction with coil spring and wishbone front suspension, provides excellent roadholding and first-class handling. Rear suspension is by semi-elliptic rear springs and "live" axle. It is a delightful car to drive, with its stubby little gear-lever which is positioned perfectly close to the driver's left or right hand (depending on whether it is a "home" or export model). Acceleration is remarkably good and it is easy to get a hundred on the clock as soon as a reasonable straight presents itself. An overdrive gear is an optional extra, and with this device installed the TR3 becomes a remarkable machine with what is in effect, a seven-speed gearbox as the overdrive can be engaged on all gears except bottom and reverse.

Its cornering powers inspire great confidence, but all this performance would be of little use if the brakes were not powerful enough to control the car in the type of emergency which can occur at high speeds. The Triumph Motor Company have been quick to appreciate the qualities of the Girling hydraulic disc brake, and have become the first quantity-production sports car to adopt it as standard equipment. Fitted to the front wheels only (the rear wheels have hydraulic drum brakes), the braking figures and the brakes' resistance to fade and fatigue are exceptionally good.

The TR3 is a very adaptable car. It can be used successfully for racing, rallying, touring and for motoring to the office. It is available with or without overdrive, knock-on wire wheels, and detachable hard coupe top. A full range of competition equipment including an undershield is available.

SPORTS CAR

Abbreviations: cyls. = cylinders.   m.m. = millimetres.   cpty. = capacity.
compression ratio.   std. = standard.   o.h.v. = overhead valves (pushrod).
s.v. = side-valves.   i.o.e. = inlet over exhaust valves.   t.s. = two-stroke.

| | | ENGINE | | | | | |
	No. of cyls.	Valve layout	Bore in m.m.	Stroke in m.m.	Cpty. in c.c.	b.h.p.	r.p.m
A.C. Ace 2-str. ...	6	o.h.c	65	100	1,991	90	4,500
A.C. Ace (Bristol eng.)	6	o.h.v.	66	96	1,971	120	5,750
Allard J2R 2-str. ...	8	o.h.v.	96.8	92	5,420	270	4,800
Alvis TC 108/G ...	6	o.h.v.	84	90	2,993	104	4,000
Aston Martin DBR1/250 ...	6	2 o.h.c.	83	76.8	2,493	—	—
Aston Martin DB2-4	6	2 o.h.c	83	90	2,922	140	5,000
Austin-Healey 100-Six	6	o.h.v.	79.4	89	2,639	102	4,600
Bentley Continental	6	i.o.e.	95.25	114.3	4,887	—	—
Berkeley	2	t-s	60	57	322	15	5,000
Buckler 90 (Ford eng.)	4	s.v.	63.5	92.5	1,172	36	4,400
Buckler DD1 ... Coventry Climax eng.	4	o.h.c.	72	66	1,098	75	6,250
Bristol 405	6	o.h.v.	66	96	1,971	105	5,000
Cooper-Climax ...	4	o.h.c.	72	66	1,098	83	6,800
Dellow Mark IIC ... (Ford eng.)	4	s.v.	63.5	92.5	1,172	36	4,400
Elva (Coventry-Climax eng.)	4	o.h.c.	72	66	1,098	83	6,800
Frazer-Nash ... Continental 2-str.	6	o.h.v.	66	96	1,971	140	5,750
Frazer-Nash ... (B.M.W. eng.)	8	o.h.v.	72	75	2,430	—	—

A.C. Aceca has coupe body and is available with A.C. (£2,063 17 0) or Bristol engine (£2,378 17 0). **Allard.** Palm Beach models available with Ford Zodiac engine (£1,576 7 0) or Jaguar 3½-litre engine (£1,951 7 0). **Aston Martin.** DB2/4 Mark II d/h Coupe £3,301 7 0. **Bentley Continental.** Also available with Park

60

b.h.p.=brake horse power.   r.p.m.=revs. per minute.   comp. ratio=
2 o.h.c.=two overhead camshafts.   o.h.c.=single overhead camshaft.
d/c=double choke.   Carbs.=carburetters.

		GEARBOX		CHASSIS DETAILS			
Comp. ratio	No. of carbs.	No. of speeds	Std. axle ratio	Chassis type	Dry weight	Fuel cpty.	Price with p. tax
8.0-1	3	4	3.64	Tubular	15 cwt.	13 g.	£1,651 3 0
8.5-1	3	4	3.91	Tubular	16½ cwt.	13 g.	£2,011 7 0
9.0-1	4 d/c	3	To choice	Tubular	19½ cwt.	—	According to specification
8.0-1	2	4	3.77	Box-section	27½ cwt.	14½ g.	£3,451 7 0
9.2-1	3 d/c	5	To choice	Tubular	—	—	Not available to the public
8.2-1	2	4	3.77	Tubular	23½ cwt.	17 g.	£3,076 7 0
8.25-1	2	4 (Plus optional overdrive)	3.91 4.1 with o'drive	Integral	21½ cwt.	12 g.	£1,144 7 0 (overdrive £69 15 ex.)
8.0-1	2	Automatic	2.92	Box-section	31 cwt.	18 g.	£7,606 7 0 Mulliner sln.
8.5-1	1	3	5.27	Plastic and aluminium pressings	5½ cwt.	3½ g.	£574 19 9
7.6-1	2	3	4.7	Tubular	8¾ cwt.	—	On application
8.8-1	2	4	To choice	Tubular	8¾ cwt.	—	On application
8.5-1	3	4 (+ overdrive)	4.22	Box-section	24¼ cwt.	16 g.	£3,586 7 0 Saloon
9.8-1	2	4	To choice	Tubular	8½ cwt.	—	On application
7.6-1	2	3	5.5 or 4.72	Tubular	11½ cwt.	—	£751 7 0 (6-volt lght.)
9.8-1	2	4	To choice	Tubular	8 cwt.	—	On application
9.0-1	3	4	To choice	Tubular	12½ cwt.	15 g.	£3,751 7 0
7.2-1	1 d/c	4	To choice	Tubular	—	17 g.	£3,751 7 0

Ward Sports Saloon or d/h Coupé £7,163 17 0.   **Dellow.** Mark IIE available with
Ford 100E engine and 12 volt lighting, £751 7 0.   **Bristol.** Type 405 available with
Convertible body, £3,676 7 0.   **Jaguar.** Also available as XK140 f/h Coupe,•
£1,711 7 0, and XK140 Convertible, £1,741 7 0.•   **Lotus.** Also available as Le

	ENGINE						
	No. of cyls.	Valve layout	Bore in m.m.	Stroke in m.m.	Cpty. in c.c.	b.h.p.	r.p.m.
Fairthorpe Electron	4	o.h.c.	72	66	1,098	71	6,600
H.W.M. Jaguar ...	6	2 o.h.c.	83	106	3,442	250	6,000
H.R.G.	4	2 o.h.c	73	89.6	1,497	110	5,750
Jaguar XK140-2str.	6	2 o.h.c.	83	106	3,442	190	5,500
Jaguar D-Type ...	6	2 o.h.c.	83	106	3,442	250	6,000
Jensen 541	6	o.h.v	87	111	3,993	130	4,000
Lagonda 3-litre Sln.	6	2 o.h.c.	83	90	2,922	140	5,000
Lister-Bristol ...	6	o.h.v.	66	96	1,971	140	5,750
Lotus Eleven Le Mans	4	o.h.c.	72	66	1,098	83	6,800
Morgan 4/4 Series 2	4	s.v.	63.5	92.5	1,172	36	4,500
Morgan Plus-Four 2-str.	4	o.h.v.	83	92	1,991	90	4,800
M.G.A. 2-str. ...	4	o.h.v.	73.025	89	1,489	68	5,500
Rover T3 ... ... Gas Turbine Engine	—	—	—	—	—	110	52,000
Sunbeam Mk. III Sln.	4	o.h.v.	81	110	2,267	80	4,400
Sunbeam Rapier ...	4	o.h.v.	76.2	76.2	1,390	67	5,400
Tojeiro Jaguar ...	6	2 o.h.c.	83	106	3,442	230	6,000
Triumph TR3 ...	4	o.h.v.	83	92	1,991	100	5,000
Turner (A35 eng.) ...	4	o.h.v.	62.9	76.2	948	34	4,750

Mans 75, £2,080 0 0, Club 2-str., £1,624 0 0, and Sports 2-str., £1,308. **Lagonda** d/h Coupe £3,376 7 0. **Morgan.** Plus-Four models also available with 4-str. and d/h coupe bodywork with Standard Vanguard or Triumph TR3 engines. **M.G.A.**

		GEARBOX			CHASSIS DETAILS			
Comp. ratio	No. of carbs.	No. of speeds	Std. axle ratio	Chassis type	Dry weight	Fuel cpty.	Price with p. tax	
8.8-1	2	4	4.44	Tubular	9¾ cwt.	10 g.	£1,049 17 0 (Mk. II engine 84 b.h.p at 6,800 rpm. £70 extra)	
9.0-1	3 d/c	4	To choice	Tubular	15 cwt.	—	On application	
—	2 d/c	4	To choice	Tubular	—	—	£1,921 7 0	
8.0-1	2	4 (+ optional overdrive)	To choice	Box-section	24 cwt.	14 g.	£1,692 12 0	
9.0-1	3 d/c	4	To choice	Tubular	21 cwt.	37 g.	£3,878 17 0	
6.8-1	3	4 (+overdrive)	3.3	Box-section	26½ cwt.	15 g.	£2,572 7 0	
8.2-1	2	4	4.56	Cruciform	31¾ cwt.	19 g.	£2,993 17 0	
9.0-1	3	4	To choice	Tubular	12 cwt.	—	On application	
9.8-1	2	4	To choice	Tubular	7⅝ cwt.	To choice	£2,155 0 0	
7.0-1	1	3	4.429	Z-section	12¾ cwt.	8 g.	£713 17 0	
8.5-1	2	4	3.73	Z-section	16½ cwt.	11 g.	£893 17 0	
8.3-1	2	4	4.3	Box-section	17½ cwt.	10 g.	£961 7 0	
—	—	Single speed	—	—	—	—	Not available to the public	
7.5-1	1	4 (+ optional overdrive)	3.9	Box-section	26¼ cwt.	10 g.	£1,148 17 0	
8.0-1	2	4 (+overdrive)	5.22	Integral	20¼ cwt.	10 g.	£1,043 17 0	
9.0-1	3 d/c	4	To choice	Tubular	15 cwt.	To choice	On application	
8.5-1	2	4 (+ optional overdrive)	3.7	Box-section	17¾ cwt.	11½ g.	£1,021 7 0	
8.3-1	2	4	4.55	Tubular	10½ cwt.	5 g.	£789 (Hardtop extra)	

with detachable hard-top, £1,035 12 0. Coupe £1,049 17 0. **Triumph TR3** Hard-top, £1,073 17 0.
* Available with automatic gearbox at extra cost.

Something new in road
books

abc

BRITISH ROADS

This is not just another book of maps and routes, but a
concise record of the history and development of British
Roads, their important place in the country's economy,
and of their service to industry. Here is explained in
fascinating detail how the lifelines of Britain serve the
thousands of cities, towns and villages, and how the
problems of overcoming the ever-increasing burden to
our roads is being met with new and faster highways.
Here also is explained the intricate, yet easy-to-follow,
system of road numbering, by which the motorist, motor-
cyclist or cyclist may easily travel the length and breadth
of the country without the aid of maps. Illustrated with
photographs and drawings—an invaluable handbook
for all who use the roads of Britain.

2s. 6d.

published and distributed by

Ian Allan Ltd

contents

abc

British Roads

J. A. Hughes

LONDON

Ian Allan Ltd

introduction

IT is not proposed to discuss, in this book, the many signs used in connection with the "Highway Code". These include signs detailing information regarding level crossings, traffic signals ahead, school, hospital, major road ahead, road narrows, hump bridge, roundabout, dual carriageway, etc. The meaning of these well-known signs is adequately given in the "Highway Code" handbook, and should be familiar to all road users. Nor is it within the scope of this book to advise travellers as to different routes and mileages between various towns. There are innumerable motoring maps and guides with both a general and local appeal, while members of those two great organizations, the A.A. and the R.A.C., are provided with not only first-class service but also excellent handbooks, maps and charts wherein advice is given as to the most desirable routes to use. This is an ABC of roads rather than of motoring.

It is hoped that this book, having attempted a survey of the geography and the history of British roads, as well as a brief explanation of the Ministry of Transport road numbering system, will serve a two-fold purpose: in the first place to aid road users in the understanding of the roads, and the value of being conversant with their numbers, so that their journeys may be undertaken with a greater comprehension, confidence and interest; in the second place to foster an interest in roads themselves, in readers of all ages, that through a new knowledge of British roads, there may be derived a new aspect of knowledge of their homeland.

J. A. H.

roads and their numbers

A CURSORY glance at a road map of Great Britain (England, Wales and Scotland) does not convey to the reader a strong impression of coherent design; rather, the inference is one of a completely arbitrary distribution of hundreds of threads in a tapestry, which, to the uninformed eye, is as formless in its complete aspect as in close detail.

Such an impression is reasonable enough, for the roads of Britain today are the results of many centuries of development. There has been no cohesive attempt to plan a national road system from the time of the Roman occupation down to the present day, although this very fact, and the anachronistic nature of medieval roads in a modern industrial economy, has eventually forced the hands of those in authority.

Industry and trade cannot function efficiently without contemporary methods of communication. On the railways, progress towards greater efficiency (both for the railways themselves and their countless users) is the keynote of the decade. The general tendency is for the pruning of "dead wood", itself a beneficial move for the main body, and development of modern techniques and modern stock, in order to keep pace with industrial and public requirements.

This progressive policy is ultimately finding its counterpart on the roads. The year 1955 heralded the announcement of new plans on a really national scale for new roads, by-passes, and widespread modernization of many existing main roads. At this stage it is not possible to sketch the future road map of Great Britain, but at least it is heartening to know that it will not be precisely the same as today's.

Is there any plan at all in the existing road pattern? This is a question which is justified, and the answer to it may help to teach road-users, and students of British geography, something of the order which exists in the apparent chaos.

Many authorities, notably Government departments, have, for their own various uses, divided Britain into regions, and while these groups of regions rarely coincide from one map to the next, similar distinct geographical regions are nearly always apparent, differing on the various maps concerned, mainly in nomenclature and marginal detail. Thus each "planner" recognizes, for example, a Metropolitan area, the "Black Country", the South Wales industrial area, or the Central lowland rift valley of Scotland as distinct and individual regions.

The nine zones

In complete contrast to this geographical method of regional demarcation, the Ministry of Transport divides Great Britain into nine road zones, the resultant map more closely resembling an old railway map than anything else. The nine zones are bounded by what we may term the nine "primary" roads: A1, A2, A3, A4, A5, A6, A7, A8 and A9, and of course the appropriate section of coastline. The only exception is in North Kent, where the Thames Estuary, and not A2, is the boundary between zones 1 and 2.

Characteristically the two focal centres are the two capitals— London and Edinburgh. It is interesting to note that the routes of A1 to A6 could be confused with some of the main railway lines: A1 with the G.N.R., A2 with the S.E.&C.R., A3 with the L.S.W.R., A4 with the G.W.R., A5 with the L.N.W.R., and A6 with a mixture of the M.R. to Manchester, and the L.N.W.R. northwards. The division of Great Britain into the nine zones is the first important thing to remember, with the two chief centres at London, where A1 to A5 commence (A6 starts at South Mimms, Herts., a few miles beyond north London), and Edinburgh, where A7, A8 and A9 commence. Having become fully familiar with the nine zones, and their boundaries, the road numbering system reveals itself to be methodically constructed, and it will be shown that if the *system* of road numbering is understood, it will go a long way towards facilitating road travel over unfamiliar country.

Every numbered road is so numbered according to its origin; i.e. if it starts in zone 1, its number will always start with the figure 1. This applies to A and B roads. However, many main roads extend beyond their zonal confines, and may in fact end three zones away from their zonal origin. There can be no argument in most cases (apart from very short local roads) as to where a road starts and where it finishes: thus A34 *starts* in Hampshire, near Winchester, and *ends* in Manchester, for A34 is a foreign road in Manchester—its number clearly indicates that it starts in zone 3 which is, roughly speaking, south and south west England.

Careful examination of the "secondary" roads (A10 to A99) and "tertiary" roads (A100 to A999) shows, moreover, a very distinct and systematic pattern which is most marked in England and Wales, but considerably less helpful in Scotland. The "secondary" roads of zone 1 are A10, A11, A12, A13, A14, A15, A16, A17, A18 and A19, and the same rule, of course, applies to all zones, with different "ten" numbers. It will be found that not only do A10 to A19 start in zone 1, as one would expect, but also that as one moves away (i.e. northwards) from London—the "birthplace" of A1—the roads have progressively higher numbers.

In other words A10 should start nearer London than, say, A16. This indeed is the case: A10 starts in the heart of London, while A16 starts at Stamford. A19, on the other hand, will start further north still—at Doncaster. To emphasize this fundamental principle, a list is given of the counties wherein A10 to A19 originate: A10 and A11, central London; A12, north east London; A13, east London; A14, Hertfordshire; A15, Huntingdonshire; A16, Lincolnshire; A17, Nottinghamshire; A18 and A19, Yorkshire— i.e. each road starts further away from London as the numbers increase (this is not always precisely true in London itself).

Zone 2 (south east England) is subject to somewhat modified rules on this point; this is largely due to the nature of the zone itself and the geography of the area. A20 to A24 start from south London like spokes of a wheel, each road starting progressively further away from A2. A25, however, is, in relation to this radial arrangement, a cross country route roughly parallel to the North Downs, while A26 to A29 are orthodox in so far as they start nearest A2 and end furthest away from London.

Zones 3, 4, 5 and 6 follow the main principle very closely, as outlined above for zone 1, while it is of interest to note some remarkable inter-zonal roads, e.g. A34, A38, A43, A45, A46, A47 and A49.

As has been mentioned, the "secondary" roads of Scotland (A70 to A99) do not closely conform to the "progressive" principle, and in their case, one can do no more than refer the reader to the tabulated lists elsewhere in this book.

The basic value of understanding the principles on which the main roads are numbered is considerable. We have shown the fundamental division of Britain into zones, and explained how the "secondary" roads normally start further away from London and/or the "primary" road, as the unit number of the "secondary" road increases from 0 to 9. As an illustration of this let us imagine a motorist wishing to travel from, say, Lancashire to South Wales.

Travelling along A6 southwards through Preston he arrives at a roundabout at Bamber Bridge where he sees, among other roads quoted—"A49 WIGAN". He can then reason as follows: zone 4 comprises the south and west Midlands, south and central Wales, etc., bounded on the south by A4; therefore A49, quoted on this signpost should have started somewhere in the west of zone 4, because 49 is the last of the "secondary" group A40-A49, and should start the furthest away from London; i.e. furthest west. This reasoning is sound, for a glance at the list of roads in zone 4 shows that A49 does, in fact, start at Ross-on-Wye, Herefordshire, whence A40 or A449 lead into various parts of South Wales. Thus by his knowledge of the basic system of road numbering our traveller can cover the distance from mid-Lancashire to Herefordshire and concern himself only with one consideration —namely to follow A49 as far as he requires.

Such assurance is certainly a source of comfort, especially to the less experienced motorist whose concentration is mainly devoted to the competent control of his vehicle, but to all road users it must be beneficial, particularly mentally, not to have to concern themselves at every junction, roundabout and signpost as to whether they ought to turn, and so on. Indeed, hesitancy at such moments can often be disastrous and many accidents have been caused through a driver not being sure whether to turn on to another road or keep straight on, particularly where a right-hand turn is involved. It is safer and simpler to know that the road along which one is travelling is definitely the right one for, perhaps fifty or more miles. Of course it may be required to make a detour to a nearby town, perhaps to avoid a poor surface and so on, in which case the driver can work out his route as required, but over long distances, the advantages of keeping to one road, confident that by so doing one's destination will be reached directly, cannot be denied.

Tertiary roads

The above remarks apply in some respects to the three-figure ("tertiary") A roads. Just as the group in zone 1 from A10 to A19 start progressively further away from London, so do the A100-A199 group in the same zone. Thus the A100-A109 group (A10x) are all to be found in London itself (except for A108, which number is in disuse following the renumbering of the Great Cambridge Road), while A190-A199 (A19x) can be found north of the Tyne and beyond, to the Edinburgh area, where A1 finishes.

Zone 2, as before, is less orthodox, although the lower numbers (A200-A240) are found in London and then the environing districts. In zones 3, 4, 5 and 6 the "progressive" principle again is followed. A traveller from Cumberland to the Northumbrian coast would, in crossing zones 5, 6 and 1 respectively, find roads numbered A59x, A69x and A19x, in that order. As mentioned earlier, a "foreign" road is easily detectable by having a number based in a different zone. A34 looks "out-of-place" in Manchester, as does A46 in Grimsby. However, it is equally possible to detect "foreign" roads within their own zone, e.g. A483, which starts at Swansea, is a stranger at Oswestry, for the A48x roads are local to South West Wales. Another good Welsh example is A525 at Rhyl having started in the Potteries, where most of the A52x group are located.

That the principle explained above may be readily apparent in practice, a table has been prepared to show the general geographical distribution of the three-figure A roads in Britain (see Appendix A). In certain cases, notably in Scotland, a group has been summarized as "various". Reference to the detailed lists of those roads so described will show that it is not possible to ascribe any specific localized area to them. The A29x group in England is another example.

It must be pointed out that some roads are definite exceptions to the normal numbering method. A598, in north London, is one of these, while A555, which was formerly the by-pass route in London from East Finchley to Hatfield, was another. However, A555 has now been renumbered to form part of A1, the original stretch of the Great North Road—extremely unsuitable for the weight of modern trunk traffic—having been "relegated" to A1000. In the normal way, one would expect to find A598 in north Cumberland, and A555 in north Cheshire. These exceptions, however, are very few in number, and are mainly confined to later additions to the general numbering scheme, in London.

Minor roads

Attention has been paid only to the main A class roads of one, two or three figures. In addition to these, there are, of course, very many other numbered roads—A roads with four figures, and B roads which may have three or four figures. These minor roads conform to the rule that their first digit will be that of the zone of origin, but they do *not* conform to the principle that the highest numbers in the zonal group are those furthest from London or Edinburgh. As these minor roads are mainly of entirely local significance, it is not proposed to consider them in detail. In more remote parts of Britain, perhaps, they assume a greater relative importance, in the absence or scarcity of major A roads, as in Anglesey and the Isle of Wight, but broadly speaking they seldom form an integral part of the road-user's journey, if it will be of any length.

signposts and their meanings

STUDY of this book will eventually familiarize the reader with the road-numbering of Great Britain's main roads, so that any excursion he may make which brings him into the vicinity of a road signpost showing numbered roads will afford an opportunity to compare what he has learnt with what he can see. This country is well served for signposts, there being, currently, a replacement and modernization scheme in hand entailing the provision of new, sometimes more elaborate, but always more informative road sign-posts. Readers familiar with central London, in particular, will have noticed the huge boards advertising selected Ring Routes and the appropriate directions to follow in order to gain access to the arterial routes radiating from the Capital. These are specially de-signed to filter the through traffic into selected roads and avoid, as far as possible, the less suitable metropolitan thoroughfares where local private and commercial traffic jeopardizes the safety and ease of flow of through vehicles—especially heavy freight lorries.

The observant reader will have noticed, in London and else-where in Britain, various devices on the road signs. It is necessary to explain the significance of these, as failure to understand the technical meaning of various signs can often mislead the traveller on to a wrong route.

The straightforward sign, for example at a cross-roads, might read as follows: at the top of the board A105 ENFIELD, to the left A406 FINCHLEY, and to the right A406 EDMONTON. Clearly this indicates that a continuation across A406, along A105, takes one on towards (in this case beyond) Enfield, while a right- or left-hand turn takes one off A105 (south-north) on to A406 (east-west) towards Edmonton or Finchley, as the case may be. It is important to note, however, that the places quoted on the road signpost—namely Enfield, Finchley and Edmonton—are not necessarily the "termini" of A105 and A406. In this case illustrated they are *not* the termini, although it is true that A105 leads to Enfield, and that parts of Finchley and Edmonton can be reached by travelling along A406. The detailed list of A roads in this book will give the complete information as to the full length of any main A road.

It is seldom that the ultimate "destination" of a main road is quoted on a signpost which is at any distance from the end of the road concerned. There are two aspects to this point, however. In a huge city such as London, it is often the adjacent or nearby suburb which is quoted on the signpost. The example given above (at Palmers Green, London) illustrates this point. Again, in central London, on the very large road signs previously mentioned, reference is made to A41, as a suitable route to Aylesbury, or perhaps Birmingham. One does not find A41, BIRKENHEAD, advertised in London, although that statement would be correct. This is due to the fact that traffic does not move strictly in accordance with road numbers, and whatever through traffic there may be between London and Birkenhead may not utilize A41 throughout (although as explained earlier, it is possible and safe to adopt such a route). The more significant reason, however, why Birkenhead is not advertised in central London as a direction along A41, is that by far the greatest bulk of traffic using A41 out of London is local or confined to the Home Counties; to cater for the immediate needs and interests of local road users, therefore, a place is indicated which is of real importance to the travellers in that district. Put another way, the average road user moving north along A41 from London is more interested to know that that road leads to Watford or Aylesbury than Birkenhead.

In the provinces, two situations may arise: in the more densely populated regions, such as the west Midlands, Lancashire, Yorkshire, South Wales, Tyneside, Lowland Scotland and so on, the towns are generally close to one another, and it is the proximity of the neighbouring urban areas which is of local commercial significance for road users. Thus, directions on road signposts normally quote neighbouring towns rather than a distant official "terminus" of some trunk road which links two nearby urban centres. In the less developed regions of Great Britain, such as north west Scotland or mid-Wales, a road may traverse many miles of country without entering any town of notable size. In such cases as these, the normal practice is to quote the first "large" town along the road, or, possibly, an even more distant town if the latter is of considerable geographical significance, affording access to other important regions; an example of this is seen in central Wales, where road signposts in the direction of England quote major border towns, such as Shrewsbury or Hereford.

An interesting point which readers can verify for themselves is that in some cases, road signposts deliberately quote information which is not strictly accurate. At Barnet, Hertfordshire, a signpost pointing north west along the original start of A6 indicated "St. Albans, Coventry and the North". It will be seen that A6 does not pass anywhere near Coventry, but this great industrial centre can readily be reached by following the erstwhile A6 to St. Albans, thence via A5 to Weedon, and finally A45 to Coventry itself. Again, in Dumfries a signpost indicated "A76 Glasgow". This will be found to be incorrect, strictly speaking, as A76 ends at Kilmarnock, but it is the normal route for Glasgow-bound traffic from Dumfries, for at Kilmarnock A77 gives a direct route to Glasgow.

Modern road signposts are very accurately designed, and are invaluable at complex road crossings, where perhaps six roads converge. The thick black "stem", which ends in the white rectangle on which road number and town are named, of course represents the road itself, and the length of these black "stems" and the angles at which other "stems" join or cross them are carefully designed to

9

leave no doubt in the traveller's mind as to which line on the sign-post indicates each particular road before him. Sometimes, particularly when it is desired to indicate clearly a through route among a maze of small streets, some strange designs appear, guiding the road user past irrelevant streets to the main route. A typical example of these unusual signs is in the Westbury Avenue area of North London, where through traffic to Cambridgeshire, etc., is cleverly directed through a host of residential streets on to A10 (Great Cambridge Road) via the Roundway.

Many people have been confused by road signposts which quote more than one road number and town in the same direction. In these cases, two practices have normally been adopted. Sometimes the road "on the spot" is quoted at the top of the white rectangle and another road, in the same rectangle, is quoted in parentheses. The significance of this should be clearly understood: the immediate road is indicated at the top of the white rectangle, and the road number in parentheses refers to another road (often a more important one) which can be reached by travelling along the immediate road. Of course when the second road is reached, another signpost will indicate the fact. It may be at a crossroads, or the immediate road may join the other road and end there.

The more usual system, however, is to show two white rectangles, one above the other (pointing in the same direction on the signpost, of course). The two rectangles are joined by a black and white check line. In this case the upper rectangle gives details of the immediate road, while the lower rectangle describes the road which can be reached further along the road quoted above it. The two towns quoted for the two roads concerned would naturally be different, and indeed would probably lie in somewhat different directions, for it would be very unusual to find two different roads from one place both leading to a common point.

This system is clearly of considerable benefit to road users, affording extra information as to the "potential" facilities along one road. In many cases, especially in large towns, the black and white check line carries only one road number and town. A moment's thought will confirm that this must lie *below* the check line, for there would be no value in indicating an immediate road "leading to" (i.e. as stated by the check line)—nowhere. The reverse, equally obviously, is not an unusual sight. The immediate road, especially, as we have said, in large towns, may not be a numbered road, but merely a reasonably wide, well-surfaced street. Its value lies not in itself as a route but because it leads to a main road. This is a valuable asset to strangers in a town who can find their way out without being obliged to keep entirely to the main street.

Nowhere is it more useful than in Preston, where the enormous passenger traffic to and from Blackpool is concentrated before splitting east and south. On the western outskirts of the town, average sized roads are advertised as affording routes to Wigan, Liverpool and the south. Indeed, such pains are taken to distribute traffic to the best advantage that there is one signpost, at least, which points westwards for Liverpool. Odd though this may at first seem, it is entirely justified, as its use obviates travel through the congested centre of Preston, leading Liverpool and southbound traffic round the western and south western outskirts of the town and thence to A59 at Penwortham Bridge.

The technique of advertising other roads which can be easily reached from the one on which one is travelling has been explained. There is, of course, a limit to what can be advertised by such methods. Thus, the "deliberate mistake" at Dumfries regarding "A76 GLASGOW" could not be replaced by the "leading to" check sign. It is necessary to direct Glasgow-bound traffic from Dumfries, and the way in which this has actually been done is certainly the best in that instance. Glasgow is a centre of infinitely greater importance than Kilmarnock, the actual terminus of A76. But to have a signpost in Dumfries (or Maxwelltown) reading "A76 KILMARNOCK" or "THORNHILL", and under it a black and white check line surmounting "A77 GLASGOW", would be extremely unsatisfactory. The motorist conversant with road signposts would expect to come across A77 within a few miles of leaving Dumfries, whereas he has to travel over sixty miles to Kilmarnock before he joins A77. It must be remembered that the "other road" which can be reached is never very far from the signpost on which it is quoted—perhaps a mile or two in rural districts, sometimes a few hundred yards in the towns. Page 45 shows a signpost quoting two "other roads" which are readily accessible from A423. The principle explained above still applies, but it must be noted that A43 is the first road which can be reached off A423, while A421 in turn leads off A43 some distance away.

Considerable confusion can arise where numbered roads run joint over a common stretch. This happens many times, but the list of roads in this book will immediately correct any mistaken impression. It must be said that some road signposts leave something to be desired in certain instances, as a main road is sometimes shown as joining another main road, with no indication that, at a further stage, the two roads concerned split along their different routes. A hurried glance at a map often fails to convey the important fact that the roads split again, particularly when they are joint for several miles, e.g. A40 and A449 between Ross-on-Wye and Raglan (almost twenty miles), A72 and A702 between Abington and Crawford, A1 and A602 between Knebworth and Stevenage, etc.

The boundary sign

In keeping with the characteristically tasteful design and presentation of road signpost information is the boundary sign (page 45). These may or may not quote the road number of the road on which they are placed. The signs are accurately placed at the administrative boundary and often quote two other towns or villages on them, one above and one below the main name of the place about to be entered. After each name there will be a remark such as 3m, 5½m, etc. The significance of this is as follows: the town or village mentioned *below* the main place is X miles behind one; in other words, one is now X miles from the previous place through which one has passed. The place mentioned *above* the main name lies X miles ahead. On these signposts, it is normally the next town or village which is quoted, and very seldom a distant town.

The reader should now be conversant with the system by which the main roads of Great Britain are numbered, the significance of the various groups of numbers, and be able to understand fully the information given on road signposts, wherever he may be. It is necessary to turn now to some discussion of the road map of Great Britain to attempt to follow the pattern of roads in different geographical environments. Reference will be made later to the first important phase of roads in Britain—namely the road map of Roman Britain.

roads through the ages

IT was pointed out earlier that there has been no coherent national plan for roads since the Roman Occupation, virtually 2,000 years ago. When the Romans conquered Britain and established their cities, they clearly realized the paramount importance of adequate communication routes. So thoroughly and effectively did they plan their roads that in the twentieth century many of our roads, including some of the most important, still use the same routes as those followed by Roman traffic, and one may speculate as to the feelings of the Roman road builders if they could return to learn that theirs was the last intelligent attempt at an integrated national road plan.

Leaving Roman Britain for the moment, we find every reason to believe that the roads themselves were allowed to deteriorate through constant usage by the animals which constituted the motive power of the Middle Ages, and the carts and wagons whose wheels carved deep ruts into the rough road surfaces. Ill-protected against the weather, roads often became impassable in times of heavy rain and storm, and the struggling efforts of beasts, vehicles and drivers to free themselves from the quagmires can hardly have left the roads in any better condition when dry weather returned.

Such was the story for many centuries—a population which, with its various localized industrial centres for woollens, iron smelting, coal mining, etc., urgently in need of (for them) modern roads and road surfaces, and yet lacking any national authority with powers to organize the general improvement which was long overdue. No doubt improvements were put into effect at the order of local authorities, perhaps new techniques were discovered for making a superior and longer lasting surface, better proof against the weight of traffic and the elements, but such improvements were almost entirely confined to the parish in which they were executed, and there was no overall authority whose primary concern was with the provision of adequate roads for the country as a whole.

Needless to say, during the medieval period new roads were "constructed" according to the needs created by new and developing centres of population, and it would be as untrue as it would be unfair to our ancestors to suggest that the road map of, say, the fourteenth century exactly resembled that of Roman Britain. The main design of the Roman roads was still very apparent, character- ized by the long straight roads linking the cities of the Roman occupation, often utilizing the high level hill ridges, as in Lincoln- shire, where Ermine Street follows the crest of the Lincoln Edge. In addition to this basically long distance pattern, many other roads added a complex pattern whose chief features were those roads constructed subsequent to the Roman occupation linking local villages and larger centres, and which normally followed the contour line, thus avoiding excessive gradients. In most cases where it was practicable, these roads utilized the slightly higher ground away from river sides and low-lying marshy areas which were liable to flooding during periods of heavy rain or snow, as well as being unhealthy for the beasts of burden. The interstices between these threads were occupied by primitive trackways and paths of local significance, leading to farms and fields. Naturally the Roman roads were not always left untouched by subsequent generations. There is evidence that bridges over rivers had not survived the years, while the stones which had been used for walls and bridges by the Romans were often appropriated for other buildings.

The modern period

As the medieval period drew to its close, eventually giving way to what is often termed the "modern" period of British history—

from the mid-eighteenth century onwards—the geographical face of Great Britain was changing although the familiar distribution of industry and population which resulted from the "Industrial Revolution" had not yet, of course, materialized. Throughout the Middle Ages, industry and commerce had been gradually increasing and this naturally resulted in a more intensive use of the roads. This commercial development, as we have seen, had no complementary scheme of progress on the roads, which by and large retained in even greater measure the inadequacies and evils of the previous centuries.

By the eighteenth century, roads which consisted merely of a moderately rough earth surface had largely become a seasonal phenomenon—for in summer, while they were notoriously dusty, they at least provided a hard, firm if not entirely smooth surface, whereas in winter it was almost the rule, rather than the exception, to find them impassable. This state of affairs could hardly have been otherwise considering their neglect and constant use for centuries. In some districts, usually in hilly country, a raised causeway was commonly found, consisting of a stone-flagged surface. These did not make for rapid movement, but they had the advantageous feature of a relatively reliable foundation on which animals and carts would not be bogged down, as on the common earth surfaces.

Amid this dolorous scene of primitive roadways whereon traffic suffered as much from the evils of the roads themselves as from the absence of a central authority empowered to remedy them, is one feature which speaks for itself of the far-sighted skill of our remote conquerors—namely that there still remained Roman road *surfaces* which had survived centuries of use. Their superiority over other roads occasioned comment from the historians of the sixteenth century.

Roads and industry

One cause of the steadily worsening condition of roads in Britain up to the eighteenth century was the fact that long-distance traffic was increasing on account of the emerging specialization of various industries in particular localities. Townships no longer found themselves self-sufficient, and news of novel materials, goods and facilities inevitably created the demand for them. In addition, the increasing complexity of manufactured products required the use of a larger variety of component materials which, because of the variegated nature of British geology and geography, it was not possible to obtain from one area. Thus the increased industrial and commercial activity meant increased traffic on roads which could not carry it. Moreover, the long-distance road users whose traffic formed an ever-increasing proportion of the total traffic on the roads were in no way liable for the upkeep of the roads they used.

Maintenance of the roads was in the hands of the local authorities, whose local needs by no means compared with the long-distance usage; consequently it is scarcely to be wondered at if some of these local authorities did not exert themselves beyond the strict requirements of the law where road maintenance was concerned.

The Turnpike Trusts

It can readily be appreciated that under conditions outlined above, road transport in Britain would rapidly cease to perform its vital function with any effectiveness. During the eighteenth century, however, an attempt was made to bring some improvement to the roads. This was done by means of the Turnpike Trusts. These consisted of bodies of men who undertook to repair and maintain certain stretches of main road in their locality. The funds for the upkeep of the roads were obtained by charging a toll on every vehicle as it entered the particular stretch of "protected" road. Each Turnpike Trust had to be approved by Act of Parliament, stating the extent of road which it proposed to maintain, and so on. One great advantage of this system was that the cost of maintenance fell on the shoulders of those who were, in fact, making use of the roads, and thus the long-distance traffic paid its due proportion, whereas previously it had been able to use the roads without paying anything in return.

At this stage the important features of the road map were first the ever-increasing importance of London as a transport focal centre, second the denser network of roads in the established industrial areas, third the much more open pattern in the agricultural regions, where roads swung through open country for miles, often passing through nowhere of note between two market towns, and fourth the definite pattern of roads from the woollen and manufacturing districts to the appropriate port. Roads in mountainous country were naturally even sparser and poorer than at the present time.

The latter half of the eighteenth century witnessed not only the work of the many Turnpike Trusts, but also that of two famous road engineers whose names are still familiar: Macadam and Telford. An interesting contrast in their work is that while Telford concentrated on the classic highway routes, such as London-Holyhead (now A5), Macadam's work was more concentrated on road improvement on a thorough scale in one particular region—e.g. the Bristol district.

The advent of the railway

While it is easy to speak with some bitterness of the lethargy and neglect which almost undermined road transport by the end of the Middle Ages, one must pause to wonder what might have happened during the nineteenth century—and what indeed would the position be today—had not the steam locomotive and the railway assumed the dominant role in inland transport. Turnpike Trusts had performed well, providing real benefits to road users on nearly all the main roads by the early nineteenth century, the Post Office was an active body in fostering the widespread improvement of main roads (primarily with a view to the more rapid carriage of mails) and one reads a general awakening of enthusiasm and a feeling of responsibility in the history of that period. There was a scheme for a new Great North Road, but this suffered the general fate when the railways came.

The phenomenal development of railways during the second half of the nineteenth century is a history in itself, the major features of which are well known, but in the shadow of its brilliance lies the story of the renewed neglect of the roads. Obviously, long-distance traffic especially was better suited for rail travel, and with the transfer of so much road traffic to rail, the Turnpike Trusts became obsolete inconveniences. The number of Trusts fell rapidly as the century progressed, finally ending in 1895. And there was still no overall organization to replace them and consummate their work.

Canals complemented, rather than competed with, the roads, but the railways gained a stranglehold which was not broken until the advent of the internal combustion engine at the start of the present century.

a survey of British roads

AT this point, prior to an examination of twentieth-century supplementation to the road map of Britain, it is advisable to pause and look again at the general pattern and characteristic features of that road map. London is clearly the focal centre of transport by both road and rail, and the main road arteries into the provinces frequently resemble in design the main railway lines, as has been described earlier. This is even true in open country, where the physical landscape does not impose restrictions on the routeing of either road or rail. Naturally, in such areas as west Lancashire or the Northumbrian coast, the proximity of the hill and mountain country to the coast forces transport routes into a narrow belt and for many miles railway and road may run side-by-side or continuously crossing and recrossing each other.

In Scotland, the English commercial influence is apparent in A1 and A6/7, whose importance is not difficult to understand. However, Glasgow and Edinburgh are two great centres in their own right.

Both are inter-connected by several routes, while their role of foci for the rest of Scotland is readily apparent. Glasgow is the centre for many roads from south-west and west Scotland—Dumfries, western Galloway, Ayrshire, the Clyde Estuary and the western highlands. In addition, Glasgow is well connected to the economically more important eastern Scotland, with A80 providing access to and from Stirling, Perth, Dundee, Aberdeen, etc. A glance at the map reveals, too, the focal nature of Edinburgh, with a radial arrangement of roads to all parts of south-east and south Scotland. Northwards, the arteries from eastern Scotland to the Capital are cruelly choked by the persistent refusal to provide funds for a road bridge over the Forth. The existing facilities consist of a ferry (Queensferry) or a wasteful circuitous route via Kincardine (Fifeshire) and A876 across the Forth. It is interesting to note the scissors-effect in Scotland, centred at Stirling, by which main roads form links between Edinburgh and west Scotland (A9 and A84) and between Glasgow and east Scotland (A80 and A9). Further north, Aberdeen is a regional centre for that part of north-east Scotland, while Inverness is another remote road centre, though hardly a regional capital.

In England and Wales (for Wales cannot claim an independent road pattern without reference to English interests) there are very many regional variations which are not allied to the overall predominance of London. Working round the country, we find in south-east England, superimposed on the radial metropolitan arteries (A2, A20-A24, A3, etc.) many roads in the Weald whose plan is primarily dictated by the geological history of the area. Such are A25, A264 and A272, all running roughly east-west, and crossed in characteristic "right angle" fashion by the coast-bound roads from London. The pattern is completed by the "holiday road", A259, which follows the south-east coast from Dover to Chichester and connects all the seaside holiday resorts between those two towns. The radial arrangement of roads from the metropolitan "hub" still exerts its influence further west where the most striking feature is the south-westerly direction of the main roads. These are crossed by some very important north-south roads which provide the Midlands with a through route to the south coast. A34 is the chief of these. So far it is noticeable that London still dominates the scene, not only in the direction of main roads, but, negatively, in the *absence* of any other road centres. This is reflected in that very many urban residents east of, say, the Somerset and Dorset borders and south of A4, tend to speak of London as "town". It is as if the whole of south-east and southern England were a semi-rural suburb of the Metropolis, although this observation is not valid for the purely rural population, where the market town dominates their activities.

Bristol and Exeter are the two centres of regional life, and therefore of roads, in the south-west. West of A37 this is very marked in contrast to the country further east. Many roads from Somerset, Dorset, Wiltshire and Gloucestershire focus on the port of Bristol, and we are reminded of the former glories of the West Country woollen trade, its iron smelting and coal mining as well as its agriculture. The importance of Bristol as a port in earlier days is equally well reflected in the road map. Although today it is not a leading British port, it maintains its role, of course, as the regional centre of the less remote parts of the "West Country". Exeter is the other great centre of the west, its maritime links being provided by Plymouth. There can be no mistaking the convergence on Exeter of the roads of the south-west peninsula, of which only A39 (to Bath) and A361 (to Taunton and the south Midlands) of major importance do not pass through it.

South Wales, of course, has very definite geographical characteristics, and the nature of the road pattern at once confirms this. There are a few through roads in north Monmouthshire, following river valleys, but in south-west Monmouthshire and east Glamorgan the roads bear eloquent testimony to the character of the country. The parallel valleys leading to the coast and the great ports of Newport and Cardiff, the sudden end of industry at the valley heads (so clearly demarcated by A465), the routes which link the ports with England, all these features speak of the region they exemplify—the South Wales coalfield. Further west, beyond Swansea and Llanelly, the roads are chiefly parallel with, or at right-angles to, the characteristic "grain" of central Wales—south-west to north-east. Roads here are sparse, for towns are widely spaced, with bare hills and high moorland between them. The industrial area of South Wales is in close commercial contact with the West Midlands, and it is to this area that we now turn.

The West Midlands is a term used here to denote the industrial heart of England, based on England's largest provincial city—Birmingham. This city is the direct focus of main roads east of A49 (which roughly follows the line of the Welsh marches), north of A40 (which demarcates in this area, the downland country of Wiltshire and the lower Severn valley centring on Gloucester and Bristol from the English plain) west and south of A5 (which, as we have seen, encloses the West Midlands in an arc from the Warwickshire/Northamptonshire boundary round to the fringes of the south Staffordshire coalfield). Within this region, the main roads from London and the Home Counties run north-westwards; some are through roads, such as A41, and pass through Birmingham, while others start within the region and focus on Birmingham or

Coventry. From the west, several roads lead from A49 (and thus central Wales) towards the Birmingham area, while there exists a close network of roads from the east and north Midlands to the Black Country. Within the latter area itself, there is, of course, a very complex cellular structure of roads which is bounded by A5, A446, A45, A456, A458 and A449. It is a typical road arrangement for a highly industrialized, densely populated region and is perhaps more marked here than in any other comparable industrial area, such as south-east Lancashire or the West Riding. This is partly due to the topography of the respective districts, for the Birmingham area lacks the high moorland spaces of the Lancashire or Yorkshire centres, where industry is of necessity confined to the valleys, leaving the intervening hills bare of road development on an intensive scale.

North Wales, apart from the north coast, is a sparsely populated area, and it is to be expected that the road map is not one of any complexity. South of Snowdonia, the majority of roads follow the valleys in the characteristic south-west—north-east direction, while in the mountainous parts of Caernarvonshire the deep glaciated valleys, running north-west—south-east are utilized, e.g. by A5 between Capel Curig and Bangor. An interesting feature of the Welsh road map is the coastal road. This can be traced from Pembrokeshire to Flintshire and consists of several different roads. It will be noted that a through road exists from Haverfordwest to Caernarvon (A487) but this does not follow the coastline entirely. The character of A487, A493 and A496 along the west coast of Wales may be compared with A55 and A548, along the popular and developing north coast, which are more comparable with the "holiday road" of south-east England, mentioned elsewhere. A noticeable feature in North Wales is the markedly increased road density at or near the English border, especially in the coalfield of Flintshire and Denbighshire.

Our survey has now reached north-west England and it can easily be realized that, as far as the road pattern is concerned, London is virtually forgotten. While it remains the national Capital, it is no longer the local or regional centre. In south-west Lancashire and north-west Cheshire, the main roads focus on Merseyside, but Liverpool is by no means the chief transport centre for any other part of Lancashire. That is a role played by Manchester, as the road map immediately reveals. From east Cheshire, Derbyshire, east and central Lancashire, the roads converge. Moreover, the great industrial regions of south and west Yorkshire have many trans-Pennine road links with Manchester, as well as their own local foci at Leeds and Bradford.

It is reasonable to state that outside the Black Country, Manchester is the most important provincial road centre in the country. Direct road links exist between Manchester and Carlisle, Leeds, Sheffield, Lincoln, London, Winchester, Chester and Liverpool, as well as innumerable places nearer at hand.

North of industrial Lancashire, A59 stands, between Preston and Harrogate, as a border-line between the urban and rural north. South of that road, the road pattern becomes progressively more complex towards the centres of Liverpool, Manchester and Sheffield, but north of it, industry gives way to the lonely Pennines, crossed by only two important roads between Skipton and Hadrian's Wall. Road centres here are truly local and there is no real road pattern. The Lake District has its own special design, determined primarily by physical geography, while in north Cumberland the transport focus on Carlisle is clearly evident. East of A6, few roads exist until the ever-narrowing Vale of York is reached. The existing roads across the north Pennines follow such "gaps" or "passes" as are there, but these are a mere relief in the general high land rather than true valleys.

Across the Pennines lies the eastern coastal plain of England, wider and more developed than its western counterpart. Here are the Newcastle and Middlesbrough industrial districts, and their local importance is once again adequately reflected in the road map. Note the different road densities east and west of a line drawn as follows: A197 Newbiggin-Morpeth; A1 Morpeth-Newcastle; A69 Newcastle-Hexham; A68 Hexham-Darlington. On the west, the wild uninhabited Pennines; on the east, the Northumberland and Durham coalfields and the Tyne and Tees urban areas.

Further south, in the agricultural and pastoral country of east Yorkshire, the main roads converge on York, which performs an interesting regional function as the agricultural and marketing capital of Yorkshire, in a region of widely spaced roads and towns. Compare this with the industrial and commercial capital of the same county—Leeds, and the surrounding area of the West Riding with its highly developed road pattern, much more closely allied to that of east Lancashire in every way than with the Vale of York and the East Riding.

Lincolnshire, an agricultural and pastoral county, apart from the iron and steel producing centre of Scunthorpe, displays a road map in keeping with its nature. Road centres are primarily the market towns—Lincoln itself, Boston, Grantham, etc. There is no density of roads where there is no density of population. Once again, study of the road pattern emphasizes the contrast between neighbouring counties: in this case between Lincolnshire and the complex area of south Yorkshire and the East Midlands from Chesterfield to

Leicestershire. This is the site of the Yorks, Derby and Notts coalfield.

The region has no real centre, for the main roads converging on such towns as Sheffield, Nottingham and Derby are as much those from other parts of England as from the coalfield itself. Note the long distance roads converging on Derby—from London, Bodmin, Nantwich, Carlisle, Thirsk and Mablethorpe.

Leicestershire is a county of varied activities—in the east the more open country bordering on Lincolnshire, with very few main roads, in the west the coalfield with a closer, yet not dense, road pattern where towns are closer together. Leicester itself is easily the largest town and houses most of the county's industry, apart from coalmining. It is also the chief road centre of the county, a feature which is by no means the rule in other counties.

East Anglia displays two characteristics in its road map. The Norfolk area clearly looks to Norwich as its road centre, although links exist with Lincolnshire, whereas further south there is no local focus, and the main roads run south-west—towards London, with Cambridge as an intermediate centre. We are now back within the metropolitan orbit, for as we travel west from Essex there are very few important exceptions to the general trend of main road direction until the Cotswolds are reached. Of course local groupings of roads can be found—such as at Bedford, Northampton or Aylesbury, but we are no longer entirely free from the grip of London.

This brief survey of Great Britain's road pattern is now complete. Its main features, without reference to specific areas, may be summarized as follows: London is the road centre (on a large scale) for all, broadly speaking, south-east Britain. Secondly, highly developed industrial areas have their own road pattern and road centres, varying in their nature according to the physical character of each particular region. Thirdly, the agricultural and pastoral regions away from metropolitan influence, in lowland Britain, normally show a loosely-knit road pattern centring on market towns. Fourthly, where there are few centres of population, either in towns or villages, as in highland Britain, the roads follow the line of least physical resistance, they are few in number and they are normally long-distance roads linking more heavily-populated areas elsewhere. Fundamentally the road mileage varies in different areas, directly with the population.

roads today

WE are now in a position to examine the latest additions and the most modern characteristics of British roads. Of recent months, public attention has been drawn, with considerable vigour, to the lamentable condition of main roads in Great Britain. The evils of our roads today lie less in the quality of their surfacing—though this is not entirely beyond reproach in some cases—than in their archaic nature. In only a handful of instances can modern trunk traffic travel over a contemporary route; a fact which seriously militates against sincere efforts by manufacturers to reduce their costs, and thus their prices, in their own and the public interest. It is discouraging to lose the fruits of production economies in costly transport, yet this frequently occurs today, particularly with the excessively high tax on fuel oil, so much of which is wasted by vehicles delayed in traffic congestion on our narrow streets.

During the twenty years preceding the 1939-45 World War several modern roads were built to facilitate the movement of the ever-increasing volume of traffic. These roads are readily identifiable to the eye, and on the map. A fine example is the "East Lancashire Road" from Walton, Liverpool, to the outskirts of Manchester (A580). Much of it consists of a dual carriageway, but at each end it becomes lost in the welter of pre-existing roads in the built-up areas of the two cities, several of which were encumbered with tram-tracks until a few years ago.

Roads such as the East Lancashire Road were built to a deliberate design—well-surfaced, well-signposted, wide—with at least two traffic lanes in each direction—and above all, they were purposely routed so as to avoid, as far as possible, all urban areas en route. Thus A580 passes to the north of St. Helens (already well-linked with Liverpool by A58 and A57) and Newton-in-Makerfield, and to the south of Leigh and Tyldesley. It is on the same level as other crossing-roads, and at junctions and cross-roads, traffic lights are usually installed.

The technique, widely employed in the U.S.A. and Germany, of fly-over crossings, tunnels, viaducts, etc., has not been generally adopted on modern British arteries, but it is anticipated that they will form a characteristic feature of roads in the future. Their use obviates traffic signals, etc., and strictly limits the number of points at which contact may be made with existing roads. Notice, too, how relatively straight is the East Lancashire Road. This not only permits faster and safer travel, but greatly facilitates the transport of very long, or outsize, loads. This is the feature which most noticeably catches one's attention on a road map.

In contrast with the original roads which have developed over the centuries, meandering from village to village, from town to town, following in many cases a winding valley or avoiding unsuitable ground, the modern arterial highways more closely resemble a main railway line—striking in almost a straight line across the countryside, less mindful of the topography and heedless of wayside villages. They are very clearly superimposed on the naturally developed social landscape, symbolizing, perhaps, the forceful, busy and high-geared element of a civilization that "has no time to stand and stare".

In London can be found several examples of well-made arterial roads; these lie in suburban rather than in central London, where the very high percentage of land already built upon largely precludes the mass demolition and temporary chaos which the construction of the new roads would necessitate. Moreover, much of the industry in London is housed away from the true central districts (apart from the industries dependent on, and adjacent to, the docks).

There will be few Londoners who are ignorant of the North Circular Road, which almost describes a semi-circular arc from Ealing to Woodford. For the greater part of its length it is a first-class route, Palmers Green being one of the few sections where a high standard is not maintained. This road carries a very large quantity of traffic, much of it industrial, and it is ironical that two factors which are inevitable should weigh against the efficiency of the road. In the first place there has arisen a host of factories on to the road; this entails frequent movements of commercial vehicles, including the parking of such vehicles, and the existence of large numbers of employees, most of whom create localized peak-hours at least twice a day and whose mass presence in a small area increases the possibility of road accidents, and also may call for the provision of a large number of peak-hour buses for transport to and from the factories, in addition to the cycles and cars which some employees may use.

Secondly, the North Circular Road is essentially a route from west to east London (or vice versa) purposely designed to enable traffic to by-pass central London on the north side. This very fact means that the road, as it exists at present, has to cross no less than eighteen important radial roads between Brentford Market and Gants Hill. At some of these eighteen places, traffic signals are in operation, but at such points as the Welsh Harp, Brent, where A5 is crossed, both roads are of such importance that considerable delay occurs. Elsewhere, as at the Cambridge, where the North Circular Road crosses A10, roundabouts have been built, but these are not easily negotiated by some of the mammoth lorries and trailers which use the "North Circular".

West London boasts two fine arterial exits: the Great West Road

(A4) and Western Avenue (A40, and previously A403). The former suffers considerably as a route for fast and trunk traffic from the growth of factories and dwellings along the roadside—an unsightly, short-sighted and suicidal phenomenon usually designated: "ribbon development." Western Avenue as yet is more fortunate in this respect, and has recently officially ousted the Uxbridge Road as the superior road to Oxford and South Wales, being happily unhindered by trolleybus routes and shopping centres.

In the east, visitors to Southend by road may have become acquainted with Eastern Avenue (from Wanstead) and the Southend Arterial Road (A127). Here are intelligently-planned roads designed with a specific purpose, a special role to play: in this case the rapid transport of people and goods from London to Southend and back. It is for these that the road caters, and as such it can, and does, avoid the villages and by-ways of south Essex, whose needs can be served by other roads, such as A13 or A129.

There is, today, so much long-distance carriage of passengers and freight by road that roads must be specially built for it. Existing roads, by their very history and origin, serve intermediate towns, usually passing through them to form the High Street. In the past, this has served for traffic which was not directly concerned with these intermediate towns, since in the past there were no vehicles capable of travelling non-stop for great distances, and the modern industrial economy which requires transport of materials from distant sources of supply had not then developed.

The twentieth century, however, brought the internal combustion engine into its own, followed by the rapid technological progress in the field of petrol and oil-driven vehicle construction which gave us the highly-mechanized factories, mass-producing ever-improving cars, lorries and public service vehicles. A vast number of these found their way on to British main roads, vehicles capable of carrying great loads over long distances. Modern British vehicles are the hallmark of a high powered, active and flourishing industrial country. British roads are the legacy of a leisurely, localized, agricultural community of the early eighteenth century. The incongruity, the anachronism is more than an interesting feature of these islands. It is rapidly developing into a national disaster.

Apart from the very few twentieth-century arterial highways, of which a few examples have been cited, the only deliberate attempt to alleviate the crushing influence of traffic congestion and the inconveniences of the existing main roads, has been the construction of by-passes in the vicinity of some urban areas. Some of these have been on a relatively large scale, such as the North Circular Road in London, Queen's Drive in Liverpool, and the Queensferry cut-off in the Wirral. Several towns and cities enjoy, however, a more localized by-pass. Coventry, Shrewsbury, Redruth, Chichester, Ormskirk, Lincoln, Chester, Nottingham, Derby, Chelmsford, Bridgend, and, near London: Dartford, Sidcup, Sutton and Guildford. These are a few random examples of towns which have been effectively by-passed to allow the free movement of traffic which does not require to visit them. In contrast, St. Albans, Staines, Stamford, Doncaster, Chepstow, Lancaster and very many market towns and industrial centres which lie on the most important roads have become veritable death-traps to road users—towns which have not been by-passed, yet carry through their tortuous, medieval streets, the life blood of a nation.

The construction of by-passes for such places as these, and the consequent elimination of some of the more notorious "black-spots" from the English landscape, has found considerable favour in responsible quarters. It is obviously an improvement in itself on the existing conditions, and yet it serves only a partial purpose. While local road users and through travellers in the particular locality must benefit from a by-pass, the inadequacies and failings of the existing road system as a whole remain unassailed.

The real answer can lie only in a thorough revision of the whole main road system, wherein, while existing main roads can be retained to play a secondary or intermediate role, the function of providing contemporary roads for to-morrow's traffic must be delegated to new first-class highways.

The co-existence of these two classes of roads is no fanciful luxury: it is a paramount requirement in a modern Britain. That the cost of providing the population with efficient roads, in an age of armed peace, would be so prohibitive as to be fatal, is perhaps a cryptic commentary on a century which has witnessed, on the one hand, unprecedented developments in technology and knowledge, and on the other, unspeakable reversions to barbarity.

the future of British roads

HITHERTO, sanction for the expenditure of large sums of money on road improvements has not been readily forthcoming. Local schemes for bettering local stretches of main road have been, perhaps reluctantly, approved, but a stalemate appeared to exist on the burning topic of a nation-wide programme for new modern highways. During 1955, however, following constant pressure from responsible bodies, a four-year plan was officially launched. Its immediate focus was on two vital routes; London to Yorkshire and Preston to Birmingham. The existing roads which roughly correspond to the line of these new highways are A1, which has several times been surveyed and analysed in all its contemporary horror by the Press, and A49/A50/A34 which pass through the centre of many large towns such as Wigan, Warrington, Newcastle-under-Lyme and Stafford without adequate by-pass facilities. Both the existing routes carry very heavy traffic, much of it industrial, and only the West Midlands-South Wales connecting roads present a picture of comparable inefficiency at the present time. Readers may have examined for themselves the plan for the two new highways, but it will be useful to look once more at the essentials of the new schemes.

The London-Yorkshire motorway will start near St. Albans, leading from the proposed, and long-awaited by-pass for that city. Thence it will pass to the west of Luton, striking north-westwards to a point north of Daventry, connecting from there to A45 which will have a dual carriageway to Birmingham. Thus far, the new motorway will serve a two-fold purpose by providing vastly improved trunk facilities to the industrial West Midlands via the Dunchurch link on A45.

Continuing north, the remainder of the motorway is not expected to be completed until after the southern section is in use. Its route will be roughly due north, avoiding Leicester and Nottingham on the western side until a point south-east of Sheffield is reached; here a spur will give access to the steel city. The main motorway will then swing in an easterly arc, avoiding the Rotherham industrial region, and end at a new Doncaster by-pass, to join A1. This road will be provided with a dual carriageway over the section north of Doncaster. Road users who are now forced to travel along A1 between London and Doncaster will readily appreciate the enormous economic value of the proposed new motorway.

On the western side of England, the Preston-Birmingham route will follow more closely the existing roads. An adequate by-pass for Preston is not available at the present time, but the pressing need for one has not been overlooked. From the future by-pass, the Birmingham motorway will run south to the west side of Wigan, then south-east to avoid Warrington on the east side, continuing south-south-east across Cheshire to the Potteries, approximately parallel to A50. The route follows the same direction past Stafford (by-pass) and so via Walsall to Birmingham. Between Warrington and Birmingham, the motorway will lie to the west of the existing roads, A50 and A34.

It is an important feature of the new motorways that access to them from existing roads will be severely limited. Where necessary, the roads will pass either under or over the existing roads, with fly-overs and under-passes at more important junctions.

A third proposal in the four-year plan is for a motorway spur from Ross-on-Wye to A38 near Tewkesbury. This will help to improve road facilities between South Wales and the West Midlands, but it cannot be considered as more than an interim gesture in this respect. The existing routes between these two centres are such that a 21-mile long road cannot effectively remedy their inadequacies.

Attention has been drawn to the lack of modern bridges over certain rivers and estuaries, and a few of these may now be considered. In Scotland, of course, the most glaring anomaly is the lack of a road bridge across the Firth of Forth. While the Forth Bridge is an essential link in the East Coast rail route, road traffic has to use the Queensferry or alternatively make a wasteful detour via Kincardine (Fife)—an unnecessary addition of some 30 miles between South Queensferry and Dunfermline, which are only six miles from each other. It has been suggested that a tunnel on the bed of the estuary would be less expensive than a bridge; whatever the final result, either would be infinitely more advantageous than the present facilities.

Further north in Scotland, a road bridge at Inverness is planned; this would obviate the detour round the head of Beauly Firth for traffic to and from Dingwall and the north. The considerable indentation of the Scottish coastline has been responsible for the original routeing of so many roads along their present circuitous paths, but today the resources of civil engineers should be equal to the task of constructing more direct links across the many estuarine waters.

English rivers have also presented uneconomical situations for road traffic. Among these are the Thames, across whose lower reaches a tunnel has been commenced from Dartford to Purfleet; the Tamar at Saltash, where serious congestion arises in the summer months at the Saltash and Torpoint ferries in the absence of a road bridge; the Mersey, where a new bridge at Widnes has long been under consideration to replace the doomed transporter bridge; the Humber at Barton-on-Humber, where there exist at present no facilities across to Yorkshire (the only conveyance in the vicinity being the ferry from New Holland to Hull); and in Wales at Conway, where the river is spanned by a handsome, but hopelessly inadequate, suspension bridge. Here, particularly in summer, chaos is never far away, for west-bound traffic is delayed at the entrance to the bridge at the toll booths and the queue of vehicles often extends back to Llandudno Junction where a further obstacle is the level crossing for the Llandudno branch. This is also in heavy use during the summer.

A proposal on a very large scale is that concerned with the crossing of Morecambe Bay. Today, south and west Cumberland suffer from a remoteness not wholly ascribable to their geographical location. While Barrow and Lancaster are only fifteen miles apart across the Bay, the road mileage between the two towns is forty, as traffic into Furness is required to travel along A6 to Levens Bridge and thence via A590 along a picturesque, but meandering route under the shadow of the mountains. In view of the resurrection of Cumbrian industry at the present time, it is imperative to improve on this route, and the plan visualizes a bridge from near Bolton-le-Sands to near Allithwaite, a new road thence to the Levens estuary which would be crossed by a new bridge parallel to the railway, whose route would be roughly followed into Ulverston. Between Ulverston and Barrow, A590 will be used. Improved connexions from the west are also included in the Furness plan: a new bridge is proposed to carry traffic from near Millom across the Duddon estuary to Roanhead, Dalton and Barrow. New roads on the mainland here, comprise Roanhead-Dalton (and thence east) and Roanhead-Barrow direct.

The above proposals will naturally divert traffic from A590 which is better utilized as a scenic, rather than an industrial, route.

During the year 1956 the following improvements have been scheduled: by-passes for the following towns and villages— Borrowash (Derbyshire); Catterick (Yorks); East Retford (Notts); Handcross (Sussex); Longton (Lancs); Neath (Glamorgan): widening of certain roads as follows—A1 Alconbury Hill, Stamford and Browney Bridge districts; A12 Woodbridge by-pass; A3 Elephant & Castle; A38 Lichfield-Burton: A34 Shirley; A40 Oxford and Park Royal; A41 Mill Hill; A45 Ryton-Coventry; A48 Llanfair Discoed; A5 Shenstone; A69 Throckley. In Scotland, improvements are to be put in hand for A82 at Dumbuck; A9 at Linlithgow, Bridge of Allan and Bridge of Don.

During the latter part of the decade, by-passes will be constructed for the following places: Doncaster (Yorks); Gateshead (Durham); Grantham (Lincs); Harlow (Essex); Lancaster; Maidenhead (Berks); Maidstone (Kent); Northwich (Cheshire); Port Talbot (Glamorgan); Preston (Lancs); St.Albans (Herts); Sandiacre-Stapleford (Derby); Staines (Middlesex). Widening and general improvement of the following roads: A13 Tilbury Docks; A3 Kingston by-pass; A34 Oxford and Stafford-Stoke; A40 underpass at Hanger Lane; A406 Edmonton; A465 Hirwaun, Brynmawr and Abergavenny; while in London improvements will be effected at the Albert Bridge, Blackwall Tunnel, Holborn/Kingsway, Notting Hill Gate, Strand and St. Giles Circus. Over the same period in the provinces, Barton Bridge (Lancs), Laira Bridge (Devon) are to be modernized, and further work will be devoted to a Huddersfield central ring road, a Manchester outer ring road and an east-west link road in the same city. In Scotland, A74 is to be widened, e.g. at Millbank, Abington and Beattock, while improvements for A77 at Malletsheugh and A80 are anticipated.

The above improvements, however, may not be undertaken as soon as was originally hoped, for the current restrictions on various forms of capital expenditure have affected the road schemes, and it may well be that the programme thus outlined will suffer unfortunate delays in execution, amounting to perhaps a few years. The latest suggestion which may have repercussions on the above schemes is the construction of approach roads to be built over railway lines from the suburbs of the cities to their centres. How far this plan will proceed, or succeed, it is difficult to say, for we have become accustomed to so many such schemes being still-born.

The various schemes detailed above form the initial move towards a modern road system for Great Britain. The task when commenced is colossal and even formidable: its cost will be in thousands of millions of pounds and it is not one which can be completed overnight. It is nonetheless essential, for if it is not undertaken and carried forward to its fulfilment, we must suffer the consequences, we must pay the price of a national paralysis on the roads. Great Britain could no more perform its social, commercial and industrial functions without the uninhibited flow of traffic along its roads than a human being could survive if the blood ceased to flow through its arteries and veins.

roads in retrospect

OUR survey of the roads of Great Britain, though by no means exhaustive, has incorporated both geographical and historical factors, which have contributed to the pattern of roads as we find them today. Historically, the development of the British road system has been briefly reviewed from medieval times to the present day, and a glimpse given of the promise of the future. To bring the wheel full circle, we cannot but focus our attention, if only for a moment, and pay our tribute to the founders of the first real British road system—the Romans. Many learned authorities have produced detailed histories of the Roman roads in Great

Britain, accounts wherein the interested reader can learn infinitely more of this heritage than is possible in this general book.

It has been found convenient to examine the road map of Roman Britain by dividing the roads into groups, each based on a particular road: (1) Watling Street; (2) Ermine Street; (3) East Anglia; (4) Icknield Way and Akeman Street; (5) Fosse Way; (6) Riknild Street; (7) Silchester and the west. Each group will be examined in turn, and reference made to the modern numbered roads which follow the same route over certain distances. In this connexion it must be remembered that where the Roman roads are described between two towns, the modern road number will be given in parentheses, to indicate that the modern road follows at least part, though not necessarily all, of the section named.

Watling Street started at Dover, whence there were branches to Richborough (formerly a port) and Lympne, and struck north-west to Canterbury (A2). This city was the road centre for roads from Thanet (Sarre Wall, A28), Richborough and Lympne (Stone Street, B2068). Watling Street then ran west-north-west to Rochester (A2), and London (A207). The line of the road in central London is probably represented by the Old Kent Road, Tabard Street and along an undeciphered route across to Westminster and Hyde Park Corner. Edgware Road, from Marble Arch to Edgware still provides a superb monument to the skill of our predecessors in the construction of a straight road. This section is now A5, from London on through St. Albans, Dunstable, Towcester, High Cross (where Fosse Way crosses) and eventually to Wroxeter, south-east of Shrewsbury. From near Cannock onwards, Watling Street ran due west, and it is noticeable how the direction of the road changes abruptly, rather than gradually in a broad curve. One reason for this is that the Romans planned their roads from elevated points, i.e. they designed the route to follow a straight line between two chosen places of higher ground, and then changed direction at a suitable point; from this point another line was drawn with another hill and so on.

Beyond Wroxeter (Roman Uriconium), Watling Street and its branches have no modern counterpart comparable to the length of A5 from London. A branch led south through Church Stretton, Leintwardine and Kenchester (near Hereford) to Abergavenny, while the main routes led north across Cheshire to Chester. This city, again, like Canterbury, was an important Roman centre, with roads to North and West Wales, Nantwich, Warrington, and the main continuation, this time east-north-east to Manchester (A556), which even in Roman times could claim a focal character in road communications. Roads radiated from Manchester to Wigan, Ribchester, Ilkley and Buxton.

The modern route of A49 and A6 from Warrington to Lancaster has its Roman counterpart, though not over precisely the same ground. From Ribchester, several roads crossed the Pennines or struck west to the Fylde. These less distinct branches north of Chester represent later additions to the main "stem" of Watling Street, and perhaps reflect successive phases of colonization as new settlements developed, as at Manchester or Ribchester. Beyond Chester, or indeed the Wroxeter area, there is no length of road of comparable single design as the section between Dover and north Staffordshire, nor have the Roman roads in the north-west left as indelible a stamp on the modern road map.

Thus the Roman Watling Street can be traced over much of its length from Kent to Cheshire, and today, for much of that distance, its route is unmistakable as the course of A2 and A5.

The second important group to be considered centres on Ermine Street. It has been suggested that this road originated at Chichester, while other authorities have found no conclusive evidence that it extended even as far south as London. However, assuming that Ermine Street did start in Roman London, its course appears to have been, due north to Braughing (Herts) (A1000). This place, now a village, was of a considerably greater significance in Roman times, for roads radiated from it to Colchester (Stane Street—A120), Chesterford (to connect with Icknield Way) and God-manchester via two different routes. One of these coincides with a section of A1, and the other with A10 through Royston. God-manchester was evidently another significant settlement, for here Ermine Street (A10) crossed the Via Devana which linked Roman centres at Cambridge and Leicester (A604). Pursuing its north-bound course, Ermine Street swung west to avoid the Fens, passing through Stilton and Stamford (A1), but beyond Colsterworth (Lincs), Ermine Street struck almost due north (B6403) along the chalk uplands to Lincoln, where a loop road from Castor which ran roughly parallel to, but east of, Ermine Street, rejoined the main route. Lincoln was, of course, a major Roman town, and here Fosse Way ended. A158 today follows an extension of the line of Fosse Way towards Wragg, while to the north-east, another road linked Lincoln and Tadcaster.

One of the most remarkable of the Roman roads is Ermine Street in the area between Lincoln and the Humber (A15) where the road travels due north along the crest of the Lincoln Edge; its emphatic influence here contrasts remarkably with the section between the Humber and the Malton/York districts where today there is little road vestige of the Roman way.

The East Riding of Yorkshire evidently enjoyed a relatively

complex road pattern, with centres at York and Malton: a cross-country road linked Tadcaster, York and Flamborough, while from York itself roads ran in all directions, including facilities for reaching the northern continuation of Ermine Street through Aldborough and on to Catterick (A1). Between the York area and Catterick two routes were available, one via Aldborough and the other via the Thirsk area, further east, and north of Catterick, the route forked again, this time permanently. Scotch Corner, today the "birthplace" of A66, represents the starting point of the Roman Road across the Pennines through Bowes and Brough to Penrith (A66) where in turn, roads radiated to the Lake District and Carlisle. The main route of Ermine Street, however, continued north, west of the present A1, through Bishop Auckland to Lanchester (branch to Tyneside) and Corbridge (B6309), just south of the famous Hadrian's Wall. The Corbridge-Bewclay locality is rich in evidence of Roman occupation, and from this area, roads linked to Berwick, the Eden Valley, Newcastle and Carlisle. The two latter places will always be associated with Hadrian's Wall, but in fact, more than one Roman road traversed the northern Pennines: Carlisle to Greenhead consisted of the Wall itself, and a separate road further south (A69); between Greenhead and Heddon-on-the-Wall, B6318 follows the line of Hadrian's Wall, while another road (Stanegate) can be traced further south, between Greenhead and Corbridge. Finally, A69 to Newcastle, and A695 to the North Sea, trace the site of the Wall east of Heddon.

North of Hadrian's Wall, the name Ermine Street is replaced by Watling Street, and is followed by part of A68 to a point slightly north-west of its junction with A696. Thence Watling Street is "lost" in the Southern Uplands, passing just east of Melrose, and heading generally north-north-east towards the Forth near Queensferry. Near Falkirk a branch crossed Scotland to the Glasgow area, while the main route swung to Perth, roughly across the same route as A9 today.

From the Scottish outposts of Roman Britain we must now revert to London, in order to commence a survey of our third group of roads—those of East Anglia. Compared with many other parts of Britain, the Roman history of this area has been less completely reconstructed, and in several instances the actual route of some roads is open to conjecture. East of Ermine Street, the main route was from London to Colchester (A12) via Chelmsford. Colchester (Camulodunum) had roads leading to Braughing via Braintree, which was linked to Chelmsford (A131), to Dunwich, a former port, Caistor St. Edmunds (via Dunwich and via a branch from Ipswich, A140) and along the main route to Castle Acre and on via Peddar's Way to the Norfolk coast near New Hunstanton. Further west, Cambridge was a local centre for roads in many directions except into the heart of the Fens; many of these roads linked Ermine Street on the west side.

Two important cross-country roads existed from East Anglia to south-west England, one of which leads from the other. The first is Icknield Way, which started near Mildenhall and ran south-west, roughly parallel with the line of A505 as far as Dunstable, where Watling Street was crossed. The same direction was followed to Tring, after which Icknield Way can be discerned under the Chiltern scarp towards Goring; it may have extended to Silchester (between Reading and Basingstoke). At Tring, Icknield Way connected with Akeman Street, the second cross-country road mentioned above. This road went through Bicester (A41)—actually the Roman town of Alchester nearby, whence another road struck north towards Watling Street (A43), and after leaving Alchester its route has been traced through the Oxfordshire countryside to Cirencester, the great Roman centre of that area. Having reached Cirencester, we may examine the focal nature of that city. Apart from Akeman Street and its East Anglian links, described above, roads led to Silchester (thence London and Chichester), and Gloucester, the gateway to South Wales at that time, as well as south-west and north-east via the great Fosse Way which is the next road to be examined.

Fosse Way is the most direct road in the country for its length, and it has been calculated that no point on it is more than six miles from a straight line joining Leicester and Bath. Its southern terminal is in the vicinity of Axminster, and the road runs north-east to South Petherton, Ilchester (A303) where a branch from Dorchester (Dorset) links it to the main stem, and along the route of A37 to Shepton Mallet and on to Bath (A367). North of Shepton Mallet a branch road went westwards to the Bristol Channel at Uphill, near Weston-super-Mare. Fosse Way continued north-east across open country to Cirencester and along the Cotswolds (A429) through Moreton-in-the-Marsh and beyond, through Warwickshire (again without lending its route to any modern road) as far as High Cross where it crossed Watling Street. Shortly after High Cross, A46 follows the line of Fosse Way into Leicester, and it is the final section from here to Lincoln that captures the admiration for Roman road builders, for throughout this length, A46 follows the same route to emphasize the undeviating straightness of the road.

Before examining the final group of Roman roads—those from London to Silchester and the south-west, one further road may be noted. This is Riknild Street, as it is sometimes called. This road ran from Fosse Way at Bourton-on-the-Water to Aldborough, Yorkshire, although the Yorkshire section has not been accurately surveyed. South-west of Birmingham, two "roots" existed—one from Bourton-on-the-Water and Alcester, and the other from Worcester (perhaps from Caerleon originally) along the route followed today by A38 in the main. Then Riknild Street ran through Lichfield (B4138, A38) and Burton-on-Trent to Derby (A38). On this course Watling Street was crossed at Wall, north of Birmingham, while at Derby roads linked with Manchester (via Buxton), the Long Eaton district, and possibly Sandbach via the Potteries and Rocester, though this has not been entirely traced. Meanwhile the main northward route of Riknild Street appears to approximate to that of A61 through Chesterfield and then north to the Rotherham area, across Wentworth Park, and again due north to Castleford and Aldborough. In this area, Riknild Street lay only a few miles west of, yet ran parallel to, Ermine Street, and it has been suggested that the proximity of the two roads hereabouts reflects the growth, in importance, of York. Access to this city from the south was required without having recourse to the Humber crossing. Thus Riknild Street was constructed to avoid the low lying land of the Humber.

The last major group of Roman roads remains now to be examined: the network of roads of southern England, starting at London. From London the road to Silchester (between Reading and Basingstoke) is roughly that of A4 and A30 as far as the southern edge of Windsor Great Park, where the Roman road can be traced turning due west and running across open country to Silchester. From Silchester roads ran north to Alchester and Tring, and south to Winchester, Chichester and Southampton. The west-bound roads ran to Speen and Cirencester, Speen and Bath (thence to the Bristol Channel, A4), and direct to Old Sarum, north of Salisbury. The Roman centre here was linked across the Downs with Winchester and Gloucestershire, northwards with Savernake and thence Cirencester, and south-westwards along the main route to Badbury, north-west of Wimborne Minster. From here a road ran south to Poole Harbour, and another north towards Shaftesbury, and the road to the west continued to Dorchester (connecting roads to Weymouth and Ilchester). Two alternative routes could be followed from here to Exeter—one via the coast (A35), the other via Honiton (A373 and A30); the routes forked at Charmouth, near Lyme Regis.

It was mentioned above that roads from Silchester ran to Speen and thence to Bath and Cirencester, and it was these two roads which led, eventually, to South Wales. The road to Cirencester continued north-west to Gloucester, where the Severn Valley route from Worcester was crossed. A road ran across Herefordshire to Hereford itself and then westwards up the Wye (A438) and so to Brecon. It may be remembered that the Abergavenny branch from Wroxeter crossed this road at Kenchester. West of Brecon a north-south road, incompletely traced, is believed to have linked Montgomeryshire with Neath, while the west-bound route proceeded to Llandovery (A40). The evidence in these parts is not exhaustive but there is reason to believe that from Llandovery, four roads radiated: to Brecon, as we have described; to Carmarthen (A483); to the Montgomery-Neath road northwards; and finally north-west to join the Sarn Helen near Lampeter. Sarn Helen is again not fully known, but it may have run from the lower valley of the Dovey, near Machynlleth, south to Carmarthen (west of which town traces of a road across Pembrokeshire to St. Davids have been discovered).

Lastly, the southern coastal roads of South Wales must be mentioned. The Severn was crossed at Gloucester and by means of a ferry between a point north-east of Avonmouth and Sudbrook. On the Welsh side, these two points were linked by a road roughly comparable to A48, which continued westwards to Caerleon and Neath (again A48). A loop existed via Usk from north of Castleford to Caerleon, while from Usk a road ran via Abergavenny to Brecon.

Those readers interested in road transport, particularly in road passenger transport should be alive to the fact that their interest, if it is confined solely to the recording of vehicle numbers, is of relatively little value, but if this aspect is one of a wider range of interests in road passenger transport, it can, of course, form a definite function in the widening of their knowledge on the subject. Thus, one of the most reliable, and interesting, means of studying regional geography is by studying bus services, particularly stage carriage services. The relationship of villages and towns to each other and generally to the region in which they exist can be understood remarkably well by a study of the bus service centres, not only on the basis of different regional companies, but also of the grouping and frequencies of services of one undertaking in any particular locality.

The same principle of a *general* understanding, rather than specialized concentration on an isolated aspect, can be equally well applied to the study of British roads. No harm can be done by recording numbered roads seen, or travelled along, but if only this is undertaken, it serves little useful purpose beyond itself.

zone I

A. No.	From	To

1   LONDON   EDINBURGH
via Hatfield, Biggleswade, Stamford, Grantham, Newark, E. Retford, Doncaster, Wetherby, Boroughbridge, Darlington, Durham (by-pass), Gateshead, Newcastle, Alnwick, Berwick-on-Tweed, Haddington

10   LONDON (City)   KINGS LYNN (Norfolk)
via Waltham Cross, Ware, Royston, Cambridge, Ely, Downham Market

11   LONDON (City)   NORWICH
via Leytonstone, Epping, Bishops Stortford, Newmarket, Thetford

12   LONDON (Leytonstone)   GREAT YARMOUTH (Norfolk)
via Romford (by-pass), Brentwood, Chelmsford (by-pass), Colchester (by-pass), Ipswich, Saxmundham, Lowestoft

13   LONDON (Aldgate)   SHOEBURYNESS (Essex)
via W. Ham, E. Ham, Rainham, Stanford-le-Hope, Pitsea, Leigh, Southend

14   ROYSTON (Herts)   ALCONBURY HILL (Hunts)
via Kneesworth, Arrington, Caxton, Godmanchester, Huntingdon

15   A1 n. of STILTON (Hunts)   NEW HOLLAND (Lincs)
via Peterborough, Bourne, Sleaford, Lincoln, Brigg, Barrow-on-Humber

16   STAMFORD (Lincs)   GRIMSBY (Lincs)
via Deeping, Spalding, Boston, Keal, Spilsby, Louth

17   NEWARK (Notts)   KINGS LYNN (Norfolk)
via Leadenham, Sleaford, Heckington, Fosdyke, Long Sutton, Sutton Bridge

18   DONCASTER (Yorks)   A46 w. of GRIMSBY (Lincs)
via Hatfield Chase, Scunthorpe (by-pass), Brigg, Melton Ross, Gt. Limber

19   DONCASTER (Yorks)   SOUTH SHIELDS (Durham)
via Selby, York, Easingwold, Thirsk, Yarm, Stockton, Easington, Sunderland

100   MONUMENT (London)   OLD KENT ROAD (London)
via Tower, Tower Bridge, Southwark

101   LIMEHOUSE (London)   ROTHERHITHE (London)
via Rotherhithe Tunnel

102   HACKNEY WICK (London)   GREENWICH (London)
via O. Ford, Bromley, Poplar, Blackwall Tunnel

103   SOUTH HOLLOWAY (London)   HORNSEY STATION (London)
via Holloway, Crouch End, Hornsey

104   ISLINGTON (London)   WOODFORD GREEN (Essex)
via Dalston, L. Clapton, Leyton Marshes, Lea Bridge, Woodford

105   NEWINGTON GREEN (London)   WALTHAM CROSS (Essex)
via Stoke Newington, Harringay, Wood Green, Palmers Green, Winchmore Hill, Enfield

106   BETHNAL GREEN (London)   LEYTON (Essex)
via Victoria Park, Hackney Wick

A No.	From	To
107	WHITECHAPEL (London)	STAMFORD HILL (London)
	via Bethnal Green, Cambridge Heath, Hackney, Clapton	
109	WHETSTONE (Middlesex)	TOTTENHAM (London)
	via Oakleigh Park, New Southgate, Bounds Green	
110	BARNET (Herts)	WOODFORD GREEN (Essex)
	via New Barnet, Oakwood, Enfield, Ponders End, Chingford	
111	POTTERS BAR (Middlesex)	EDMONTON (Middlesex)
	via Hadley Wood, Cockfosters, Southgate, Palmers Green	
112	SILVERTON (Essex)	WALTHAM ABBEY (Essex)
	via Plaistow, Stratford, Leyton, Walthamstow, Chingford	
113	LEYTONSTONE (Essex)	ONGAR (Essex)
	via Snaresbrook, South Woodford, Woodford Bridge, Chigwell, Abridge	
114	PLAISTOW (Essex)	WHIPPS CROSS (Essex)
	via Forest Gate, Wanstead	
115	HACKNEY WICK (London)	STRATFORD (Essex)
116	MANOR PARK (Essex)	SOUTH WANSTEAD (Essex)
	via Wanstead Flats	
117	NORTH WOOLWICH (Essex)	WANSTEAD FLATS (Essex)
	via Beckton, East Ham, Manor Park	
118	STRATFORD (Essex)	GIDEA PARK (Essex)
	via Forest Gate, Ilford, Seven Kings, Goodmayes, Chadwell Heath, Romford	
119	e. HERTFORD	BISHOPS STORTFORD (Essex)
	via Ware, Widford, Much Hadham	
120	PUCKERIDGE (Herts)	MARKS TEY (Essex)
	via L. Hadham, Bishops Stortford, Gt. Dunmow, Braintree, Coggeshall	
121	WALTHAM CROSS (Essex)	All s. of LOUGHTON (Essex)
	via Waltham Abbey, Loughton	
122	EPPING (Essex)	CHELMSFORD (Essex)
	via N. Weald, Chipping Ongar, High Ongar, Writtle	
123	UPNEY (Essex)	CHIGWELL (Essex)
	via Barking, Ilford, Gants Hill, Barkingside, Fairlop	
124	CANNING TOWN (Essex)	HORNCHURCH (Essex)
	via E. Ham, Barking, Becontree Heath	
125	RAINHAM (Essex)	ROMFORD (Essex)
	via Elm Park, Hornchurch	
126	AVELEY (Essex)	TILBURY (Essex)
	via W. Thurrock, Grays, L. Thurrock	
127	GIDEA PARK (Essex)	SOUTHEND (Essex)
	via E. Horndon, Nevendon, Prittlewell	
128	TILBURY (Essex)	ONGAR (Essex)
	via Chadwell, E. Horndon, Ingrave, Brentwood, Kelvedon Hatch	
129	SHENFIELD (Essex)	HADLEIGH (Essex)
	via Billericay, Grays Hill, Wickford, Rayleigh	

A. No.	From	To

130 A129 ne. of RAYLEIGH (Essex)   TRUMPINGTON (Cambs)
via Rettendon, Chelmsford, Gt. Dunmow, Thaxted, Saffron Walden, Gt. Chesterford

131 L. WALTHAM (Essex)   SUDBURY (Suffolk)
via Braintree, H. Garret, Halstead, Ballingdon

133 CLACTON-ON-SEA (Essex)   SUDBURY (Suffolk)
via Weeley, Colchester, Bures, Gt. Cornard

134 COLCHESTER (Essex)   A10 s. of KINGS LYNN (Norfolk)
via Nayland, Sudbury, Bury St. Edmunds, Thetford, Mundford, Stokeferry

136 A133 n. of CLACTON (Essex)   PARKESTON (Essex)
via Thorpe-le-Soken, Gt. Oakley, Dovercourt

137 COLCHESTER (Essex)   IPSWICH (Suffolk)
via Ardleigh, Brantham, Wherstead

138 ERWARTON BAY, opp. HARWICH (Essex) A137 s. of IPSWICH (Suffolk)
via Chelmondiston, Woolverstone

140 CLAYDON (Suffolk)   A149 s. of CROMER (Norfolk)
via Yaxley, L. Stratton, Norwich, Aylsham, Roughton

141 n. of BUCKDEN (Hunts)   GUYHIRNE (Cambs)
via Huntingdon, Warboys, Chatteris, Doddington, March

142 NEWMARKET (Suffolk)   CHATTERIS (Cambs)
via Fordham, Soham, Ely, Witchford, Mepal

143 HAVERHILL (Suffolk)   GREAT YARMOUTH (Norfolk)
via Bury St. Edmunds, Botesdale, Diss, Harleston, Bungay, Gorleston

144 A12 s. of HALESWORTH (Suffolk)   s. of NORWICH
via Halesworth, Ilketshall, St. John, Bungay, Brooke

145 n. of BLYTHBURGH (Suffolk)   BECCLES (Norfolk)
via Sotherton, Brampton, Shadingfield, Weston

146 LOWESTOFT (Suffolk)   NORWICH
via Barnby, Beccles, Loddon, Thurton

148 MUNDESLEY (Norfolk)   S. WOOTTON (Norfolk)
via Cromer, Holt, Fakenham, Rudham, Harpley

149 GREAT YARMOUTH (Norfolk)   KINGS LYNN (Norfolk)
via Caister, Statham, N. Walsham, Cromer, Sheringham, Wells, New Hunstanton

151 BOURNE (Lincs)   FLEET HARGATE (Lincs)
via Pinchbeck West, Spalding, Fulney, Whaplade, Holbeach

152 GOSBERTON (Lincs)   DONINGTON (Lincs)
via Quadring

153 HONINGTON (Lincs)   LOUTH (Lincs)
via Wilsford, Sleaford, Billinghay, Coningsby, Horncastle, Scamblesby

155 TUMBY (Lincs)   W. KEAL (Lincs)
via Mareham-le-fen, Revesby, E. Kirkby

A No.	From	To
156	A57 w. of SAXILBY (Lincs)	GAINSBOROUGH (Lincs)
	via Fenton, Torksey, Marton, Gate Burton, Lea	
157	WRAGBY (Lincs)	MALTBY-LE-MARSH (Lincs)
	via Barkwith, Burgh-on-barn, Louth, Withern, Strubby	
158	LINCOLN	SKEGNESS (Lincs)
	via Langworth, Wragby, Horncastle, Partny, Burgh-le-marsh	
159	GAINSBOROUGH (Lincs)	SCUNTHORPE (Lincs)
	via Blyton, Scotter, Messingham, Frodingham	
160	nr. MELTON ROSS (Lincs)	BARROW-ON-HUMBER (Lincs)
	via Croxton, Wootton, Thornton Curtis	
161	BECKINGHAM (Notts)	GOOLE (Yorks)
	via Walkeringham, Misterton, Epworth, Crowle, Swinefleet	
162	BROTHERTON (Yorks)	TADCASTER (Yorks)
	via S. Milford, Sherburn-in-Elmet, Towton	
163	A19 n. of SELBY (Yorks)	GT. DRIFFIELD (Yorks)
	via Bubwith, Holme, Mkt. Weighton, Bamton, Kirkburn	
164	HULL	GT. DRIFFIELD (Yorks)
	via Anlaby, Willerby, Beverley, Watton, Cranswick	
165	HULL	BURNISTON (Yorks)
	via Skirlaugh, Leven Beeford, Bridlington, Muston, Scarborough	
166	A1079 e. of YORK	BRIDLINGTON (Yorks)
	via Gate Helmsley, Wetwang, Gt. Driffield, Burton Agnes, Carresby	
167	GREEN HAMMERTON (Yorks)	s. of DARLINGTON (Durham)
	via Boroughbridge, Topcliffe, Northallerton, Gt. Smeaton, Croft	
168	TOPCLIFFE (Yorks)	NORTHALLERTON (Yorks)
	via Thirsk, Thornton-le-Street	
169	MALTON (Yorks)	A171 w. of WHITBY (Yorks)
	via Pickering, Sleights	
170	THIRSK (Yorks)	SEAMER (Yorks)
	via Helmsley, Kirby Moorside, Pickering, Brompton, Ayton	
171	SCARBOROUGH (Yorks)	MIDDLESBROUGH (Yorks)
	via Scalby, Whitby, Guisborough, Ormesby	
172	A19 ne. of NORTHALLERTON (Yorks)	MIDDLESBROUGH (Yorks)
	via Ingleby Cross, Stokesley, Marton	
173	STOKESLEY (Yorks)	BROTTON (Yorks)
	via Gt. Ayton, Guisborough, Skelton	
174	WHITBY (Yorks)	THORNABY-ON-TEES (Yorks)
	via Lythe, Hinderwell, Loftus, Saltburn, Normanby, Ormesby	
175	NORMANBY (Yorks)	MIDDLESBROUGH (Yorks)
	via South Bank	
177	STOCKTON-ON-TEES (Durham)	DURHAM
	via Thorpe Thewles, Sedgefield, Shincliffe	

A No.	From	To
178	nr. STOCKTON-ON-TEES (Durham)	W. HARTLEPOOL (Durham)
	via Port Clarence, Seaton Carew	
179	A19 w. of HART (Durham)	W. HARTLEPOOL (Durham)
	via Hart	
181	DURHAM	A19 w. of CASTLE EDEN (Durham)
	via Byers Garth, Running Water	
182	EASINGTON (Durham)	A184 e. of GATESHEAD (Durham)
	via Hetton-le-Hole, Houghton-le-spring, Washington	
183	CHESTER-LE-STREET (Durham)	S. SHIELDS (Durham)
	via Sunderland, Whitburn, Marsden	
184	n. SUNDERLAND (Durham)	GATESHEAD (Durham)
	via E. Boldon, W. Boldon, Felling	
185	S. SHIELDS (Durham)	FELLING (Durham)
	via Jarrow, Heworth	
186	NEWCASTLE-ON-TYNE	WALLSEND (Northumb)
	via Walker, Hebburn	
187	WALLSEND (Northumb)	N. SHIELDS (Northumb)
	via Willington	
188	A191 e. of BENTON SQ. (Northumb)	EARSDON (Northumb)
189	n. NEWCASTLE-ON-TYNE	BEDLINGTON (Northumb)
	via W. Moor, Shankhouse Row	
190	A189 w. of SEGHILL (Northumb)	SEATON SLUICE (Northumb)
	via Seghill	
191	LONGBENTON (Northumb)	WHITLEY BAY (Northumb)
	via Benton Square	
192	TYNEMOUTH (Northumb)	MORPETH (Northumb)
	via Earsdon, Holywell	
193	TYNEMOUTH (Northumb)	BEDLINGTON (Northumb)
	via Whitley Bay, Hartley, Blyth	
196	s. of MORPETH (Northumb)	ASHINGTON (Northumb)
	via Guide Post	
197	MORPETH (Northumb)	NEWBIGGIN-BY-SEA (Northumb)
	via Pegswood, Bothal, Ashington, Woodhorn	
198	A1 w. of DUNBAR (E. Lothian)	A1 w. of PRESTONPANS (E. Lothian)
	via Whitekirk, N. Berwick, Gullane, Aberlady, Longniddry, Prestonpans	
199	PORTOBELLO (Midlothian)	LEITH (Midlothian)
	via Seafield	

● *Thanet Way, Kent, showing wide separation of carriageways to avoid dazzle at night.*

● *A model of a fly-over roundabout, where the motorway passes over an all-purpose road.*

● *One of Britain's few remaining Toll Gates, where tolls are still levied—at Swinford, Nr. Oxford.* [Fox Photos

● *This narrow street at Ledbury is part of the A449 from the Midlands to the industrial area of South Wales.* [Br. Road Federation Ltd.

● *The A6, England to Scotland, is routed through the back streets of Lancaster.*   [Br. Road Federation Ltd.

● *An estimated 10,000 vehicles a day pass through Markyate on the A5 London to the Midlands.*   [Br. Road Federation Ltd.

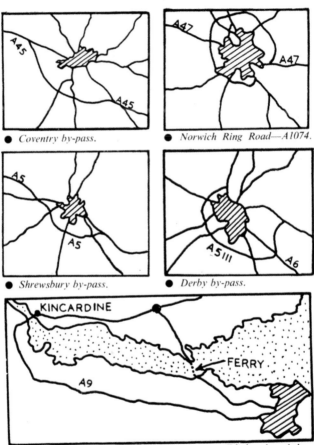

● *Coventry by-pass.*

● *Norwich Ring Road—A1074.*

● *Shrewsbury by-pass.*

● *Derby by-pass.*

● *Crossing the Firth of Forth—traffic between Edinburgh and the north has to use the ferry at Queensferry, or make the long detour via Kincardine (Fife).*

● This type of road sign is to be found in many parts of rural Britain. Illustrated is the sign at Nantlle Village in Caernarvonshire. In addition to marking the boundary, it indicates that the village is 3¼ miles beyond Penygroes, while Rhyd-ddu lies 4 miles ahead.

● A more common sight is this type of sign at the approach to a roundabout on the Oxford by-pass. The black and white check indicates that the roads beneath it lead off the immediate road (A423) some distance along it.

45

● *The A1, London to Edinburgh, as it passes through the centre of Doncaster.* [M.O.I.

● *Out into the country goes the A30, Hounslow to Lands End, shown here near Stockbridge.* [M.O.I.

● *En route from Southampton to Exeter—the A35 entering Bournemouth Square.*

● *The Mickleham by-pass, a fast dual-carriage motorway between Leatherhead and Dorking, in Surrey.*

● One of London's exits—leading off to the top right is the *Great West Road* at *Brentford, which takes traffic on its way to Bristol via Slough, Reading, Chippenham and Bath.*

[Camera Press

zone 2

A. No.	From	To
2	LONDON	DOVER (Kent)

via Eltham, Dartford (by-pass), Rochester, Chatham, Sittingbourne, Faversham, Canterbury

| 20 | LONDON (New Cross) | FOLKESTONE (Kent) |

via Sidcup, Farningham, Wrotham, Maidstone, Charing, Ashford

| 21 | LONDON (Lewisham) | HASTINGS (Sussex) |

via Bromley, Sevenoaks, Tonbridge, Robertsbridge, Battle

| 22 | PURLEY (Surrey) | EASTBOURNE (Sussex) |

via Godstone, E. Grinstead, Uckfield, Hailsham, Willingdon

| 23 | LONDON (Westminster) | BRIGHTON (Sussex) |

via Brixton, Croydon, Redhill, Crawley (by-pass), Handcross, Sayers Common

| 24 | LONDON (Clapham) | WORTHING (Sussex) |

via Morden, Ewell, Leatherhead (by-pass), Dorking (by-pass), Horsham, Washington

| 25 | A20 nr. WROTHAM (Kent) | MERROW, nr. GUILDFORD (Surrey) |

via Ightham, Westerham, Godstone, Redhill, Reigate, Dorking

| 26 | MAIDSTONE (Kent) | LEWES (Sussex) |

via Tonbridge, Tunbridge Wells, Marefield, Uckfield

| 27 | PEVENSEY (Sussex) | A36 nr. WHITEPARISH (Wilts) |

via Lewes, Brighton, Hove, Arundel, Chichester (by-pass), Havant, Fareham, Swaythling, Romsey

| 28 | MARGATE (Kent) | n. of HASTINGS (Sussex) |

via Westgate-on-Sea, Canterbury, Chilham, Ashford, Tenterden, Rolvenden

| 29 | BEARE GREEN (Sussex) | BOGNOR REGIS (Sussex) |

via Five Oaks, Billingshurst, Pulborough, Houghton, Westgate

| 200 | LONDON BRIDGE | GREENWICH (London) |

via Bermondsey, Rotherhithe, Deptford

| 201 | SOUTHWARK (London) | BLACKFRIARS (London) |

via Elephant & Castle, Blackfriars Bridge

| 202 | NEW CROSS (London) | VICTORIA (London) |

via Peckham, Camberwell, Kennington

| 203 | TULSE HILL (London) | VAUXHALL (London) |

via Brixton, Stockwell

| 205 | WOOLWICH (London) | SHEPHERDS BUSH (London) |

via Eltham, Catford, Tulse Hill, Clapham, Battersea, Kensington

| 206 | GREENWICH (London) | DARTFORD (Kent) |

via Woolwich, Plumstead, Abbey Wood, Erith

| 207 | KIDBROOKE (London) | DARTFORD (Kent) |

via Shooters Hill, Welling, Bexleyheath, Crayford

A. No.	From	To
208	ELTHAM (London) *via* Mottingham, Chislehurst, Petts Wood	nr. ORPINGTON (Kent)
209	w. of WELLING (Kent) *via* Welling	ABBEY WOOD (London)
210	ELTHAM (London) *via* Blackfen	w. of BEXLEY (Kent)
211	ELTHAM (London) *via* New Eltham, Sidcup	FOOTS CRAY (Kent)
212	CATFORD (London) *via* Sydenham, Crystal Palace, Thornton Heath	W. CROYDON (Surrey)
213	SYDENHAM (London) *via* Penge, Norwood Jct., Selhurst	W. CROYDON (Surrey)
214	WICKHAM (Kent) *via* Elmers End, Crystal Palace, Streatham, Tooting Bec	WANDSWORTH (London)
215	SHIRLEY (Kent) *via* Norwood Jct., Upper Norwood, Tulse Hill, Herne Hill, Camberwell	ELEPHANT & CASTLE (London)
216	STREATHAM (London)	N. MITCHAM (Surrey)
217	A23 n. of CRAWLEY (Sussex) *via* Reigate, Kingswood, Sutton (by-pass), Mitcham, Tooting, Wandsworth	FULHAM (London)
218	S. WIMBLEDON (Surrey) *via* Southfields	WANDSWORTH (London)
219	S. WIMBLEDON (Surrey) *via* Wimbledon, Putney, Hammersmith, Shepherds Bush, White City	WILLESDEN JCT. (London)
220	BEXLEYHEATH (Kent) *via* Bursted Wood	ERITH (Kent)
221	HURST (Kent) *via* Danson Park	BEXLEYHEATH (Kent)
222	E. CROYDON (Surrey) *via* Addiscombe, Elmers End, Bromley, Chislehurst, Sidcup	BEXLEY (Kent)
223	CRAYFORD (Kent) *via* N. Cray, St. Pauls Cray, St. Mary Cray, Orpington	GREEN STREET GREEN (Kent)
224	FOOTS CRAY (Kent) *via* St. Mary Cray, Orpington (by-pass), Chelsfield	HALSTEAD (Kent)
225	DARTFORD (Kent) *via* Darenth, Sutton-at-Hone, Farningham, Eynsford, Otford	SEVENOAKS (Kent)
226	CRAYFORD (Kent) *via* Dartford, Swanscombe, Northfleet, Gravesend, Chalk	STROOD (Kent)
227	GRAVESEND (Kent) *via* Meopham, S. Street, Wrotham, Borough Green, Ightham	TONBRIDGE (Kent)
228	HOO (Kent) *via* Strood, Cuxton, Snodland, Ledbourne, W. Malling	MEREWORTH (Kent)

A. No.	From	To
229	ROCHESTER (Kent) *via* Maidstone, Staplehurst, Cranbrook, Hawkhurst, Sedlescombe	A28 n. of. HASTINGS (Sussex)
230	CHATHAM (Kent)	HORSTED (Kent)
232	ORPINGTON (Kent) *via* W. Wickham, Shirley, Croydon, Waddon, Carshalton, Cheam	EWELL (Surrey)
233	BROMLEY COMMON (Kent) *via* Keston Mark, Leaves Green, Biggin Hill	WESTERHAM (Kent)
234	CRYSTAL PALACE (Kent) *via* Penge	BECKENHAM (Kent)
235	THORNTON HEATH (Surrey) *via* Croydon	PURLEY (Surrey)
236	COLLIERS WOOD (Surrey) *via* Mitcham Common	CROYDON (Surrey)
237	MITCHAM COMMON (Surrey) *via* Mitcham Jct., Hackbridge, Wallington	COULSDON (Surrey)
238	S. WIMBLEDON (Surrey) *via* Raynes Park, Coombe	KINGSTON (Surrey)
239	MORDENHALL PARK (Surrey) *via* Mitcham Station	MITCHAM COMMON (Surrey)
240	BURGH HEATH (Surrey) *via* Ewell, Tolworth	SURBITON (Surrey)
241	EPSOM (Surrey)	A240 nr. TATTENHAM CORNER (Surrey)
242	A23 n. of REDHILL (Surrey)	REIGATE (Surrey)
243	LEATHERHEAD (Surrey) *via* Chessington Park	SURBITON (Surrey)
244	A243 n. of LEATHERHEAD (Surrey) *via* Oxshott, Esher, Hersham, Walton-on-Thames, Halliford, Feltham	A315 w. of HOUNSLOW (Middlesex)
245	LEATHERHEAD (Surrey) *via* Stoke d'Abernon, Cobham, Byfleet, Sheerwater	A320 n. of WOKING (Surrey)
246	s. of LEATHERHEAD (Surrey) *via* Gt. Bookham, Effingham, Horsley, E. Clarendon, Merrow	GUILDFORD (Surrey)
247	ALBURY DOWNS (Surrey) *via* W. Clarendon, Send, O. Woking	WOKING (Surrey)
248	nr. ALBURY DOWNS (Surrey) *via* Albury, Chilworth	A3100 s. of GUILDFORD (Surrey)
249	MAIDSTONE (Kent) *via* Detting, Bobbing, Iwade, W. Minster	SHEERNESS (Kent)
250	W. MINSTER (Kent) *via* Minster	EASTCHURCH (Kent)
251	ne. of ASHFORD (Kent) *via* Kennington, Boughton Amph, Leaveland, Sheldwich	FAVERSHAM (Kent)

A. No.	From	To
252	CHARING (Kent) *via* Paddock, Challock Lees	CHILHAM (Kent)
253	SARRE (Kent) *via* Gore Str., St. Lawrence	RAMSGATE (Kent)
254	MARGATE (Kent) *via* St. Peters	RAMSGATE (Kent)
255	MARGATE (Kent) *via* Upton, Broadstairs	RAMSGATE (Kent)
256	ST. PETERS (Kent) *via* Haire, Cliffsend, Richborough, Sandwich, Eastry	EWELL (Kent)
257	CANTERBURY (Kent) *via* Wingham, Ash	SANDWICH (Kent)
258	DOVER (Kent) *via* Ringwould, Walmer, Deal, Shalden	SANDWICH (Kent)
259	DOVER (Kent) *via* Folkestone, Hythe, Rye, Hastings, Eastbourne, Brighton, Worthing, Bognor	CHICHESTER (Sussex)
260	BROOME PARK (Kent) *via* Denton, Selstead, Hawkinge	FOLKESTONE (Kent)
261	NEW INN GREEN (Kent) *via* Pedling	HYTHE (Kent)
262	A28 n. of TENTERDEN (Kent) *via* Biddenden, Sissinghurst, Goudhurst	LAMBERHURST (Kent)
263	nr. PEMBURY (Kent)	TUNBRIDGE WELLS (Kent)
264	TUNBRIDGE WELLS (Kent) *via* Groombridge, Hartfield, Forest Row, E. Grinstead, Crawley, Horsham	A29 w. of HORSHAM (Sussex)
265	HAWKHURST (Kent) *via* Hurst Green, Burwash, Cross-in-hand, Ringmer	LEWES (Sussex)
266	A267 s. of TUNBRIDGE WELLS (Kent) *via* Wadhurst, Ticehurst	A21 n. of HURST GREEN (Sussex)
267	TUNBRIDGE WELLS (Kent) *via* Frant, Mayfield, Five Ashes, Cross-in-hand, Hellingly	HORSEBRIDGE (Sussex)
268	A21 w. of HAWKHURST (Kent) *via* Hawkhurst, Newenden, Northiam, Beckley, Peasemarsh	RYE (Sussex)
269	BATTLE (Sussex) *via* Catsfield, Ninfield, Sidley Green	BEXHILL (Sussex)
270	SIDLEY (Sussex)	A259 e. of BEXHILL (Sussex)
271	NINFIELD (Sussex) *via* Windmill Hill, Gardner Street	HORSEBRIDGE (Sussex)
272	A265 e. of UCKFIELD (Sussex) *via* Uckfield, Haywards Heath, Billingshurst, Midhurst, Petersfield, Winchester	STOCKBRIDGE (Hants)
273	A22 w. of HORSEBRIDGE (Sussex) *via* Laughton	RINGMER (Sussex)

A. No.	From	To
275	WYCH CROSS (Sussex)	NEWHAVEN (Sussex)
	via Chailey, Offham, Lewes, Rodmall, Southease	
279	HANDCROSS (Sussex)	L. BEEDING (Sussex)
280	FINDON (Sussex)	ANGMERING STN. (Sussex)
	via Clapham, Angmering	
281	U. BEEDING (Sussex)	GUILDFORD (Surrey)
	via Henfield, Cowfield, Horsham, Bramley, Shalford	
283	NEW SHOREHAM (Sussex)	MILFORD (Surrey)
	via Steyning, Pulborough, Petworth, N. Chapel	
284	HOUGHTON (Sussex)	LITTLEHAMPTON (Sussex)
	via Arundel, Lyminster	
285	PETWORTH (Sussex)	CHICHESTER (Sussex)
	via Duncton, U. Waltham, W. Hampnett	
286	W. WITTERING (Sussex)	MILFORD (Surrey)
	via Chichester, Mid Lavant, W. Dean, Midhurst, Haslemere	
287	A286 s. of HASLEMERE (Surrey)	A30 e. of BASINGSTOKE (Hants)
	via Hindhead, Farnham, Odiham, North Warnborough	
288	HILSEA (Hants)	PORTSMOUTH (Hants)
	via Copnor, Milton, Eastney, Southsea	
289	Links A2 and A228 n. of STROOD (Kent)	
290	CANTERBURY (Kent)	WHITSTABLE (Kent)
	via Blean	
291	STURRY (Kent)	HERNE BAY (Kent)
	via Herne, Eddington	
295	A271 e. of HORSEBRIDGE (Sussex)	HAILSHAM (Sussex)
296	DARTFORD (Kent)	SWANSCOMBE (Kent)
297	MORDEN (Surrey)	BELMONT (Surrey)
	via St. Helier, Sutton	
298	WIMBLEDON CHASE (Surrey)	A3 w. of RAYNES PARK (Surrey)
	via Raynes Park	
299	A2 e. of FAVERSHAM (Kent)	nr. ST. NICHOLAS-AT-WADE (Kent)
	passes s. of Whitstable and Herne Bay	

zone 3

3	LONDON	PORTSMOUTH (Hants)
	via Putney, Esher, Guildford (by-pass), Petersfield, Cosham	
30	HOUNSLOW (Middlesex)	LANDS END (Cornwall)
	via Staines, Basingstoke, Stockbridge, Salisbury, Shaftesbury, Yeovil, Chard, Honiton, Exeter, Okehampton, Launceston, Redruth, Bodmin, Penzance	

A. No.	From	To
31	GUILDFORD (Surrey)	BERE REGIS (Dorset)

31 GUILDFORD (Surrey)   BERE REGIS (Dorset)
   via Farnham, Alton, Winchester, Romsey, Ringwood, Wimborne Minster

32 GOSPORT (Hants)   READING (Berks)
   via Fareham, W. Meon, Alton, Odiham, Hook, Swallowfield.

33 SOUTHAMPTON   RISELEY COMMON (Berks)
   via Chandlers Ford, Winchester (by-pass), Basingstoke, Sherfield Loddon

34 s. WINCHESTER (Hants)   MANCHESTER
   via Newbury, Abingdon, Oxford, Stratford, Birmingham, Walsall, Cannock, Stafford, Newcastle-under-Lyme, Congleton, Wilmslow

35 SOUTHAMPTON   EXETER (Devon)
   via Lyndhurst, Bournemouth, Bere Regis, Dorchester, Bridport, Lyme Regis

36 TOTTON, nr. SOUTHAMPTON   w. BATH (Somerset)
   via Landford, Salisbury, Wilton, Warminster, Beckington

37 DORCHESTER (Dorset)   BRISTOL
   via Stratton, Yeovil, Ilchester, W. Lydford, Shepton Mallet, Pensford

38 BODMIN (Cornwall)   DERBY
   via Liskeard, Plymouth, Buckfastleigh, Exeter, Taunton, Bridgwater, Bristol, Gloucester, Tewkesbury, Worcester, Bromsgrove, Birmingham, Lichfield, Burton-on-Trent

39 FALMOUTH (Cornwall)   nr. BATH (Somerset)
   via Truro, Wadebridge, Camelford, Bideford, Barnstaple, Minehead, Bridgwater, Glastonbury, Wells

300 ELEPHANT & CASTLE (London)   SOUTHWARK BRIDGE (London)
   via Southwark Bridge Road

301 ELEPHANT & CASTLE (London)   STRAND (London)
   via Waterloo Road

302 ELEPHANT & CASTLE (London)   HYDE PARK CORNER (London)
   via Westminster, Victoria

303 nr. MICHELDEVER (Hants)   A30 w. of YARCOMBE (Devon)
   via Andover, Amesbury, Wincanton, Ilchester, Ilminster

304 HYDE PARK (London)   FULHAM (London)
   via S. Kensington, Walham Green

305 WANDSWORTH (London)   KEMPTON PARK (Middlesex)
   via Putney, Mortlake, Richmond, Twickenham, Hanworth

306 ROEHAMPTON (London)   HAMMERSMITH (London)
   via Barnes

307 nr. ESHER (Surrey)   KEW BRIDGE (London)
   via Long Ditton, Surbiton, Kingston, Ham, Richmond, Kew

308 CHELSEA (London)   s. of MARLOW (Bucks)
   via Putney, Kingston, Hampton Court, Staines, Windsor, Maidenhead

309 nr. ESHER (Surrey)   TWICKENHAM (Middlesex)
   via Thames Ditton, Hampton Court, Teddington

A. No.	From	To
310	HAMPTON WICK (Middlesex) *via* Teddington, Twickenham	ISLEWORTH (Middlesex)
311	HAMPTON (Middlesex) *via* Fulwell	TWICKENHAM (Middlesex)
312	BUSHY PARK (Middlesex) *via* Feltham, London Airport, Harlington, Yeading, Northolt	HARROW (Middlesex)
313	TEDDINGTON (Middlesex) *via* Hampton Hill	A312 e. of HANWORTH (Middlesex)
314	HANWORTH (Middlesex) *via* Hounslow Heath, Whitton	HOUNSLOW (Middlesex)
315	KEW BRIDGE (Middlesex) *via* Isleworth, Hounslow	E. BEDFONT (Middlesex)
316	TURNHAM GREEN (London) *via* Chiswick, Mortlake, Twickenham, Whitton	nr. HANWORTH (Middlesex)
317	HERSHAM (Surrey) *via* Weybridge	CHERTSEY (Surrey)
318	BYFLEET (Surrey) *via* Newhaw, Addlestone	CHERTSEY (Surrey)
319	ADDLESTONE (Surrey) *via* Ottershaw, Chobham	WEST END, nr. BISLEY (Surrey)
320	STAINES (Middlesex) *via* Chertsey, Ottershaw, Woking	GUILDFORD (Surrey)
321	GUILDFORD (Surrey) *via* Stoughton, Pirbright, Frimley Green, Sandhurst, Wokingham, Twyford	HENLEY-ON-THAMES (Oxon)
322	RICKFORD (Surrey) *via* Bisley, Bagshot	BRACKNELL (Berks)
323	GUILDFORD (Surrey) *via* Normandy, Ash	nr. FARNHAM (Surrey)
324	WOKING (Surrey) *via* Brookwood, Pirbright, Ash	ALDERSHOT (Hants)
325	n. of PETERSFIELD (Hants) *via* Greatham, Farnham, Aldershot, Farnborough	BAGSHOT HEATH (Surrey)
327	FRIMLEY (Surrey) *via* Yateley, Eversley, Shinfield	READING (Berks)
328	NEW EGHAM (Surrey) *via* O. Windsor, Datchet	WINDSOR (Berks)
329	A30 nr. SUNNINGDALE (Berks) *via* Ascot, Bracknell, Wokingham, Reading, Wallingford	SHILLINGFORD (Oxon)
330	A30 on CHOBHAM COMMON (Surrey) *via* Ascot, Winkfield, Holyport	A308 s. of MAIDENHEAD (Berks)
331	WINDSOR (Berks) *via* Datchet	A4 w. of COLNBROOK (Bucks)

A. No.	From	To
332	A322 n. of BAGSHOT (Surrey)	A413 n. of GERRARDS CROSS (Bucks)
	via Ascot, Windsor, Slough, Gerrards Cross	
333	WYRING (Hants)	A34 s. of WINCHESTER (Hants)
	via Wickham, Bishops Waltham, Twyford	
334	A333 n. of WICKHAM (Hants)	BITTERNE (Hants)
	via Botley	
335	SWAYTHLING (Hants)	s. of TWYFORD (Hants)
	via Eastleigh, Albrook	
336	SWAYTHLING (Hants)	SOUTHAMPTON
	via St. Denys	
337	CADNAM (Hants)	e. of CHRISTCHURCH (Hants)
	via Lyndhurst, Brockenhurst, Lymington, Milton	
338	SOMERFORD (Hants)	A420 sw. of OXFORD
	via Ringwood, Fordingbridge, Salisbury, Boscombe Down, Hungerford, Wantage	
339	ALTON (Hants)	NEWBURY (Berks)
	via Lasham, Basingstoke, Kingsclere	
340	n. of BASINGSTOKE (Hants)	PANGBOURNE (Berks)
	via Tadley, Aldermaston, Englefield, Tidmarsh	
341	ENSBURY (Hants)	nr. WIMBORNE MINSTER (Hants)
	via Kinson, Canford Magna	
342	WEYHILL, nr. ANDOVER (Wilts)	A4 w. of CALNE (Wilts)
	via Ludgershall, Upavon, Rughall, Devizes	
343	A30 e. of SALISBURY (Wilts)	NEWBURY (Berks)
	via Wallop, Andover, Hurstbourne Tarrant	
344	STONEHENGE (Wilts)	HEYTESBURY (Wilts)
	via Rollestone, Shrewton, Chuterne St. Mary	
345	SALISBURY (Wilts)	nr. SWINDON (Wilts)
	via Amesbury, Enford, Upavon, Pewsey, Marlborough	
346	nr. LUDGERSHALL (Wilts)	MARLBOROUGH (Wilts)
	via Collingbourne Ducis, Collingbourne Kingston, Burbage	
347	BOURNEMOUTH (Hants)	TRICHETTS CROSS (Dorset)
	via Winton, Moordown, Ensbury, Parley	
348	POOLE (Dorset)	TRICHETTS CROSS (Dorset)
	via Branksome, W. Howe, Longham	
349	POOLE (Dorset)	WIMBORNE MINSTER (Dorset)
	via Fleets Corner, Oakley	
350	POOLE (Dorset)	CHIPPENHAM (Wilts)
	via Spettisbury, Blandford Forum, Shaftesbury, Warminster, Melksham	
351	LYTCHETT MINSTER (Dorset)	SWANAGE (Dorset)
	via Sandford, Wareham, Corfe Castle, Herston	

A. No.	From	To

352 WAREHAM (Dorset)   SHERBORNE (Dorset)
via Wool, Broadmayne, Dorchester, Cerne Abbas, Long Burton

353 A352 nr. WARMWELL (Dorset)   WEYMOUTH (Dorset)
via Poxwell, Osmington, Preston

354 SALISBURY (Wilts)   PORTLAND (Dorset)
via Coombe Bissett, Blandford Forum, Puddletown, Dorchester, Weymouth

356 GRIMSTONE (Dorset)   w. of S. PETHERTON (Somerset)
via Maiden Newton, S. Perrott, Crewkerne, Lopan

357 DURWESTON (Dorset)   w. of WINCANTON (Somerset)
via Shillingstone, Lydlinch, Stalbridge, Templecombe

358 A35 n. of AXMOUTH (Devon)   WILLITON (Somerset)
via Musbury, Axminster, Chard, Beauchamp, Taunton, Crowcombe

359 YEOVIL (Somerset)   A361 w. of FROME (Somerset)
via Marston Magna, Sparkford, Bruton, Wanstrow

360 SALISBURY (Wilts)   DEVIZES (Wilts)
via Shrewton, Tilshead, W. Lavington, Potterne

361 ILFRACOMBE (Devon)   BANBURY (Oxon)
via Barnstaple, Bampton, Taunton, Frome, Devizes, Swindon, Chipping Norton

362 WARMINSTER (Wilts)   FARRINGTON GURNEY (Somerset)
via Bugley, Frome, Buckland Denham, Radstock, Midsomer Norton

363 YARNBROOK (Wilts)   BATHFORD (Somerset)
via Woodmarsh, Trowbridge, Bradford

365 A361 w. of DEVIZES (Wilts)   BOX (Wilts)
via Bowerhill, Melksham, Shaw, Atworth

366 TROWBRIDGE (Wilts)   A362 se. of RADSTOCK (Somerset)
via Farleigh Hungerford, Norton St. Philip, Faulkland

367 OAKHILL (Somerset)   BATH (Somerset)
via Stratton-on-the-Fosse, Radstock, Peasedown, St. John

368 MARKSBURY (Somerset)   BANWELL (Somerset)
via Chelwood, Compton Martin, Blagdon, Sandford

370 E. BRENT (Somerset)   BRISTOL
via Bleadon, Weston-super-mare, Worle, Congresbury, Long Ashton

371 WINCANTON (Somerset)   e. of WESTON-S-MARE (Somerset)
via Castle Cary, Shepton Mallet, Wells, Draycott, Cheddar, Banwell

372 nr. W. CAMEL (Somerset)   BRIDGWATER (Somerset)
via L. Sutton, Lamport, Othery, Weston Zoyland

373 nr. CHARMOUTH (Dorset)   S. MOLTON (Devon)
via Axminster, Honiton, Cullompton, Willand, Tiverton, Witheridge

374 w. of PLYMPTON (Devon)   A38 w. of TIDEFORD (Cornwall)
via Crown Hill, St. Budeaux, Saltash, Tideford

375 HONITON (Devon)   SIDFORD (Devon)
via Sidbury

A. No.	From	To

376 NEWTON POPPLEFORD (Devon)   EXMOUTH (Devon)
via Colaton Raleigh, E. Burleigh, Budleigh Salterton

377 EXMOUTH (Devon)   BARNSTAPLE (Devon)
via Topham, Exeter, Crediton, Eggesford, Bishops Tawton

379 EXETER (Devon)   PLYMOUTH (Devon)
via Dawlish, Teignmouth, Torquay, Paignton, Dartmouth, Kingsbridge

380 A38 s. of KENNFORD (Devon)   TORQUAY (Devon)
via Kingsteinton, Newton Abbot, Kingskerswell

381 TEIGNMOUTH (Devon)   KINGSBRIDGE (Devon)
via Kingsteinton, Newton Abbot, Totnes, Halwell

382 NEWTON ABBOT (Devon)   WHIDDON DOWN (Devon)
via Bovey Tracy, Moreton Hampstead, Sandypark

383 NEWTON ABBOT (Devon)   BICKINGTON (Devon)

384 TOTNES (Devon)   s. of LAUNCESTON (Cornwall)
via Ashburton, Two Bridges, Tavistock, Milton Abbot

385 PAIGNTON (Devon)   s. of S. BRENT (Devon)
via Collaton St. Mary, Totnes, Avon Wick

386 PLYMOUTH (Devon)   NORTHAM (Devon)
via Yelverton, Tavistock, Okehampton, Hatherleigh, Gt. Torrington, Bideford

387 A38 w. of ST. GERMANS (Cornwall)   POLPERRO (Cornwall)
via Hessenford, E. Looe, W. Looe

388 PLYMOUTH (Devon)   LANDCROSS (Devon)
via Saltash, Callington, Launceston, Holsworthy, Monkleigh

389 BODMIN (Cornwall)   PADSTOW (Cornwall)
via Egloshayle, Wadebridge, St. Issey, Little Petherick

390 TAVISTOCK (Devon)   REDRUTH (Cornwall)
via Callington, Liskeard, Lostwithiel, St. Austell, Truro

391 A30 s. of BODMIN (Cornwall)   ST. AUSTELL (Cornwall)
via Trescoll, Bugle, Treverbyn

392 nr. FRADDON (Cornwall)   NEWQUAY (Cornwall)
via White Cross, St. Columb Minor

393 REDRUTH (Cornwall)   nw. of PENRYN (Cornwall)
via Lannor, Ponsanooth

394 nw. of PENRYN (Cornwall)   LONGROCK, nr. MARAZION (Cornwall)
via Helston, Ashton, Marazion

395 A30 w. of LAUNCESTON (Cornwall)   A39 n. of CAMELFORD (Cornwall)
via Hallworthy, Davidstow

396 n. of EXETER (Devon)   DUNSTER (Somerset)
via Tiverton, Bampton, Exton, Cutcombe

399 BLACKMOOR STN. (Devon)   ILFRACOMBE (Devon)
via Seven Ash, Combe Martin, Hele

A. No.	From	To
4	LONDON	AVONMOUTH (Glos.)

via Hounslow, Slough, Maidenhead, Reading, Newbury, Hungerford, Marlborough, Calne, Chippenham, Bath, Bristol

| 40 | LONDON | GOODWICK, nr. FISHGUARD (Pembr.) |

via Beaconsfield, High Wycombe, Wheatley, Oxford, Burford, Cheltenham, Gloucester, Ross, Monmouth, Abergavenny, Brecon, Llandovery, Carmarthen, Haverfordwest

| 41 | LONDON | BIRKENHEAD (Cheshire) |

via Cricklewood, Watford, Tring, Aylesbury, Banbury, Warwick, Birmingham, Wolverhampton, Newport, Whitchurch, Chester

| 43 | n. of OXFORD | STAMFORD (Lincs) |

via Brackley, Towcester, Northampton, Kettering, Duddington

| 44 | CHIPPING NORTON (Oxon) | ABERYSTWYTH (Cards) |

via Moreton-in-the-Marsh, Evesham, Pershore, Worcester, Leominster, Kington, New Radnor, Rhayader, Llangurig

| 45 | BIRMINGHAM | FELIXSTOWE (Suffolk) |

via Coventry (by-pass), Dunchurch, Daventry, Northampton, Wellingborough, Higham Ferrers, St. Neots, Cambridge, Newmarket, Bury St. Edmunds, Stowmarket, Ipswich

| 46 | BATH (Somerset) | GRIMSBY (Lincs) |

via Nailsworth, Stroud, Cheltenham, Stratford, Warwick, Coventry, Leicester, Newark, Lincoln, Market Rasen, Caistor

| 47 | BIRMINGHAM | GREAT YARMOUTH (Norfolk) |

via Coleshill, Nuneaton, Hinckley, Leicester, Uppingham, Peterborough, Wisbech, Kings Lynn, Swaffham, E. Dereham, Norwich, Acle

| 48 | nr. GLOUCESTER | CARMARTHEN |

via Lydney, Chepstow, Newport, Cardiff, Bridgend, Aberavon, Neath, Morriston, Hendy

| 49 | ROSS-ON-WYE (Hereford) | BAMBER BRIDGE (Lancs) |

via Hereford, Leominster, Ludlow, Church Stretton, Shrewsbury, Whitchurch, Tarporley, Warrington, Ashton, Wigan

| 400 | TRAFALGAR SQUARE (London) | ARCHWAY (London) |

via Camden Town, Kentish Town, Tufnell Park

| 401 | PICCADILLY (London) | ISLINGTON (London) |

via Soho, Bloomsbury, Clerkenwell

| 402 | STAMFORD BROOK (London) | SHEPHERDS BUSH (London) |

via Goldhawk Road

| 404 | PADDINGTON (London) | A4 w. of MAIDENHEAD (Berks) |

via Willesden, Harrow, Rickmansworth, Amersham, High Wycombe, Marlow

| 405 | KINGSWOOD, WATFORD (Herts) | A1 s. of HATFIELD (Herts) |

via Kingswood, St. Albans by-pass

A. No.	From	To

406 EALING (Middlesex)   WOODFORD (Essex)
via Park Royal, Neasden, Brent, Finchley, New Southgate, Edmonton

407 HARLESDEN (London)   CHILDS HILL (London)
via Church End, Willesden, Willesden Green, Cricklewood

408 LONDON AIRPORT   UXBRIDGE (Middlesex)
via Harmondsworth, W. Drayton, Yiewsley, Cowley

409 HARROW (Middlesex)   BUSHEY HEATH (Middlesex)
via Harrow and Wealdstone, Harrow Weald

410 PINNER (Middlesex)   STANMORE (Middlesex)
via Hatch End, Harrow Weald

411 LEAVESDEN (Herts)   BARNET (Herts)
via Watford, Oxhey, Bushey Heath, Elstree, Arkley

412 IVER HEATH (Bucks)   ST. ALBANS (Herts)
via Denham, Rickmansworth, Watford

413 A40 s. of GERRARDS CROSS (Bucks)   A43 s. of TOWCESTER (N'hants)
via Amersham, Wendover, Aylesbury, Winslow, Buckingham

414 APSLEY END (Herts)   MALDON (Essex)
via St. Albans, Hatfield, Hertford, Sawbridgeworth, Chelmsford

415 DORCHESTER (Oxon)   WITNEY (Oxon)
via Clifton Hampden, Abingdon, Frilford, Brighthampton, Ducklington

416 AMERSHAM (Bucks)   BERKHAMSTEAD (Herts)
via Chesham Bois, Chesham, Ashley Green

417 STREATLEY (Berks)   HOPE-UNDER-DINMORE (Hereford)
via Wantage, Faringdon, Fairford, Cirencester, Gloucester, Ledbury

418 A40 e. of WHEATLEY (Oxon)   BEDFORD
via Thame, Aylesbury, Leighton Buzzard, Woburn, Ridgmont, Ampthill

419 HUNGERFORD (Berks)   A38 nr. QUEDGLEY (Glos)
via Aldbourne, Swindon, Cricklade, Cirencester, Stroud

420 BRISTOL   OXFORD
via Marshfield, Chippenham, Wootton Bassett, Swindon, Faringdon

421 WESTON-ON-THE-GREEN (Oxon)   BUCKINGHAM
via Bicester, Newton Purcell, Tingewick

422 WORCESTER   A428 w. of BEDFORD
via Alcester, Stratford, Eatington, Banbury, Buckingham, Wolverton

423 A4 w. of MAIDENHEAD (Berks)   s. of TAMWORTH (Staffs)
via Henley, Dorchester, Oxford, Deddington, Banbury, Southam, Coventry

424 BURFORD (Oxon)   A44 w. of MORETON-IN-THE-MARSH (Glos)
via Fifield, Stow-in-the-wold

425 DAVENTRY (Northants)   WARWICK
via Staverton, L. Shuckbrugh, Southam, Leamington

426 DUNCHURCH (Warwick)   LEICESTER
via Rugby, Brownsover, Lutterworth, Blaby, Aylestone

A. No.	From	To
427	A45 w. of DUNCHURCH (Warwick)	OUNDLE (Northants)

via Rugby, Swinford, N. Kilworth, Lubenham, Mkt. Harborough, Corby, Waldon

| 428 | BINLEY, nr. COVENTRY | A1 s. of ST. NEOTS (Hunts) |

via Rugby, Crick, Northampton, Turvey, Bedford, Roxton

| 429 | CHIPPENHAM (Wilts) | LONGBRIDGE, nr. WARWICK |

via Malmesbury, Cirencester, Stow-in-the-wold, Moreton-in-the-marsh, Eatington

| 431 | BATH (Somerset) | BRISTOL |

via Kelston, Bitton, Hanham

| 432 | BRISTOL | O. SODBURY (Glos) |

via Downend, Coalpit Heath, Yate, Chipping Sodbury

| 433 | DUNKIRK (Glos) | nr. BURFORD (Oxon) |

via Didmarton, Tetbury, Cirencester, Bibury, Aldsworth

| 434 | MALMESBURY (Wilts) | NAILSWORTH (Glos) |

via Brokenborough, Tetbury, Avening

| 435 | CIRENCESTER (Glos) | BIRMINGHAM |

via Colesborne, Cheltenham, Evesham, Alcester, Studley

| 436 | A417 s. of CHELTENHAM (Glos) A 44 w. of CHIPPING NORTON (Oxon) |

via Dowdeswell, Naunton, Stow-in-the-wold, Adlestrop

| 438 | TODDINGTON STN. (Glos) | BRECON |

via Tewkesbury, Ledbury, Tarrington, Hereford, Willersley, Hay

| 439 | NORTON, nr. EVESHAM (Worcs) | STRATFORD-ON-AVON |

via Harvington, Salford Priors, Bidford

| 440 | PERSHORE (Worcs) | GT. MALVERN (Worcs) |

via Defford, Upton-on-Severn, Hanley Castle, Rhydd

| 441 | DUNNINGTON (Warwick) | BIRMINGHAM |

via Weethley, Astwood, Bank, Redditch, Alvechurch, Kings Norton

| 442 | KIDDERMINSTER (Worcs) | A41 at PREES HEATH (Salop) |

via Quatt, Bridgnorth, Sutton Maddock, Wellington, Crudgington, Hodnet

| 443 | WORCESTER | NEWNHAM (Worcs) |

via Holt Heath, L. Witley, Gt. Witley, Stockton-on-Teme

| 444 | A452 n. of LEAMINGTON (Warwick) | BURTON-ON-TRENT (Staffs) |

via Stoneleigh, Coventry, Longford, Bedworth, Nuneaton, Twycross, Castle Gresley

| 445 | WARWICK | nr. RYTON-ON-DUNSMORE (Warwick) |

via Leamington, Bubbenhall

| 446 | A452 s. of COLESHILL (Warwick) | A51 nr. LICHFIELD (Staffs) |

via Coleshill

| 447 | WOLVEY (Warwick) | TONGE (Leics) |

via Hinckley, Stapleton, Cadeby, Ibstock, Swannington

| 448 | A435 n. of ALCESTER (Warwick) | KIDDERMINSTER (Worcs) |

via Crabbs Cross, Bromsgrove, Chaddesley Corbett

A. No.	From	To
449	NEWPORT (Mon)	STAFFORD

449 NEWPORT (Mon)   STAFFORD
via Caerleon, Usk, Monmouth, Ross, Ledbury, Malvern, Worcester, Kidderminster, Wolverhampton

450 TORTON (Worcs)   nr. STOURBRIDGE (Worcs)
via Harvington, Stokenbridge

451 GT. WITLEY (Worcs)   STOURBRIDGE (Worcs)
via Dunley, Stourport, Kidderminster

452 A41 s. of LEAMINGTON (Warwick)   A5 nr. BROWNHILLS (Staffs)
via Leamington, Kenilworth, Stone Bridge, Castle Bromwich, Erdington, Brownhills

453 BIRMINGHAM   NOTTINGHAM
via Sutton Coldfield, Tamworth, Measham, Ashby-de-la-Zouch, Longeaton

454 nr. SUTTON COLDFIELD (Warwick)   BRIDGNORTH (Worcs)
via Aldridge, Walsall, Willenhall, Wolverhampton, Hilton, Roughton

456 BIRMINGHAM   BRIMFIELD (Hereford)
via Halesowen, Hagley, Kidderminster, Bewdley, Newnham, Tenbury

457 BIRMINGHAM   SEDGLEY (Staffs)
via Smethwick, Oldbury, Tipton

458 HALESOWEN (Worcs)   A487 nr. DOLGELLEY (Merion)
via Stourbridge, Bridgnorth, Much Wenlock, Shrewsbury, Welshpool, Mallwyd

459 A38 n. of BROMSGROVE (Worcs)   WOLVERHAMPTON
via Romsley, Halesowen, Dudley, Sedgley, Blakenhall

460 WOLVERHAMPTON   CANNOCK (Staffs)
via Bushbury, L. Saredon

461 STOURBRIDGE (Worcs)   LICHFIELD (Staffs)
via Brierley Hill, Dudley, Wednesbury, Walsall, Rushall, Shire Oak

462 W. BROMWICH (Staffs)   n. L. SAREDON (Staffs)
via Wednesbury, Darlaston, Willenhall, New Invention

463 WILLENHALL (Staffs)   s. of WOLVERHAMPTON
via Bilston, Ettingshall

464 A41 at KINGSWOOD COMMON (Staffs)   A5 nr. OAKENGATES (Salop)
via Boningdale, Shifnal

465 BROMYARD (Hereford)   NEATH (Glam)
via Hereford, Pontrilas, Abergavenny, Brynmawr, Dowlais, Merthyr, Hirwain

466 A49 s. of HEREFORD   CHEPSTOW (Mon)
via St. Leonards, Monmouth, Llandego, Tintern, St. Arvans

467 NEWPORT (Mon)   BRYNMAWR (Brecon)
via Risca, Abercarn, Crumlin, Abertillery, Blaina

468 NEWPORT (Mon)   NANTGARW (Glam)
via Bassaleg, Machin, Caerphilly

A. No.	From	To

469 CARDIFF   RHYMNEY BRIDGE STN. (Glam)
via Caerphilly, Maes-y-Cwmmer, Bargoed, Rhymney

470 CARDIFF   BRECON
via Whitchurch, Nantgarw, Pontypridd, Treharris, Merthyr, Nant-ddu

471 USK (Mon)   LLANVIHANGEL-NIGH-USK (Mon)
via Trostry, Kerneys Commander

472 USK (Mon)   A470 nr. TREHARRIS (Glam)
via Pontypool, Crumlin, Newbridge, Maes-y-Cwmmer, Nelson

473 PONTYPRIDD (Glam)   LALESTON (Glam)
via Llantrisant, Llanharan, Pencoed, Coychurch, Bridgend

474 NEATH (Glam)   AMMANFORD (Carm)
via Pontardawe, Gwaen-cae-gurwen, Glanamman, Pontamman

475 LAMPETER (Cards)   NEWCASTLE EMLYN (Carm)
via Llanwnen, Llanwenog, Prengwyn, Llandyfriog

476 LLANELLY (Carm)   LLANDILO (Carm)
via Llannon, Cross Hands, Carmel

477 ST. CLEARS (Carm)   PEMBROKE DOCK
via Llandowror, Red Roses, Begelly, Redberth, Milton

478 TENBY (Pemb)   CARDIGAN
via Begelly, Narberth, Llandissilio, Crymmych Arms, Bridell

479 A40 nr. CRICKHOWELL (Brecon)   RHAYADER (Radnor)
via Cwmdu, Talgarth, Llynwen, Builth Wells, Newbridge-on-Wye

480 A438 w. of HEREFORD   LYONSHALL (Hereford)
via Creden Hill, Yazor, Moorhampton, Woonton, Bryncure

481 BUILTH WELLS (Radnor)   LLANFIHANGEL-NANT-MELAN (Radnor)
via Llanelwedd, Hundred House

482 LLANWRDA (Carm)   ABERAYRON (Cards)
via Hafod Bridge, Lampeter, Llanfihangel Ystrad, Llanerch Aeron

483 SWANSEA (Glam)   CHESTER
via Hendy, Ammanford, Llandovery, Builth Wells, Llandrindod Wells, Newtown, Welshpool, Oswestry, Wrexham

484 A483 n. of SWANSEA (Glam)   CARDIGAN
via Loughor, Llanelly, Kidwelly, Carmarthen, Newcastle Emlyn

485 CARMARTHEN   A487 s. of ABERYSTWYTH (Cards)
via Lampeter, Tregaron, Llanfihangel, Lledrod, Llanilar

486 A484 s. of LLANDYSSUL (Cards)   SYNOD (Cards)
via Llandyssul, Clawddmelyn

487 HAVERFORDWEST (Pemb)   CAERNARVON
via St. Davids, Fishguard, Cardigan, Aberayron, Aberystwyth, Machynlleth,
Dolgelley, Beddgelert

488 PENYBONT (Radnor)   SHREWSBURY
via Knighton, Clun, Minsterley, Gt. Hanwood

A. No.	From	To
489	A49 n. of CRAVEN ARMS (Salop)	MACHYNLLETH (Montgom)

489 A49 n. of CRAVEN ARMS (Salop)　　　　MACHYNLLETH (Montgom)
via Church Stoke, Newtown, Caerswys, Tafolwern

490 CHURCH STOKE (Salop)　　　　　　　LLANFYLLIN (Montgom)
via Chirbury, Welshpool, Bwlch-y-ciban

491 FINSTALL, nr. BROMSGROVE (Worcs)　A449 nr. KINGS WINFORD (Staffs)
via Bromsgrove, Bell End, Wardsley

492 LLANGURIG (Montgom)　　　　　　　NEWTOWN (Montgom)
via Llanidloes, Llandinam, Penstrowed

493 MACHYNLLETH (Montgom)　　　　　　DOLGELLEY (Merion)
via Pennal, Aberdovey, Towyn, Llanegryn, Capel Arthog

494 DOLGELLEY (Merion)　　　　　　　　QUEENSFERRY (Ches)
via Llanuwchllyn, Bala, Derwen, Ruthin, Mold

495 A458 w. of LLANFAIR CAEREINION (Montgom)
　　　　　　　　　　　　　　A525 w. of WHITCHURCH (Salop)
via Meifod, Llanyblodwel, Oswestry, Whittington, Ellesmere

496 LLANELLTYD (Merion)　　　　　　　LLANDUDNO (Caerns)
via Barmouth, Harlech, Maentwrog, Blaenau Festiniog, Bettws-y-coed, Llan-rwst, Deganwy

497 PENRHYNDEUDRAETH (Merion)　　　　NEVIN (Caerns)
via Portmadoc, Criccieth, Llanystumdwy, Pwllheli, Bodfean

498 PEN-Y-GWRHYD INN (Caerns)　　　　TREMADOC (Caerns)
via Beddgelert, Aberglaslyn

499 ABERSOCH (Caerns)　　　　　　　　BANGOR (Caerns)
via Pwllheli, Llanaelhaiarn, Clynnog Fawr, Llanwnda, Caernarvon, Port Dinorwic

zone 5

5 LONDON (Marble Arch)　　　　　　　HOLYHEAD
via Edgware, St. Albans, Dunstable, Towcester, Atherstone, Wellington, Shrewsbury (by-pass), Chirk, Llangollen, Corwen, Bettws-y-coed, Bangor

50 HOCKLIFFE (Beds)　　　　　　n. of WARRINGTON (Lancs)
via Woburn, Newport Pagnell, Northampton, Leicester, Coalville, Ashby-de-la-Zouch, Burton-on-Trent, Uttoxeter (by-pass), Longton, Stoke, Burslem, Tunstall, Knutsford

51 A5 s. of TAMWORTH (Staffs)　　　　　CHESTER
via Tamworth, Lichfield, Rugeley, Colwich, Weston-on-Trent, Stone, Nant-wich, Tarporley, Tarvin.

52 NANTWICH (Ches)　　　　　　　　　MABLETHORPE (Lincs)
via Newcastle-under-Lyme, Stoke, Ashbourne, Derby, Stapleford, Notting-ham, Bingham, Grantham, Donington, Boston, Skegness

A. No.	From	To

53 n. of SHREWSBURY — BUXTON (Derby)
via Shawbury, Hodnet, Market Drayton, Newcastle-under-Lyme, Stoke, Burslem, Leek

54 TARVIN (Ches) — BUXTON (Derby)
via Kelsall, Winsford, Middlewich, Holmes Chapel, Congleton

55 CHESTER — LLANDEGAI, nr. BANGOR (Caerns)
via Hawarden, Northop, Holywell, St. Asaph, Abergele, Colwyn Bay, Conway, Penmaenmawr, Llanfairfechan

56 CHESTER — A59 w. of SKIPTON (Yorks)
via Frodsham, Stockton Heath, Altrincham, Sale, Manchester, Bury, Edenfield, Rawtenstall, Burnley, Brierfield, Nelson, Colne, Earby

57 LIVERPOOL — LINCOLN
via Prescot, Rainhill, Warrington, Irlam, Manchester, Hyde, Glossop, Sheffield, S. Anston, Worksop, E. Markham, Saxilby

58 PRESCOT (Lancs) — WETHERBY (Yorks)
via St. Helens, Ashton-in-Makerfield, Hindley, Bolton, Bury, Heywood, Rochdale, Littleborough, Ripponden, Sowerby Br., Halifax, Leeds, Bardsey

59 LIVERPOOL — YORK
via Maghull, Ormskirk, Rufford, Preston, Samlesbury, Whalley, Clitheroe, Chatburn, Gisburn, Skipton, Bolton Bridge, Harrogate, Knaresborough

501 PADDINGTON (London) — CITY (London)
via Marylebone, Euston, Kings Cross, City Road

502 CAMDEN TOWN (London) — HENDON (London)
via Chalk Farm, Hampstead, Golders Green

503 CAMDEN TOWN (London) — WOODFORD (Essex)
via Holloway, Harringay, Tottenham, Walthamstow

504 W. HENDON (London) — S. TOTTENHAM (London)
via Hendon, Finchley, E. Finchley, Muswell Hill, Wood Green

505 DUNSTABLE (Beds) — nr. GT. ABINGTON (Cambs)
via Luton, Hitchin, Letchworth, Baldock, Royston

507 AMPTHILL (Beds) — BUNTINGFORD (Herts)
via Clophill, Shefford, Henlow, Baldock, Cottered

508 nr. STONY STRATFORD (Bucks) — MARKET HARBOROUGH (Leics)
via Roade, Northampton, Brixworth, Lamport

509 NEWPORT PAGNELL (Bucks) — KETTERING (Northants)
via Olney, Bozeat, Wollaston, Wellingborough, Isham

510 WELLINGBOROUGH (N'hants) — A604 e. of KETTERING (N'hants)
via Finedon

512 ASHBY-DE-LA-ZOUCH (Leics) — LOUGHBOROUGH (Leics)
via Grace Dien Priory

513 nr. TAMWORTH (Staffs) — STAFFORD
via Alrewas, Armitage, Rugeley, Milford

A. No.	From	To

514 CASTLE GRESLEY STN., nr. SWADLINCOTE (Derby)   DERBY
via Swadlincote, Ticknall, Melbourne, Swarkeston, Chellaston

515 A51 nw. of LICHFIELD (Staffs)   BUXTON (Derby)
via Kings Bromley, Yoxall, Sudbury, Clifton, Ashbourne, Parsley Hay

516 SUDBURY (Derby)   DERBY
via Hilton, Etwall, Mickleover

517 ASHBOURNE (Derby)   BELPER (Derby)
via Hulland, Turnditch

518 nr. WELLINGTON (Salop)   UTTOXETER (Staffs)
via Donnington, Newport, Gnosall, Stafford, Weston-on-Trent

519 NEWPORT (Salop)   NEWCASTLE-UNDER-LYME (Staffs)
via Littleworth, Eccleshall

520 ECCLESHALL (Staffs)   LEEK (Staffs)
via Stone, Meir, Cheddleton

521 BLYTHEMARSH (Staffs)   KINGSLEY and FROGHALL STN. (Staffs)
via Cheadle

522 U. TEAN (Staffs)   WETLEYROCKS (Staffs)
via Cheadle

523 A52 at CALTONMOOR HOUSE (Staffs)   HAZELGROVE STN. (Ches)
via Waterhouses, Leek, Rushton, Macclesfield, Poynton

524 A515 n. of ASHBOURNE (Derby)   A6 w. of ROWSLEY (Derby)
via Grangemill, Winster

525 NEWCASTLE-UNDER-LYME (Staffs)   RHYL (Denbigh)
via Madeley, Woore, Audlem, Whitchurch, Bangor, Wrexham, Coedpoeth, Ruthin, Denbigh, St. Asaph

527 NEWCASTLE-UNDER-LYME (Staffs)   CONGLETON (Ches)
via Longport, Tunstall, Knypersley, Biddulph

528 SHREWSBURY (Salop)   MARCHWIEL (Denbigh)
via Albrighton, Cockshutt, Ellesmere, Overton

529 HINSTOCK (Salop)   NANTWICH (Ches)
via Market Drayton, Adderley, Audlem

530 A525 at DODDS GREEN (Ches)   MIDDLEWICH (Ches)
via Sound, Nantwich, Minshull Vernon Stn.

531 A525 at MADELEY HEATH (Staffs)   A52 at BALTERLEY HEATH (Ches)
via Wrinehall, Betley

532 A530 w. of CREWE (Ches)   A534 e. of CREWE (Ches)
via Crewe

533 RODE HEATH (Ches)   RUNCORN (Ches)
via Sandbach, Middlewich, Northwich, Halton

534 CONGLETON (Ches)   WREXHAM (Denbigh)
via Sandbach, Wheelock, Crewe, Nantwich, Faddiley, Farndon, Holt

A. No.	From	To
535	HOLMES CHAPEL (Ches) *via* Twemlow Green, Chelford	ALDERLEY EDGE (Ches)
536	CONGLETON (Ches) *via* Eaton, Warren	MACCLESFIELD (Ches)
537	KNUTSFORD (Ches) *via* Chelford, Henbury-cum-Pexall, Macclesfield, Cat and Fiddle	A54 sw. of BUXTON (Derby)
538	ALTRINCHAM (Ches) *via* Ringway, Morley, Wilmslow, Prestbury	nr. PRESTBURY (Ches)
539	A525 w. of WHITCHURCH (Salop) *via* Hanmer, Overton, Ruabon, Acrefair	LLANGOLLEN (Denbigh)
540	CHESTER *via* Hinderton, Heswall, Thurstaston, West Kirby	HOYLAKE (Ches)
541	WREXHAM (Denbigh) *via* Caergwrle, Mold, Nannerch, Bodfari, Trefnant	ST. ASAPH (Denbigh)
542	LLANGOLLEN (Denbigh) *via* Valle Crucis, Pentre-bwlch	A525 sw. of LLANDEGLA (Denbigh)
543	PENTRE FOELAS (Denbigh) *via* Bylchau, Denbigh	A541 nr. BODFARI (Denbigh)
544	BYLCHAU (Denbigh) *via* Llansannan	LLANFAIR TALHAIARN (Denbigh)
545	MENAI BRIDGE (Anglesey)	BEAUMARIS (Anglesey)
546	COLWYN BAY (Denbigh) *via* Llandrillo-yn-rhos	LLANDUDNO (Caerns)
547	RHUDDLAN (Denbigh) *via* Morfa Rhuddlan	A55 e. of ABERGELE (Denbigh)
548	CHESTER *via* Queensferry, Flint, Bagillt, Mostyn, Prestatyn, Rhyl, Abergele, Llanfair Talhaiarn	LLANRWST (Denbigh)
549	BROUGHTON (Flint) *via* Buckley	MOLD (Flint)
550	HOOTON (Ches) *via* Shotwick, Queensferry, Hawarden, Hope	CAERGWRLE (Flint)
551	nr. HESWALL (Ches) *via* Thingwall, Woodchurch, Upton, Moreton, Wallasey	NEW BRIGHTON (Ches)
552	BIRKENHEAD (Ches) *via* Prenton	ARROWE PARK (Ches)
553	HOYLAKE (Ches) *via* Moreton, Bidston, Claughton	BIRKENHEAD (Ches)
554	SEACOMBE (Ches) *via* Egremont	NEW BRIGHTON (Ches)
556	A54 nr. DELAMERE (Ches) *via* Northwich, Lostock Gralam, Mere	A56 sw. of ALTRINCHAM (Ches)

A. No.	From	To
557	nr. FRODSHAM (Ches) *via* Clifton, Higher Runcorn	RUNCORN (Ches)
558	nr. HALTON (Ches) *via* Moore	A56 s. of WARRINGTON (Lancs)
559	LOSTOCK GRALAM (Ches) *via* Budworth, Frandley	STRETTON (Ches)
560	ALTRINCHAM (Ches) *via* Cheadle, Stockport, Woodley, Gee Cross	MOTTRAM-IN-LONGDENDALE (Ches)
561	LIVERPOOL *via* Dingle, Aigburth	GARSTON (Lancs)
562	LIVERPOOL *via* Wavertree, Woolton, Halebank, Widnes, Penketh	nr. WARRINGTON (Lancs)
565	LIVERPOOL *via* Bootle, Crosby, Ainsdale, Southport, Mere Brow	TARLETON (Lancs)
566	WALTON (Liverpool) *via* Orrell Park, Bootle	SEAFORTH (Liverpool)
567	LIVERPOOL *via* Bootle, Litherland, Maghull, Lydiate, Halsall	SCARISBRICK (Lancs)
568	WIDNES (Lancs) *via* Farnworth	SUTTON (Lancs)
569	A568 nr. FARNWORTH (Lancs)	RAINHILL STOOPS (Lancs)
570	BOLD HEATH (Lancs) *via* Sutton, St. Helens, Rainford, Ormskirk, Scarisbrick	SOUTHPORT (Lancs)
571	ST. HELENS (Lancs) *via* Carr Mill, Billinge, Pemberton	WIGAN (Lancs)
572	ST. HELENS (Lancs) *via* Newton-in-Makerfield, Lowton, Leigh, Boothstown, Worsley	SWINTON (Lancs)
573	WINWICK (Lancs) *via* Golborne, Abram, Platt Bridge, Ince	WIGAN (Lancs)
574	WARRINGTON (Lancs) *via* Padgate, Culcheth, Glazebury	LEIGH (Lancs)
575	STRETFORD (Lancs) *via* Patricroft, Worsley, Walkden	FARNWORTH (Lancs)
576	MANCHESTER *via* Crumpsall, Rhodes	MIDDLETON (Lancs)
577	BOOTHSTOWN (Lancs) *via* Tyldesley, Atherton, Hindley, Wigan, Upholland, Skelmersdale	ORMSKIRK (Lancs)
578	LEIGH (Lancs) *via* Westleigh	HINDLEY GREEN (Lancs)
579	LEIGH (Lancs) *via* Atherton, Daub Hill	BOLTON (Lancs)

A. No.	From	To
580	LIVERPOOL *via* Walton, Haydock, Lowton, Astley	IRLAMS O' TH' HEIGHT (Lancs)
581	nr. RUFFORD (Lancs) *via* Croston, Euxton	CHORLEY (Lancs)
582	BAMBER BRIDGE (Lancs) *via* Lostock Hall, Middleforth Green	PENWORTHAM (Lancs)
583	BLACKPOOL (Lancs) *via* Marton, Kirkham (by-pass), Lea	PRESTON (Lancs)
584	LEAGATE, NEWTON (Lancs) *via* Freckleton, Warton, Lytham St. Annes	N. BLACKPOOL (Lancs)
585	KIRKHAM (Lancs) *via* Wesham, Gt. Singleton, Thornton	FLEETWOOD (Lancs)
586	BLACKPOOL (Lancs) *via* Poulton-le-Fylde, Gt. Eccleston, St. Michaels-on-Wyre	A6 s. of GARSTANG (Lancs)
587	BLACKPOOL (Lancs) *via* Layton, Bispham, Cleveleys	FLEETWOOD (Lancs)
588	nr. SKIPPOOL (Lancs) *via* Hambleton, Stalmine, Pilling Stn., Cockerham, Conder Green	LANCASTER
589	HEYSHAM (Lancs) *via* Morecambe, Torrisholme	LANCASTER
590	BARROW-IN-FURNESS (Lancs) *via* Dalton, Ulverston, Greenodd, Backbarrow, Newby Bridge, Lindale	LEVENS BRIDGE (Westm)
591	BOTHEL (Cumb) *via* Bewaldeth, Keswick, Dunmail Raise, Ambleside, Windermere, Staveley	KENDAL (Westm)
592	NEWBY BRIDGE (Lancs) *via* Bowness, Kirkstone, Glenridding, Pooley Bridge, Yanwath	K. ARTHUR'S TABLE, PENRITH (Cumb)
593	BROUGHTON (Lancs) *via* Torver, Coniston	AMBLESIDE (Westm)
594	MARYPORT (Cumb) *via* Cockermouth, Bassenthwaite Lake Stn., Keswick, Motherby, Greystoke	PENRITH (Cumb)
595	DALTON (Lancs) *via* Broughton, Bootle, Egremont, Whitehaven, Cockermouth, Bothel, Thursby	CARLISLE (Cumb)
596	A595 s. of WORKINGTON (Cumb) *via* Workington, Maryport, Aspatria, Wigton	nr. THURSBY (Cumb)
597	WORKINGTON (Cumb) *via* Gt. Clifton	BRIDGEFOOT STN. (Cumb)
598	HAMPSTEAD (London) *via* Golders Green, Finchley	N. FINCHLEY (Middx)
599	BLACKBROOK (Lancs) *via* Haydock	A49 s. of HAYDOCK (Lancs)

zone 6

A. No.	From	To
6	SOUTH MIMMS (Middx)	CARLISLE (Cumb)
	via Luton, Bedford, Kettering, Leicester, Derby, Bakewell, Stockport, Manchester, Preston, Lancaster, Kendal, Penrith	
60	LOUGHBOROUGH (Leics)	DONCASTER (Yorks)
	via Nottingham, Mansfield, Worksop, Tickhill	
61	DERBY	THIRSK (Yorks)
	via Ripley, Alfreton, Chesterfield, Sheffield, Barnsley, Wakefield, Leeds, Harrogate, Ripley, Ripon	
62	MANCHESTER	LEEDS
	via Oldham, Huddersfield, Liversedge, Birstall	
63	LEEDS	HULL
	via W. Garforth, Hambleton, Selby, Howden, Elloughton	
64	LEEDS	SCARBOROUGH (Yorks)
	via Tadcaster, York, Malton, Sherburn, Seamer	
65	LEEDS	KENDAL (Westm)
	via Yeadon, Ilkley, Skipton, Settle, Ingleton, Kirkby Lonsdale	
66	PENRITH (Cumb)	SCOTCH CORNER (Yorks)
	via Appleby, Brough, Stainmore, Bowes	
67	BOWES (Yorks)	MIDDLESBROUGH
	via Barnard Castle, Gainford, Darlington, Stockton, Thornaby-on-Tees	
68	DARLINGTON (Durham)	EDINBURGH
	via St. Helen, Auckland, Tow Law, Corbridge, Jedburgh, Lauder, Dalkeith	
69	CARLISLE (Cumb)	NEWCASTLE-UPON-TYNE
	via Brampton, Haltwhistle, Hexham, Corbridge, Heddon	
600	BEDFORD	WELWYN (Herts)
	via Cotton End, Shefford, Hitchin, Codicote	
602	HITCHIN (Herts)	HODDESDON (Herts)
	via Stevenage, Stapleford, Hertford	
603	BEDFORD	CAMBRIDGE
	via Sandy, Potton, Barton	
604	nr. KETTERING (Northants)	HARWICH (Essex)
	via Thrapston, Huntingdon, Cambridge, Haverhill, Halstead, Colchester, Elmstead Market, Wix, Ramsey	
605	HIGHAM FERRERS (Northants)	WHITTLESEY (Lincs)
	via Thrapston, Oundle, Warmington, Peterborough	
606	W. BRIDGEFORD (Nottingham)	STAMFORD (Lincs)
	via U. Broughton, Nether Broughton, Melton Mowbray, Oakham	
607	SYSTON, nr. LEICESTER	nr. LINCOLN
	via Melton Mowbray, Grantham, Barkston, Leadenham, Coleby	

A. No.	From	To
608	DERBY	ANNESLEY (Notts)
	via Smalley, Heanor, Langley Mill, Brinsley, Underwood	
609	NOTTINGHAM	SMALLEY COMMON (Derby)
	via Wollaton, Trowell	
610	AMBERGATE JCT. (Derby)	NUTHALL (Notts)
	via Ripley, Codnor, Langley Mill, Eastwood, Kimberley	
611	NOTTINGHAM	A57 at DARLTON (Notts)
	via Hucknall Torkard, Annesley, Mansfield, Ollerton, Tuxford	
612	NOTTINGHAM	SOUTHWELL (Notts)
	via Carlton, Burton Joyce, Lowdham, Thurgarton	
613	NOTTINGHAM	ALFRETON (Derby)
	via Nuthall, Greasley, Underwood, Selston, Pyebridge	
614	NOTTINGHAM (ring)	A163 w. of MKT. WEIGHTON (Yorks)
	via Redhill, Ollerton, Blyth, Bawtry, Finningley, Thorne, Howden	
615	ALFRETON (Derby)	MANSFIELD (Notts)
	via Sutton-in-Ashfield	
616	NEWARK (Notts)	HUDDERSFIELD (Yorks)
	via Ollerton, Clowne, Eckington, Sheffield, Langsett, Honley	
617	KELHAM (NEWARK) (Notts)	CHESTERFIELD (Derby)
	via Southwell, Farnsfield, Mansfield, Pleasley, Heath, Hasland	
618	PLEASLEY (Derby)	ROTHERHAM (Yorks)
	via Scarcliffe, Clowne, Swallow Nest, Whiston	
619	BAKEWELL (Derby)	WORKSOP (Notts)
	via Baslow, Chesterfield, Staveley, Barlborough	
620	WORKSOP (Notts)	A631 w. of GAINSBOROUGH (Lincs)
	via Ranby, E. Retford, N. Wheatley, S. Wheatley, Saundby	
621	BASLOW (Derby)	SHEFFIELD
	via Totley, Millhouses	
622	BAKEWELL (Derby)	HATHERSAGE (Derby)
	via Hassop, Calver, Grindleford, Eyam Woodlands	
623	A624 s. of CHAPEL-EN-LE-FRITH (Derby)	ROWSLEY (Derby)
	via Peak Forest, Stony Middleton, Calver, Baslow, Beeley	
624	BUXTON (Derby)	GLOSSOP (Derby)
	via Chapel-en-le-Frith, Hayfield	
625	WHALEYBRIDGE (Derby)	SHEFFIELD
	via Chapel-en-le-Frith, Castleton, Hope, Hathersage	
626	STOCKPORT (Ches)	GLOSSOP (Derby)
	via Marple, Charlesworth	
627	ASHTON-U-LYNE (Lancs)	EDENFIELD (Lancs)
	via Oldham, Royton, Rochdale, Wolstenholme	
628	HOLLINGWORTH-IN-LONGDENDALE (Ches)	PONTEFRACT (Yorks)
	via Woodhead, Penistone, Barnsley, Hemsworth, Ackworth	

A. No.	From	To

629 ROTHERHAM (Yorks)   SKIPTON (Yorks)
via Penistone, Shepley, Huddersfield, Elland, Halifax, Keighley

630 SHEFFIELD   nr. DONCASTER (Yorks)
via Tinsley, Rotherham, Conisbrough, Warmsworth

631 TINSLEY, ROTHERHAM (Yorks)   A157 w. of LOUTH (Lincs)
via Maltby, Bawtry, Gainsborough, Glentham, Mkt. Rasen, Judford Magna

632 CHESTERFIELD (Derby)   CUCKNEY (Notts)
via Calow, Bolsover, U. Langwith, Nether Langwith

633 ROTHERHAM (Yorks)   A61 n. of BARNSLEY (Yorks)
via Rawmarsh, Wath-upon-Dearne, Wombwell, Ardsley

634 MALTBY (Yorks)   BARNBY MOOR (Yorks)
via Oldcoates, Blyth

635 MANCHESTER   nr. DONCASTER (Yorks)
via Ashton-u-Lyne, Mossley, Holmfirth, Barnsley, Darfield, Marr

636 DENBY DALE (Yorks)   WAKEFIELD (Yorks)
via Scissett, Clayton West Stn.

637 BARUGH, BARNSLEY (Yorks)   A642 at FLOCKTON MOOR (Yorks)
via Darton, W. Bretton, Flockton

638 ODSAL, BRADFORD   A1 n. of DONCASTER (Yorks)
via Cleckheaton, Heckmondwike, Dewsbury, Wakefield, N. Elmsall

639 STOURTON, LEEDS   A1 at BARNSDALE BAR (Yorks)
via Oulton, Methley, Castleford (by-pass), Pontefract, E. Hardwick

640 ROCHDALE (Lancs)   HUDDERSFIELD (Yorks)
via Milnrow, New Hey, Denshaw, Scammonden

641 HUDDERSFIELD (Yorks)   BRADFORD
via Brighouse, Low Moor, Wibsey

642 A629 nr. ALMONDBURY (Yorks)   A1 nr. ABERFORD (Yorks)
via Middlestown, Hirbury, Wakefield, Oulton, Garforth

643 A640 at OUTLANE (Yorks)   LEEDS
via Rastrick, Brighouse, Cleckheaton, Birstall, Churwell

644 DENHOLME (Yorks)   DEWSBURY (Yorks)
via Queensbury, Hipperholme, Brighouse, Mirfield

645 nr. WAKEFIELD (Yorks)   SNAITH (Yorks)
via Purston Jaglin, Pontefract, Knottingley

646 HALIFAX (Yorks)   BURNLEY (Lancs)
via Hebden Bridge, Todmorden, Cornholme

647 HALIFAX (Yorks)   LEEDS
via Queensbury, Bradford, Farsley, Bramley

649 HIPPERHOLME (Yorks)   LIVERSEDGE (Yorks)
via Bailiff Bridge

650 WAKEFIELD (Yorks)   KEIGHLEY (Yorks)
via E. Ardsley, Adwalton, Bradford, Saltaire, Bingley

A. No.	From	To
651	A650 nr. BIRKENSHAW (Yorks) *via* Birkenshaw, Gomersal	HECKMONDWIKE (Yorks)
652	GOMERSAL (Yorks) *via* Birstall, Batley	DEWSBURY (Yorks)
653	DEWSBURY (Yorks) *via* W. Ardsley, Beeston	LEEDS
654	TINGLEY (Yorks) *via* Thorpe-on-the-hill, Rothwell	OULTON (Yorks)
655	A638 sw. of WAKEFIELD (Yorks) *via* Warmfield, Normanton, Whitwood	CASTLEFORD (Yorks)
656	CASTLEFORD (Yorks) *via* Ledstone Stn.	A1 s. of ABERFORD (Yorks)
657	BRAMLEY (Yorks) *via* Calverley, Idle	SHIPLEY (Yorks)
658	BRADFORD *via* Eccleshill, Yeadon, Pool	A61 s. of HARROGATE (Yorks)
659	BURLEY-IN-WHARFEDALE (Yorks) *via* Otley, Pool, Harewood, Collingham, Boston Spa	TADCASTER (Yorks)
660	LEEDS *via* Headingley, Bramhope	OTLEY (Yorks)
661	HARROGATE (Yorks) *via* Spofforth	WETHERBY (Yorks)
662	MANCHESTER *via* Clayton, Droylsden	ASHTON-U-LYNE (Lancs)
663	NEWTON HEATH, MANCHESTER *via* Holmwood, Chadderton, Royton	NEW HEY (Lancs)
664	MANCHESTER *via* Blackley, Middleton, Castleton	ROCHDALE (Lancs)
665	MANCHESTER *via* N. Manchester, Prestwich, Whitefield	RADCLIFFE (Lancs)
666	IRLAMS O' TH' HEIGHT (Lancs) *via* Pendlebury, Farnworth, Bolton, Darwen, Blackburn	A59 n. of BLACKBURN (Lancs)
667	WHITEFIELD (Lancs) *via* Bingley	FARNWORTH (Lancs)
668	RADCLIFFE (Lancs) *via* Black Lane Stn.	A58 s. of AINSWORTH (Lancs)
669	MIDDLETON (Lancs) *via* Greenhill, Chadderton	OLDHAM (Lancs)
670	ASHTON-U-LYNE (Lancs) *via* Mossley	A62 at STANDEDGE MOOR (Yorks)
671	ROCHDALE (Lancs) *via* Whitworth, Bacup, Burnley, Padiham, Read	WHALLEY (Lancs)

A. No.	From	To
672	OLDHAM (Lancs) *via* Moorside, Denshaw, Booth, Rishworth	RIPPONDEN (Yorks)
673	A6 s. of CHORLEY (Lancs) *via* Adlington, Horwich	BOLTON (Lancs)
674	CHORLEY (Lancs) *via* Heapey, Wheelton, Feniscowles	BLACKBURN (Lancs)
675	WALTON-LE-DALE (Lancs) *via* H. Walton, Hoghton, Withnell, Belmont, Bolton (by-pass)	A58 e. of BOLTON (Lancs)
676	BOLTON (Lancs) *via* Bradshaw, Holcombe Brook, Ramsbottom	EDENFIELD (Lancs)
677	5-BARRED GATE INN, SAMLESBURY (Lancs) *via* Blackburn, Knuzden	HASLINGDEN (Lancs)
678	BLACKBURN (Lancs) *via* Rishton, Clayton-le-moors, Altham	PADIHAM (Lancs)
679	BLACKBURN (Lancs) *via* Accrington	BURNLEY (Lancs)
680	n. EDENFIELD (Lancs) *via* Haslingden, Accrington, Clayton-le-moors	A671 nr. WHALLEY (Lancs)
681	HASLINGDEN (Lancs) *via* Rawtenstall, Waterfoot, Bacup	TODMORDEN (Yorks)
682	NELSON (Lancs) *via* Barrowford, Gisburn, Nappa	HELLIFIELD (Yorks)
683	LANCASTER *via* Caton, Hornby, Melling, Casterton, Middleton	SEDBERGH (Yorks)
684	KENDAL (Westm) *via* Sedbergh, Garsdale, Hawes, Leyburn, Bedale, Northallerton	A19 e. of NORTHALLERTON (Yorks)
685	KENDAL (Westm) *via* Tebay, Kirkby Stephen, Brough Sowerby	BROUGH (Westm)
686	EAMONT BRIDGE, PENRITH (Cumb) *via* Langwathby, Melmerby, Alston	HAYDON BRIDGE (Northumb)
687	nr. TUNSTALL (Lancs) *via* Burton-in-Lonsdale	nr. INGLETON (Yorks)
688	BARNARD CASTLE (Durham) *via* Staindrop, W. Auckland	BISHOP AUCKLAND (Durham)
689	A68 w. of CROOK (Durham) *via* Crook, Bishop Auckland, Sedgefield, Greatham	W. HARTLEPOOL (Durham)
690	CROOK (Durham) *via* Willington, Brancepeth, Durham, Houghton-le-Spring	SUNDERLAND (Durham)
691	A68 w. of CONSETT (Durham) *via* Benfieldside, Leadgate, Lanchester	DURHAM
692	CASTLESIDE (Durham) *via* Consett, Leadgate, Burnopfield	GATESHEAD (Durham)

A. No.	From	To
693	nr. LEADGATE (Durham) *via* Annfield Plain, Stanley, Pelton	CHESTER-LE-STREET (Durham)
694	SHOTLEY BRIDGE (Durham) *via* Ebchester, Lintzford, Blaydon	NEWCASTLE-UPON-TYNE
695	BROOMHAUGH (Northumb) *via* Prudhoe, Crawcrook, Newcastle, Wallsend	N. SHIELDS (Northumb)
696	A68 nr. OTTERBURN (Northumb) *via* Otterburn, Belsay, Ponteland	NEWCASTLE-UPON-TYNE
697	LAUDER (Berwick) *via* Greenlaw, Eccles, Coldstream, Wooler, Longhorsley	A1 n. of MORPETH (Northumb)
698	HAWICK (Roxburgh) *via* Crailing, Kelso, Birgham, Coldstream	BERWICK-ON-TWEED
699	SELKIRK *via* Maxton, Kelso, Eccles, Swinton	BERWICK-ON-TWEED

zone 7

	From	To
7	EDINBURGH *via* Dalkeith, Stow, Galashiels, Selkirk, Hawick, Langholm, Longtown	CARLISLE (Cumb)
70	EDINBURGH *via* Currie, Carnwath, Douglas, Muirkirk, Cumnock	AYR
71	EDINBURGH *via* Calder, Newmains, Stonehouse, Strathaven, Galston, Kilmarnock	IRVINE (Ayr)
72	GALASHIELS (Selkirk) *via* Innerleithen, Peebles, Blyth Bridge, Biggar, Lanark, Dalsert	A74 se. of HAMILTON (Lanark)
73	ABINGTON (Lanark) *via* Roberton, Lanark, Carluke, Newmains, Newhouse, Airdrie	CUMBERNAULD (Dumbarton)
74	A7 n. of CARLISLE (Cumb) *via* Gretna, Ecclefechan, Lockerbie, Crawford, Lesmahagow, Hamilton	GLASGOW
75	GRETNA (Dumfries) *via* Annan, Dumfries, Castle Douglas, Creetown, Newton Stewart, Glenluce	STRANRAER (Wigton)
76	DUMFRIES *via* Thornhill, Sanquhar, New Cumnock, Mauchline, Hurlford	KILMARNOCK (Ayr)
77	PORTPATRICK (Wigton) *via* Stranraer, Ballantrae, Girvan, Maybole, Ayr, Kilmarnock, Fenwick	GLASGOW
78	MONKTON (Ayr) *via* Irvine, W. Kilbride, Largs, Wemyss Bay, Inverkip	GOUROCK (Renfrew)

A. No.	From	To
701	A7 s. of EDINBURGH	DUMFRIES
	via Penicuik, Blyth Bridge, Broughton, Moffat, Kirkpatrick Juxta	
702	EDINBURGH	DALRY (Kirkcud)
	via Carlops, W. Linton, Biggar, Culter, Crawford, Thornhill, Moniaive	
703	A702 s. of EDINBURGH	PEEBLES
	via Milton Bridge, Penicuik, Leadburn, Eddleston	
704	A71 w. of W. CALDER (Midlothian) A706 n. of WILSONTOWN (Lanark)	
	via Ruska, Blinkbonny	
705	MID CALDER (W. Lothian) A8 w. of WHITBURN (W. Lothian)	
	via Livingston, Blackburn, Whitburn	
706	LANARK	BO'NESS (W. Lothian)
	via Wilsontown, Whitburn, Armadale, Linlithgow	
707	w. of SELKIRK A72 nr. ACHIESTEEL (Selkirk)	
	via Roelees, Yair House	
708	SELKIRK	MOFFAT (Dumfries)
	via Yarrowford, Gordon Arms, St. Mary's Loch	
709	LANGHOLM (Dumfries)	DUMFRIES
	via Lockerbie, Lochmaben, Torthorwald	
710	DUMFRIES A75 nw. of HAUGH OF URR (Kirkcud)	
	via New Abbey, Kirkbean, Colvend, Dalbeattie, Haugh of Urr	
711	MAXWELLTOWN (Dumfries) A75 n. of KIRKCUDBRIGHT	
	via Beeswing, Dalbeattie, Palnackie, Dundrennan, Kircudbright	
712	CROCKETFORD (Kirkcud) A75 e. of NEWTON STEWART (Wigton)	
	via Corsock, Balmaclellan, New Galloway	
713	CASTLE DOUGLAS (Kirkcud)	AYR
	via Crossmichael, Ken Bridge, Dalry, Carsphairn, Dalmellington	
714	PORT WILLIAM (Wigton)	GIRVAN (Ayr)
	via Wigtown, Newton Stewart, Bargrennan, Barrhill, Pinwherry	
715	A75 w. of GLENLUCE (Wigton) A716 n. of SANDHEAD (Wigton)	
	via Whitehill	
716	DRUMMORE (Wigton) A77 s. of STRANRAER (Wigton)	
	via Ardwell, Sandhead, Stoneykirk, Lochans	
718	STRANRAER (Wigton) n. of KIRKCOLM (Wigton)	
	via St. Mary's Croft, Kirkcolm	
719	A77 s. of TURNBERRY (Ayr) A77 ne. of KILMARNOCK (Ayr)	
	via Turnberry, Dunure, Ayr, Whitletts, Galston	
721	A72 sw. of BLYTH BRIDGE (Peebles)	GLASGOW
	via Elsrickle, Carnwath, Carluke, Wishaw, Motherwell, Bellshill, Mt. Vernon	
722	NEWMAINS (Lanark)	WISHAW (Lanark)
	via Cambusnethan	
723	MUIRKIRK (Ayr)	NEWHOUSE (Lanark)
	via Strathaven, Hamilton, Motherwell, Newarthill	

A. No.	From	To
724	A776 w. of HAMILTON (Lanark) *via* Cambuslang, Rutherglen	GLASGOW
725	BOTHWELL (Lanark) *via* Bellshill	COATBRIDGE (Lanark)
726	A74 n. of LESMAHAGOW (Lanark) *via* Strathaven, E. Kilbride, Busby, Clarkston, Murlet, Paisley	ERSKINE FERRY (Renfrew)
727	CLARKSTON (Renfrew) *via* Cathcart, Queens Park	GLASGOW
728	CATHCART (Lanark) *via* S. Glasgow	GLASGOW
730	RUTHERGLEN (Lanark)	GLASGOW
734	HURLFORD (Ayr)	RICCARTON (Ayr)
735	KILMARNOCK (Ayr) *via* Kilmaurs, Stewarton, Dunlop	LUGTON (Ayr)
736	IRVINE (Ayr) *via* Auchentiber, Lugton, Barrhead, Murlet	A77 nr. QUEENS PK. (Glasgow)
737	KILWINNING (Ayr) *via* Dalgarven, Dalry, Beith, Howwood, Johnstone, Paisley	IBROX (Glasgow)
738	STEVENSTON (Ayr) *via* Saltcoats	ARDROSSAN (Ayr)
741	PAISLEY (Renfrew) *via* Renfrew	RENFREW FERRY
742	BANKFOOT (Renfrew) *via* Ravenscraig Stn.	GREENOCK (Renfrew)
743	RAVENSTRUTHER (Lanark)	LANARK
744	A72 w. of LANARK *via* Auchenheath	A74 n. of LESMAHAGOW (Lanark)
745	CASTLE DOUGLAS (Kirkcud) *via* Buittle, Dalbeattie, Auchenskeoch	A710 w. of KIRKBEAN (Kirkcud)
746	A714 s. of WIGTOWN *via* Kirkinner, Sorbie, Whithorn	A747 s.w. of WHITHORN (Wigton)
747	A746 sw. of WHITHORN (Wigton) *via* Craiglemine, Monreith, Port William, Longforth	GLENLUCE (Wigton)
748	Links A75 and A715 west of Glenluce (Wigton)	
749	E. KILBRIDE (Lanark) *via* Nerston, Burnside Stn.	RUTHERGLEN (Lanark)
750	WHITHORN (Wigton)	ISLE OF WHITHORN (Wigton)
751	A75 e. of STRANRAER (Wigton)	INNERMESSAN (Wigton)
755	KIRKCUDBRIGHT *via* Kirkchrist, Boreland	A75 se. of GATEHOUSE OF FLEET (Kirkcud)
757	WHITEHILL (Wigton) *via* E. Galdenoch, W. Galdenoch	A77 s. of STRANRAER (Wigton)

A. No.	From	To
758	MAUCHLINE (Ayr) *via* Cairngillan, Whitletts	AYR
759	KILMARNOCK (Ayr) *via* Gatehead, Parkthorn, Loans	TROON (Ayr)
760	A737 sw. of HOWWOOD (Renfrew) *via* Lochwinnoch, Kilbirnie	A78 s. of LARGS (Ayr)
761	w. PAISLEY (Renfrew) *via* Linwood, Bridge of Wier, Kilmacolm	e. PORT GLASGOW
762	A71 n. of KIRKCUDBRIGHT *via* Ringford, Laurieston, New Galloway	A713 n. of DALRY (Kirkcud)
763	CAMBUSLANG (Lanark) *via* Carmyle	s. of TOLCROSS (Lanark)
764	nr. PORTPATRICK (Wigton) Knock of Maize, Portslogan	KNOCKALDIE (Wigton)
765	PINWHERRY (Ayr) *via* Colmonell	A77 n. of BALLANTRAE (Ayr)
766	PENICUIK (Mid Lothian)	A702 at NINE MILE BARN (Mid Lothian)
767	MID CALDER (W. Lothian)	UPHALL (W. Lothian)
768	ESKBANK (Mid Lothian) *via* Lasswade, Loanhead	A701 n. of MILTON BRIDGE (Mid Lothian)
769	BALMACLELLAN (Kirkcud)	A702 e. of DALRY (Kirkcud)
775	BELLSHILL (Lanark) *via* Mossend, Holytown, Bothwell Church	NEWHOUSE (Lanark)
776	HAMILTON (Lanark) *via* High Blantyre	A749 n. of E. KILBRIDE (Lanark)

zone 8

	From	To
8	EDINBURGH *via* Corstorphine, Murraygate, Kirk O' Shotts, Newhouse, Glasgow, Govan, Renfrew, Langbank, P. Glasgow, Greenock	GOUROCK (Renfrew)
80	A8 e. of GLASGOW *via* Stepps, Cumbernauld, Dennyloanhead, Denny, Dunipace	ST. NINIANS (Stirling)
81	GLASGOW *via* Maryhill, Strathblane, Bravall, P. of Monteith	CALLANDER (Perth)
82	GLASGOW *via* Duntocher, Balloch, Tarbet, Crianlarich, Tyndrum, Kinlochleven, F. William, Spean Bridge, Invergary, F. Augustus, L. Ness,	INVERNESS

A. No.	From	To

83 TARBET (Dunbarton) CAMPBELTOWN (Argyll)
via Arrochar, Inverary, Lochgilphead, Ardrishaig, Tarbert

84 LOCHEARNHEAD (Perth) STIRLING
via Callander, Doune, Blair Drummond

85 OBAN (Argyll) DUNDEE
via Taynuilt, Dalmally, Crianlarich, Lochearnhead, Comrie, Crieff, Perth

86 SPEAN BRIDGE (Inverness) NEWTONMORE (Inverness)
via Glen Spean, Tulloch, L. Laggan, Laggan

87 INVERGARRY (Inverness) KYLE OF LOCHALSH (R and Crom)
via L. Garry, Cluanie, Invershiel, Ardelve, Auchtertyre

89 A8 e. of BATHGATE (W. Lothian) GLASGOW
via Bathgate, Armadale, Airdrie, Coatbridge, Baillieston, Parkhead

800 BATHGATE (W. Lothian) A706 n. of ARMADALE (W. Lothian)
via Balbardie

801 A706 s. of LINLITHGOW (W. Lothian) LAURIESTON (Stirling)
via Bowhouse Stn., Redding

803 GLASGOW CAMELON (Falkirk)
via Springburn, Bishopbriggs, Kirkintilloch, Kilsyth, Dennyloanhead

806 A814 w. of GLASGOW A82 at GT. WESTERN RD. STN. (Glasgow)
via Scotstounhill Stn.

807 A803 sw. of KIRKINTILLOCH (Dunbarton) A81 nr. MILNGAVIE (Dunbarton)
via Balmore, Robinsfield

809 A82 at GT. WESTERN RD. STN. (Glasgow) S. DRYMEN (Dunbarton)
via Bearsden, Dualt

810 n. of BEARSDEN (Dunbarton) O. KILPATRICK (Dunbarton)
via Duntocher

811 BALLOCH (Dunbarton) STIRLING
via Drymen, Buchlyvie

812 DUMBARTON BALLOCH (Dunbarton)
via Renton, Alexandria

814 GLASGOW ARROCHAR (Dunbarton)
via Clydebank, O. Kilpatrick, Dumbarton, Helensburgh, Garelochhead

815 A83 at n. L. FYNE (Argyll) L. STRIVEN, w. of INNELLAN (Argyll)
via Strachur, L. Eck, Kirn, Dunoon, Innellan

816 LOCHGILPHEAD (Argyll) OBAN (Argyll)
via Kilmartin, Kilmelfort, Kilninver

819 INVERARY (Argyll) A85 w. of DALMALLY (Argyll)
via Cladich

820 DOUNE (Perth) DUNBLANE (Perth)

821 A81 se. of ABERFOYLE (Perth) A84 w. of CALLANDER (Perth)
via Trossachs, L. Venacher

A.No.	From	To
822	GREENLOANING (Perth) *via* Brado, Muthill, Crieff, Gilmerton, Amulree	DUNKELD (Perth)
823	A822 s. of CRIEFF (Perth) *via* Gleneagles, Yetts of Muckhart, Rumbling Bridge, Dunfermline, Rosyth	N. QUEENSFERRY (Fife)
824	GLENEAGLES HOTEL (Perth)	AUCHTERARDER (Perth)
826	A822 ne. of Amulree (Perth) *via* Glen Cochill	ABERFELDY (Perth)
827	A85 sw. of KILLIN (Perth) *via* Killin, L. Tay, Kenmore, Aberfeldy	BALLINLUIG JCT. (Perth)
828	CONNEL BRIDGE (Argyll) *via* L. Creran, Portnacroish, Duror, Ballachulish	BRIDGE OF COE (Argyll)
830	A82 ne. of F. WILLIAM (Inverness) *via* L. Eil, Glenfinnan, Arisaig, Morar	MALLAIG (Inverness)
831	DRUMNADROCHIT (Inverness) *via* Glen Urquhart, Strath Glass, Struy Kilmorack	A9 s. of BEAULY (Inverness)
832	BRAEMORE LODGE (R and Crom) *via* Dundonnell, Gairloch, L. Maree, Achnasheen, Contin, Fortrose	CROMARTY
833	A831 w. of DRUMNADROCHIT (Inverness) *via* Glen Convinth, Kiltarlity	A9 s. of BEAULY (Inverness)
834	CONTIN (R and Crom) *via* Strathpeffer, Fodderty	DINGWALL (R and Crom)
835	nr. GARVE (R and Crom) *via* Braemore Lodge, Ullapool, Knockan, Elphin	LEDMORE (Suther)
836	A9 sw. of ALNESS (R and Crom) *via* Bonar Bridge, Lairg, Altnaharra, Tongue, Strathy, Thurso, Castletown	JOHN O' GROATS
837	INVERAN (Suther) *via* Oykell Bridge, Ledmore, Inchademff, L. Assynt	LOCHINVER (Suther)
838	A836 n. of LAIRG (Suther) *via* L. Shin, L. More, Laxford Bridge, Durness, L. Eriboll	TONGUE (Suther)
839	ROSEHALL (Suther) *via* Lairg, Strath Fleet	THE MOUND (Suther)
841	se. of ARRAN *via* Lamlash, Brodick, Corrie, Catacol, Machrie	FEORLINE (Arran)
843	FEORLINE (Arran) *via* Corriecravie, Kilmory, Bennan	A841 in se. ARRAN
844	KILNGARTH (Bute) *via* Kerrycroy, Ardencraig, Rothesay, P. Bannatyne, Scalspie	A845 nr. SCALSPIE BAY (Bute)
845	ROTHESAY (Bute) *via* Meikle Grenoch	KILNGARTH (Bute)
846	ARDBEG (Islay) *via* Bowmore, Bridgend, Ballygrant, Feolin Ferry, Craighouse, Lagg	ARDLUSSA (Jura)

A. No.	From	To
847	BRIDGEND (Islay) *via* Blackrock, P. Charlotte	PORTNAHAVEN (Islay)
848	SALEN (Mull) *via* Tobermory, Kilmore	CALGARY (Mull)
849	SALEN (Mull) *via* L. na Keal, L. Scridain, Bunessan	FIONPHORT (Mull)
850	KYLEAKIN (Skye) *via* Broadford, Sligachan, Glen Varragill, Portree, Edinbain	DUNVEGAN (Skye)
851	BROADFORD (Skye) *via* Kinloch, I. Ornsay, Kilmore, Kilbeg	ARMADALE (Skye)
852	I. ORNSAY (Skye)	e. coast, opp. LIGHTHOUSE (Skye)
853	ARMADALE (Skye) *via* Ardvasar	CALLIGARRY (Skye)
854	BROADFORD (Skye)	BROADFORD BAY (Skye)
855	PORTREE (Skye) *via* Staffin, Kilmaluag, Linacro	UIG (Skye)
856	n. of PORTREE (Skye) *via* Borve, Snizort	UIG (Skye)
857	STORNOWAY (Hebrides) *via* Laxdale, Barvas, Borve, Galson, Cross	HEBOST (Hebrides)
858	STORNOWAY (Hebrides) *via* Garynahine, Callerrish, Breasclete, Shawbost	BARVAS (Hebrides)
859	STORNOWAY (Hebrides) *via* Laxay, Balallan, Tarbert, Borvemore, Obbe	RODEL (Hebrides)
860	follows the coast of GT. CUMBRAE ISLAND	
861	w. end of L. EIL (Inverness) *via* L. Eil, L. Linnhe, Glen Tarbert, Strontian, L. Sunart	SALEN (Argyll)
862	A82 s. of F. AUGUSTUS (Inverness) *via* White Bridge, L. Garth, Dores	INVERNESS
863	SLIGACHAN (Skye) *via* Drynoch, Bracadale, Kensalroag	DUNVEGAN (Skye)
864	A863 n. of KENSALROAG (Skye)	A850 e. of DUNVEGAN (Skye)
865	LOCHMADDY (Hebrides) *via* Tigharry, Grinsay, Creagorry, Carnan Inn	LOCHBRISDALE (Hebrides)
866	STORNOWAY (Hebrides) *via* Melbost, Garrabost	PORTNAGURAN (Hebrides)
867	LOCHMADDY (Hebrides)	A865 n. of CARINISH (Hebrides)
869	A870 sw. of SCALASAIG (Colonsay)	s. coast of COLONSAY
870	SCALASAIG (Colonsay)	ne. of KILORAN (Colonsay)
871	SCALASAIG (Colonsay)	nr. KILORAN (Colonsay)

A. No.	From	To
873	BLAIR DRUMMOND (Perth) *via* Thornhill	A81 w. of P. of MONTEITH (Perth)
875	A81 n. of STRATHBLANE (Stirling) *via* Killcarn, Balfron	A811 s. of ABERFOYLE (Perth)
876	BONNYBRIDGE (Stirling) *via* Larbert, Bellsdyke, Road Bridge	KINCARDINE (Fife)
879	GLASGOW *via* Summerston Stn.	A807 e. of MILNGAVIE (Dunbarton)
880	A815 n. of SANDBANK (Argyll) *via* Kilmun, Strone, Blairmore	ARDENTINNY (Argyll)
881	STRATH CHURCH (Skye) *via* Torran, L. Slapin	ELGOL (Skye)
882	SCRABSTER (Caithness) *via* Thurso, Watten	WICK (Caithness)
883	DENNY (Stirling)	LARBERT JCT. (Stirling)
884	A861 e. of STRONTIAN (Argyll) *via* Gleann Geal, Claggan	LOCHALINE (Argyll)
885	SANDBANK (Argyll)	DUNOON (Argyll)
886	STRACHUR (Argyll) *via* L. Fyne, Otter Ferry, Kilfinan	TIGHNABRUICH (Argyll)
887	CLUANIE INN (R and Crom) *via* L. Cluanie, Glen Moriston	INVERMORISTON (Inverness)
888	ERSARY (Barra-Hebrides) *via* Castlebay, Borve	ERSARY (Barra-Hebrides)
889	LAGGAN BRIDGE (Inverness) *via* Breakachy	n. of DALWHINNIE (Inverness)
890	AUCHTERTYRE (R and Crom) *via* Strome Ferry, Joanstown, Glen Carron	ACHNASHEEN (R and Crom)
891	A803 ne. of KIRKINTILLOCH (Dunbarton) *via* Milton, Lennoxtown	STRATHBLANE (Stirling)
892	CALLANDER (Perth)	A821 e. of L. VENACHAR (Perth)
894	A837 n. of INCHNADAMFF (Suther) *via* Unapool, Kylesku Ferry, Kylestrome, Scourie	LAXFORD BRIDGE (Suther)
895	n. of GEORGEMAS JCT. (Caithness) *via* Mybster, Achavanich	LATHERON (Caithness)
897	A836 se. of MELVICH (Suther) *via* Strath Halladale, Forsinard, Kinbrace, Strath Ullie	HELMSDALE (Suther)
899	A8 e. of BROXBURN (W. Lothian) *via* Broxburn, Uphall	A8 w. of UPHALL (W. Lothian)

A. No.	From	To

9   A8 w. of EDINBURGH   JOHN O' GROATS
via Linlithgow, Falkirk, Stirling, Dunblane, Perth, Dunkeld, Pitlochry, Blair Atholl, Aviemore, Inverness, Dingwall, Tain, Bonar Bridge, Golspie, Helmsdale, Lybster, Wick

90   EDINBURGH   PERTH
via Queensferry, Inverkeithing, Cowdenbeath, Kinross, Glenfarg

91   CAUSEWAYHEAD (Stirling)   ST. ANDREWS (Fife)
via Tillicoultry, Dollar, Milnathort, Strathmiglo, Cupar

92   INVERKEITHING (Fife)   FRASERBURGH (Aberdeen)
via Burntisland, Kirkcaldy, Cupar, Dundee (+ ferry), Arbroath, Montrose, Stonehaven, Aberdeen, Ellon

93   PERTH   ABERDEEN
via Blairgowrie, Bridge of Cally, Braemar, Balmoral, Ballater, Aboyne, Banchory, Peterculter

94   PERTH   STONEHAVEN (Kincardine)
via Coupar Angus, Meigle, Glamis, Forfar, Brechin, Laurencekirk

95   A9 n. of AVIEMORE (Inverness)   A98 w. of BANFF
via Grantown-on-Spey, Bridge of Avon, Aberlour, Craigellachie, Keith

96   A9 e. of INVERNESS   ABERDEEN
via Nairn, Forres, Elgin, Fochabers, Keith, Huntly, Oyne, Inverurie, Kintore, Bucksburn

97   CAMBUS O' MAY (Aberdeen)   BANFF
Logie Coldstone, Mossat, Rhynie, Huntly, Aberchirder

98   FOCHABERS (Moray)   FRASERBURGH (Aberdeen)
via Cullen, Portsoy, Banff, Macduff, Tyrie

901   LEITH (Mid Lothian)   GRANTON (Mid Lothian)
via Newhaven, Trinity

902   A8 w. of EDINBURGH   LEITH (Mid Lothian)
via Barnton, Mains

903   A902 s. of GRANTON (Mid Lothian)   GRANTON (Mid Lothian)

904   FALKIRK   S. QUEENSFERRY (W. Lothian)
via Grangemouth, Bo'ness

905   A9 s. of GRANGEMOUTH (Stirling)   STIRLING
via Bellsdyke, Airth, Throsk Platform

906   DUNFERMLINE (Fife)   INVERKEITHING (Fife)
via Broomhall, Limekilns, Rosyth

907   STIRLING   A92 n. of KIRKCALDY (Fife)
via Alloa, Clackmannan, Carnock, Dunfermline, Crossgates

908   ALLOA (Clackm)   TILLICOULTRY (Clackm)
via Sauchie, Devonside

A. No.	From	To
909	COWDENBEATH (Fife)	BURNTISLAND (Fife)
910	COWDENBEATH (Fife) *via* Lochgelly, Auchterderran, Greenhead	KIRKCALDY (Fife)
911	MILNATHORT (Kinross) *via* Balgedie, Portmoak, Leslie, Markinch	WINDYGATES (Fife)
912	A90 ne. of GLENFARG (Perth) *via* Gateside, Strathmiglo, Falkland	FALKLAND RD. STN. (Fife)
913	A90 se. of BRIDGE OF EARN (Perth) *via* Abernethy, Newburgh	CUPAR (Fife)
914	FALKLAND RD. STN. (Fife) *via* Fernie Castle, Moonzie, Kilmany, Wormit	NEWPORT (Fife)
915	KIRKCALDY (Fife) *via* Collatown, Windygates, Largo, Lathanes	ST. ANDREWS (Fife)
916	WINDYGATES (Fife) *via* Kennoway, Craigrothie	CUPAR (Fife)
917	LARGO (Fife) *via* Elie, St. Monance, Pittenween, Anstruther	CRAIL (Fife)
918	ST. ANDREWS (Fife) *via* Kingsbarns	CRAIL (Fife)
919	GUARD BRIDGE STN. (Fife) *via* Leuchars	A92 nw. of LEUCHARS (Fife)
920	DUFFTOWN (Banff) *via* Strath Isla	KEITH (Banff)
921	A917 e. of LARGO (Fife) *via* Collinsburgh, Spalefield	A918 n. of CRAIL (Fife)
923	DUNKELD (Perth) *via* Blairgowrie, Coupar Angus, Muirhead	DUNDEE
924	PITLOCHRY (Perth) *via* Moulin, Cotterton, Kirkmichael	BRIDGE OF CALLY (Perth)
926	RATTRAY (Perth) *via* Ruthven, Kirriemuir	FORFAR (Angus)
927	A923 nw. of DUNDEE *via* Newtyle, Meigle	ALYTH (Angus)
928	A929 n. of DUNDEE *via* Glamis	KIRRIEMUIR (Angus)
929	DUNDEE *via* Todhills	FORFAR (Angus)
930	DUNDEE *via* Broughty Ferry, Monifieth, Carnoustie, Panbride	MUIRDRUM (Angus)
932	FORFAR (Angus) *via* Guthrie Stn.	FRIOCKHEIM (Angus)

A. No.	From	To
933	ARBROATH (Angus) *via* Gowanbank, Friockheim	BRECHIN (Angus)
934	A933 n. of FRIOCKHEIM (Angus) *via* Maryton Church	A92 sw. of MONTROSE (Angus)
935	BRECHIN (Angus)	MONTROSE (Angus)
937	n. MONTROSE (Angus) *via* Hillside Stn., Marykirk	LAURENCEKIRK (Kincardine)
938	CARRBRIDGE (Inverness) *via* Duthie	DULNAN BRIDGE (Inverness)
939	BALMORAL (Aberdeen) *via* Corgarth, Tomintoul, Grantown-on-Spey, Dava	NAIRN
940	DAVA (Moray) *via* Edinkillie	FORRES (Moray)
941	RHYNIE (Aberdeen) *via* Cabrach, Dufftown, Rothes, Elgin	LOSSIEMOUTH (Moray)
942	A98 s. of RATHVEN (Banff) *via* Rathven, Portessie, Portknockie	A98 w. of CULLEN (Banff)
943	A957 e. of BANCHORY (Kincardine) *via* Kirkton of Durris	A92 s. of ABERDEEN
944	MOSSAT (Aberdeen) *via* Alford, Waterton, Elrick	ABERDEEN
947	ABERDEEN *via* Bucksburn, O. Meldrum, Turriff, Plaidy	MACDUFF (Banff)
948	ELLON (Aberdeen) *via* Mill of Elrick, New Deer, Cuminestown, Monquhitter	A947 se. of TURRIFF (Aberdeen)
950	A98 n. of NEW PITSLIGO (Aberdeen) *via* New Pitsligo, Mintlaw, Longside	PETERHEAD (Aberdeen)
952	O. BIRNESS (Aberdeen) *via* Bogbrae, Peterhead, Inverquinzie, Crimond	A92 s. of RATHEN (Aberdeen)
955	KIRKCALDY (Fife) *via* Pathhead, Dysart, E. Wemyss, Methil, Leven	A915 n. of LEVEN (Fife)
956	A92 n. of NEWTON HILL (Kincardine) *via* Nigg, Torry	ABERDEEN
957	BANCHORY (Kincardine) *via* Mowtie	STONEHAVEN (Kincardine)
958	FORFAR (Angus)	MUIRDRUM (Angus)
959	ANSTRUTHER (Fife) *via* Spalefield, Dunino	A918 se. of ST. ANDREWS (Fife)
960	KIRKWALL (Orkney)	w. of DEERNESS (Orkney)
961	KIRKWALL (Orkney) *via* St. Marys, I. of Burray	ST. MARGARETS HOPE (Orkney)

A. No.	From	To
964	KIRKWALL (Orkney) *via* Kirkbister, Orphir	WAITH BRIDGE (Orkney)
965	KIRKWALL (Orkney) *via* Finstown	STROMNESS (Orkney)
966	FINSTOWN (Orkney) *via* Woodwick, Evie	BIRSAY (Orkney)
967	BIRSAY (Orkney) *via* Twatt	STROMNESS (Orkney)
968	LERWICK (Shetland) *via* Sound, Quarff, Cunningsburgh, Levenwick, Virkie	GRUTNESS (Shetland)
969	LERWICK (Shetland)	SWALLOWAY (Shetland)
970	nr. LERWICK (Shetland) *via* Girlesta, Catfirth, Voe, Brae, Collafirth	ISBISTER (Shetland)
971	A970 nr. LERWICK (Shetland) *via* Huxter, Tresta, Bixter, Sandness	MELBY (Shetland)
972	INVERGOWRIE (Angus) *via* Dundee by-pass	A92 e. of DUNDEE
973	BALMORAL (Aberdeen)	A93 w. of BANCHORY (Kincardine)
974	A97 n. of DINNET (Aberdeen) *via* Tarland, Midmar, Echt, Garlogie	A944 w. of ABERDEEN
975	A92 s. of ELLON (Aberdeen) *via* Newburgh, Ytham Ferry, Chapelhill, Port Errol	A952 s. of PETERHEAD (Aberdeen)
977	KINCARDINE (Fife) *via* Blaingore, Fossoway	KINROSS
979	A97 n. of RHYNIE (Aberdeen) *via* Kennethmont, Rothney, Insch Stn.	OYNE (Aberdeen)
980	BANCHORY (Kincardine) *via* Torphins, Lumphanan, Alford Ch.	BRIDGE OF ALFORD (Aberdeen)
981	INVERURIE (Aberdeen) *via* O. Meldrum, Methlick, New Deer, Strichen, Memsie	FRASERBURGH (Aberdeen)
983	FALKLAND (Fife) *via* Dunshelt, Auchtermuchty	A913 se. of NEWBURGH (Perth)
984	DUNKELD (Perth) *via* Caputh, Banchry	A923 nw. of COUPAR ANGUS (Perth)
985	KINCARDINE (Fife) *via* Low Torry, Torryburn	A906 s. of DUNFERMLINE (Fife)
986	e. of FINSTOWN (Orkney) *via* Dounby	TWATT (Orkney)
990	A98 s. of PORTGORDON (Banff) *via* Portgordon, Buckie	RATHVEN (Banff)
994	CAIRNEYHILL (Fife) *via* Crossford	DUNFERMLINE (Fife)

APPENDIX A

Ferries in England, Wales and Scotland.

AN interesting feature of road travel in Britain is the ferry over certain rivers, estuarine waters and between neighbouring coastal towns. Some of these are well-known, for example the Thames ferry between Tilbury and Gravesend, the Mersey ferry between Liverpool and Birkenhead or the ferries from the Hampshire coastal towns to the Isle of Wight. There are many others, however, less familiar even to the well-travelled road-user, and for the information of those interested in bettering their knowledge of Britain's highways and byways, and also to fore-warn travellers who might have occasion to seek out, or maybe avoid the lesser-known road ferries, we detail below a list of forty-seven of the more important ferries, of which twenty-five are in England and Wales, and no less than twenty-two in Scotland, despite the less developed road pattern of that country. Reference is also made to the roads which are involved at each ferry. In this respect, only the road *numbers* will be quoted if the roads concerned are among the lists elsewhere in this book, or if the roads are purely of local significance.

The following list commences at London (Thames) and the ferries are arranged "clockwise" thereafter. The list also includes some tunnels, etc.

	Ferry between	River, etc., crossed	Road(s) affected
1	Woolwich—N. Woolwich	R. Thames	A117, A205
2	Tilbury—Gravesend	R. Thames	A126, A227
3	Portsmouth—Fishbourne (I.O.W.)	Spithead	—
4	Portsmouth—Gosport	Portsmouth Harbour	A3, A32
5	Southampton—Woolston	R. Itchen	A33, A3025
6	Southampton—Cowes (I.O.W.)	Solent	—
7	Cowes—E. Cowes (I.O.W.)	R. Medina	A3020, A3021
8	Lymington—Yarmouth (I.O.W.)	Solent	—
9	Sandbanks—Shell Bay (Purbeck)	Poole Harbour	—
10	Dartmouth—Kingswear	R. Dart	A379, each side
11	Dartmouth—Old Rock	R. Dart	—
12	Torpoint—Devonport	Hamoaze (R. Tamar)	A38, each side
13	Saltash—St. Budeaux	Hamoaze (R. Tamar)	A388, each side

	Ferry between	River, etc., crossed	Road(s) affected
14	Fowey—Bodinnick	R. Fowey	——
15	King Harry—Philleigh	R. Fal	B3289, each side
16	Pilning Stn.—Severn Tunnel Jct.	R. Severn	B.R.(W.R.)
17	Beachley—Aust	R. Severn	——
18	Neyland—Pembroke Dock	Milford Haven Harbour	A477, B4325
19	Birkenhead—Liverpool	R. Mersey	A41, A57
20	Birkenhead—Liverpool	R. Mersey	Queensway Tunnel
21	Widnes—Runcorn (transporter)	R. Mersey,	A557, A569
22	Windermere	L. Windermere	——
23	Wemyss Bay—Rothesay	Firth of Clyde	——
24	Gourock—Dunoon	Firth of Clyde	——
25	Erskine—Old Kilpatrick	R. Clyde	A726, A814
26	Renfrew—Yoker	R. Clyde	A741, A814
27	Linthouse—Whiteinch	R. Clyde	——
28	Govan—Partick	R. Clyde	——
29	Greenock—Hafton (not in use)	R. Clyde	——
30	Colintraive—Rhubodach (Bute)	Kyles of Bute	B8000, each side
31	Cuan (linking Seil and Luing Is.)	Cuan Sound	——
32	Connel Bridge	Loch Etive	A85, A828
33	Ballachulish	Loch Leven	A828, A82
34	Corran—Ardgour	Loch Linnhe	A82, A861
35	Mallaig—Armadale (Skye) not in use	Sound of Sleat	A830, A851
36	Glenelg—Kylerhea (Skye) not in use	Kyle Rhea	——
37	Kyle of Lochalsh—Kyleakin	Loch Alsh	A87, A850
38	Strome	Loch Carron	A890, each side
39	Strome via rail—alternative facility	Kyle of Lochalsh—Strathcarron	——
40	Kylesku	Loch Glendhu	A894, each side
41	Kessock	Beauly Firth	——
42	Dundee—Newport	Firth of Tay	A92, each side
43	Granton—Burntisland	Firth of Forth	——
44	Queensferry	Firth of Forth	A90, each side
45	N. Shields—S. Shields	R. Tyne	A695, A19
46	Middlesbrough (transporter)	R. Tees	A178, A172
47	Hull—New Holland	R. Humber	A165, A15